BUDDHISM IN SOUTH ASIA

Dr. Shiv Charan Pipal

PRASHANT PUBLISHING HOUSE
DELHI-110094

Published by :
Prashant Publishing House
C-34, 28 Foota Road, Gali-3,
West Karwal Nagar, Delhi-110094
Phone : 011-22963970, Mob. : 9810396373
e-mail.: prashantpublishinghouse@gmail.com

Buddhism in South Asia
Reserved
First Published 2015

ISBN 978-93-80565-55-2

PRINTED IN INDIA
Published by Mr. R.K. Jha M/s Prashant Publishing House and Published at H.S. Offset House Press, Delhi.

Preface

The History of Buddhism spans from the 6th century BCE to the present, starting with the birth of the Buddha Siddhartha Gautama. This makes it one of the oldest religions practiced today. Throughout this period, the religion evolved as it encountered various countries and cultures, adding to its original Indian foundation Hellenistic as well as Central Asian, East Asian, and Southeast Asian cultural elements. In the process, its geographical extent became considerable so as to affect at one time or another most of the Asian continent. The history of Buddhism is also characterized by the development of numerous movements and schisms, foremost among them the Theravada, Mahayana and Vajrayana traditions, punctuated by contrasting periods of expansion and retreat.

In the early centuries of the Common Era, the people in various parts of Southeast Asia came to know of Buddhism as a result of increased contact with the Indian merchants who had come to the region to trade. These merchants not only established trading stations in Southeast Asia, but also brought their religions and cultures with them. Under their influence, the local people began to practise a mixture of Buddhism and Hinduism, while retaining at the same time many of their old beliefs and customs.

This book contains the fundamental and basic information of subject and the selection of contents makes it an appropriate book for the students.

—*Author*

Contents

Preface

1. Introduction 1
2. Buddhism Religions in Asia 27
3. Buddhism in India 51
4. Teachings of the Buddha 81
5. The Ethics of Buddhism 121
6. The Philosophy of Buddhism 149
7. Buddhism in Bangladesh 187
8. Tibetan Buddhism 198
9. Chinese Buddhism 214
10. Buddhism in Bhutan 264
11. Buddhist Texts 282

Bibliography 301

Index 303

1

Introduction

The History of Buddhism spans from the 6th century BCE to the present, starting with the birth of the Buddha Siddhartha Gautama. This makes it one of the oldest religions practiced today. Throughout this period, the religion evolved as it encountered various countries and cultures, adding to its original Indian foundation Hellenistic as well as Central Asian, East Asian, and Southeast Asian cultural elements. In the process, its geographical extent became considerable so as to affect at one time or another most of the Asian continent. The history of Buddhism is also characterized by the development of numerous movements and schisms, foremost among them the Theravada, Mahayana and Vajrayana traditions, punctuated by contrasting periods of expansion and retreat.

WHAT IS BUDDHISM?

IT seems to be very appropriate and even necessary at the outset to draw a well-defined line of demarcation between what is understood as Hinayana Buddhism and what is known as Mahayana Buddhism.

Most people imagine that there is only one school of Buddhism and that one school is no other than the Buddhism they have learned from the Buddhist books written or compiled or translated by Western Orientalists--Orientalists who are in many respects prejudiced against the doctrine which they propose to study most impartially. Owing to these unhappy circumstances, the outsiders are either generally ignorant or altogether misinformed of the true character of Buddhism. For what is understood by the Western people as Buddhism is no more than-one of its main divisions, which only partially expresses the spirit of its founder.

I said here "divisions," but it may be more proper to say "stages of development." For Buddhism, like so many other religions, has gone through several stages of development before it has attained the present state of perfection among the Oriental nations. And it will be evident to you that if we catch only a glimpse of an object and try to judge the whole from this transient impression, we place ourselves in a most awkward position, and shall be at a loss how to extricate ourselves from it. Therefore, let me try in the beginning to take a comprehensive view of the subject we here propose to expound.

Properly speaking, Hinayana Buddhism is a phase of Mahayana Buddhism. The former is preparatory for the latter. It is not final, but merely a stepping stone which leads the walker to the hall of perfect truth. Hinayanism is therefore more or less pessimistic, ascetic, ethical (to be distinguished from religious), and monastical. It fails to give a complete satisfaction to a man's religious yearnings. It does not fully interpret the spirit of Buddha. The Buddhism now, prevailing in Ceylon, Burma, and Siam may be considered to be betraying in a certain way a Hinayana tendency.

The Buddhism of present Japan, on the other hand, is Mahayanistic. It is more comprehensive, more religious, more humanistic, and more satisfying to the innermost needs of the religious consciousness. It cannot be said to be absolutely free from superstition, error, prejudice, etc., for it is a constantly growing, ever-living faith which knows no ossification or fossilization.

Some pious people are apt to consider their religious belief to be absolutely fixed and unchanging since the dawn of human consciousness; but they have forgotten, in my opinion, the fact that the human mind is still keeping on unfolding itself, that it has not yet exhausted all its possibilities, that it is constantly coming to a clearer consciousness as to its own nature, origin, and destiny. But what I firmly believe is that in the Buddhism of Japan today are epitomized all the essential results reached through the unfolding of the religious consciousness during the past twenty or thirty centuries of Oriental culture.

In a word, what has been known in the West as the teaching of Buddha does not represent it in its true, unadulterated colour, for it is Hinayanistic in tendency; that is, it is exclusive and not comprehensive, narrow and limited, and not all absorbing and assimilating. What I propose to expound in this lecture tonight is the Mahayana Buddhism, so called by Buddhist scholars of the East.

Let me point out in this connection what is most characteristic of Buddhism as distinguished from any other religion. I refer to a predominant tendency of Buddhism toward intellectuality, and it seems to me that the reason why Buddhism is always ready to stand before the tribunal of science and let her pass a judgment upon its merits or demerits is due to this intellectual tenor.

It goes without saying that the intellect does not constitute the most essential element of religion, but we must not forget that a religious system too much given up to sentimentalism (understanding it in its purely psychological sense) is generally prone to accede to unwarranted mysticism, ignoring altogether the legitimate claim of the intellect. Buddhism is fortunately saved from this grievous blunder, and always endeavours not to give a free rein to the wantonness of imagination and the irrationality of affection. Love without enlightenment excludes, discriminates, and contradicts itself. Love is not love unless it is purified in the mill of spiritual insight and intellectual discrimination.

What are, then, the fundamental teachings of Buddhism? I deem it best to consider it from two standpoints, ethical and philosophical, or practical and speculative, or affective and intellectual. The philosophical or speculative is preparative for the ethical or practical, for religion is not a system of metaphysics which plays with verbalism and delights in sophistry, but its aim is pre-eminently practical and spiritual. It must bear fruit in this our everyday life.

To begin with the metaphysical side of Buddhism:

(1) We Buddhists believe that as far as phenomenality goes, things that exist are all separate and discrete, they are

subject to the law of individuation and therefore to that of limitation also. All particular things exist in time and space and move according to the law of cause and effect, not only physically but morally. Buddhism does not, though sometimes understood by Western people to do so, advocate the doctrine of emptiness or annihilation. It most assuredly recognizes the multitudinousness and reality of phenomena. This world as it is, is real, not void. This life as we live it, is true, and not a dream.

(2) We Buddhists believe that all these particular things surrounding us come from one ultimate source which is all-powerful, all-knowing, and all-loving. The world is the expression or manifestation of this reason or spirit or life, whatever you may designate it. However diverse, therefore, things are, they all partake of the nature of the ultimate being. Not only sentient beings, but non-sentient beings, reflect the glory of the Original Reason. Not only man but even the lower animals and inorganic substances manifest the divinity of their source. To use the Christian term, God, it 1 is visible and audible not only in one of its highest manifestations, whom Christians call Jesus Christ, but also in the meanest and most insignificant piece of stone lying in a deserted field. God's splendour is seen not only in the Biblical lilies, but also in the mud and mire from which they grow. The melody of divine reason is heard not only in the singing of a bird or in the composition of an inspired musician, but also in the "slums of life" as Emerson phrases it.

(3) This recognition of the oneness of things naturally leads to our third belief, that the one is the many and the many is the one. God does not dwell in the heavens. It does not direct its affairs in a closed office situated somewhere outside this world. It did not create heaven and earth out of nothingness. According to Buddhism, it is a serious error to seek God outside this life, outside this universe. It is living right among ourselves and directing the course of things according to its innate destiny. Though Buddhists refuse to have God walk out of us, they do not identify

> it with the totality of existence, they are not willing to cast their lot with pantheists so called. God is immanent, surely enough, but it is greater than the totality of things. For the world may pass away, the universe may be shaken out of its foundation, but God will remain and will create a new system out of the former ruins. The ashes of existence will never be scattered to the winds, but they will gather themselves in the ever designing hand of God and build themselves up to a new order of things, in which it is ever shining with its serene radiance.

To sum up the first part of this discourse, what may be called the metaphysical phase of Buddhism is to recognize (1) the reality of the phenomenal world, (2) the existence of one ultimate reason, and (3) the immanence of this reason in the universe.

Now to come to the practical side of Buddhism: The aim of Buddhism, to state it briefly, is to dispel the clouds of ignorance and to make shine the sun of enlightenment. We are selfish because we are ignorant as to the nature of self. We are addicted to the gratification of the passions, because we are ignorant as to the destiny of humanity. We are quarrelsome and want to make ourselves powerful and predominant at the expense of our fellow-beings, because we are ignorant of the ultimate reason of the universe. Buddhists do not recognize any original sin, but acknowledge the existence of ignorance, and insist on its total removal as the surest means of salvation.

Let us, therefore, all be enlightened as to the statement made before. Let us know that we are all one in the reason of the universe, that the phenomenal world is real only to the extent it manifests reason, that egoism has no absolute sway in this life, for it destroys itself when it tries to preserve itself through its arrogant assertion, and that perfect peace is only attained when I recognize myself in you and you in me. Let us all be enlightened as to these things, and our ignorance and egoism are forever departed; the wall that divides is destroyed, and there is nothing which prevents us from loving Our enemies; and the source of divine love is open in our hearts, the eternal current of sympathy has now found its unobstructed path. This is the reason why Buddhism is called the religion of enlightenment. Now that we stand on this eminence of religious sanctity, we know what Buddhist practical faith is. It is threefold: W to cease from wrong-doing, (2) to promote goodness, and (3) to enlighten the ignorant. Buddhist ethics is the simplest thing to Practise in the world. It has nothing mysterious, nothing superstitious, nothing idolatrous, nothing supernatural. Stop doing anything wrong, which is against the reason of things; do whatever is good, which advances the course of reason in this life; and finally help those who are still behind and weary of life to realize enlightenment: and here is Buddhism in a nutshell. It has nothing to do with prayer and worship and singing and what not. Our simple everyday life of love and sympathy is all that is needed to be a good Buddhist.

I was once asked whether there was such a thing as religious life particularly. To which my answer was simple enough: "Attend to Your daily business, do all you can for the promotion of goodness in this world, and out of fullness of heart help your fellow-beings to gain the path of enlightenment. Outside of this there cannot be anything to be specially called a religious life."

In the latter part of the T'ang Dynasty in China, there was a famous poet-statesman who is known in Japanese as Hak-Rak-Ten. He learned that there resided in his district a Buddhist monk greatly noted for his saintly life and scholarly learning. The governor went to see him, intending to discuss some deeply religious topics. As soon as he was ushered into the pretence of the monk, he inquired what was thought by the saint to be the most fundamental teaching of Buddhism. The monk immediately replied that it is the teaching of all enlightened ones to cease doing anything evil, to promote goodness, and to purify one's own heart.

Hak-Rak-Ten was nonplused to receive such a commonplace instruction from the mouth of such a scholarly personage professing the faith of Buddha; for he secretly expected to have something highly metaphysical and profoundly speculative, which would naturally lead them to further philosophizing and contentless abstraction. The poet-statesman therefore retorted: "This is what every child of three summers is familiar with. I desire on the other hand what is most abstruse, most essential, most vital in Buddhism."

The monk, however, coldly replied: "Every child of three summers may know what I said now, but even a silvery-haired man of eighty winters finds it difficult to put the Buddhist instruction into the practice of everyday life."

And it is said that thereupon the Governor reverentially bowed and went home wiser.

What is philosophical in Buddhism is no more than a preliminary step toward what is practical in it. Every religion, if it deserves the name, must be essentially practical and conducive to the promotion of the general welfare and to the realization of Reason. Though intellectualism is one of the most characteristic features of Buddhism, making it so distinct from any other religious system, it never forgets the fact that our religious consciousness ever demands something concrete, that which is visible to our senses, that which is observable in our everyday life. Religion does not necessarily consist in talking on such subjects as the continuation after death of individual personality, original sin committed by some mythical personages, the last judgment to be given by an unknown quantity, a special historical revelation which takes place in a congested brain, and what not.

At least, practical Buddhism does not trouble itself with solving these problems through speculation or imagination or sophistry. Let those theologians who delight in abstraction and supernaturalism discuss them to their hearts' content, for that is their profession. We, plain ordinary Buddhists, will keep on removing selfishness, seeking the light that is everywhere, practising lovingkindness that does not contradict or discriminate. Says an ancient sage, "The Way is near, and thou seekest it afar." Why, then, shall we ever attempt to walk away from the path which extends right in front of us, so wide and well paved?

EARLY BUDDHISM

Before the royal sponsorship of Ashoka the Great in the 3rd century BCE, Buddhism is to have remained a relatively minor phenomenon, and the historicity of its formative events is poorly established. Two formative councils are supposed to have taken place, although our knowledge of them is based on much later accounts. The councils tend to explain the formalization of the Buddhist doctrine, and the various subsequent schisms inside the Buddhist movement.

1st Buddhist Council (5th c. BCE)

The first Buddhist council was held soon after the death of the Buddha under the patronage of king Ajatashatru of the Magadha empire, and presided by a monk named Mahakasyapa, at Rajagriha (today's Rajgir). The objective of the council was to record the Buddha's sayings (sutra) and codify monastic rules (vinaya): Ananda, one of the Buddha's main disciples and his cousin, was called upon to recite the discourses of the Buddha, and Upali, another disciple, recited the rules of the vinaya. These became the basis of the Pali Canon, which has been the orthodox text of reference throughout the history of Buddhism.

2nd Buddhist Council (383 BCE)

The second Buddhist council was convened by King Kalasoka and held at Vaishali, following conflicts between the traditional schools of Buddhism and a more liberal interpretational movement called the Mahasanghikas. The traditional schools considered the Buddha as a human being who reached enlightenment, which could be most easily attained by monks following the monastic rules and practicing the teaching for the sake of overcoming suffering and attaining Arahantship. The secessionist Mahasangikas, however, tended to consider this approach too individualistic and selfish. They considered the objective of becoming an arhat insufficient, and instead proposed that the only true goal was to reach full Buddhahood, in a sense opening the way to future Mahayana thought. They became proponents of more relaxed monastic rules, which could appeal to a large majority of monastic and lay people (hence their name the "great" or "majority" assembly). The council ended with the rejection of the Mahasanghikas. They left the council and maintained themselves for several centuries in northwestern India and Central Asia according to Kharoshti inscriptions found near the Oxus and dated c. 1st century CE.

Ashokan Proselytism (c. 261 BCE)

The Mauryan emperor Ashoka the Great (273–232 BCE) converted to Buddhism after his bloody conquest of the territory of Kalinga (today's Orissa) in eastern India. Regretful of the horrors brought by the conflict, the king decided to renounce violence, and propagate the faith by building stupas and pillars urging for the respect of all animal life, and enjoining people to follow the Dharma. Perhaps the finest example of these is the Great Stupa in Sanchi, India (near Bhopal). It was constructed in the third century BCE and later enlarged. Its carved gates, called Tohans, are considered among the finest examples of Buddhist art in India. He also built roads, hospitals, resthouses, universities and irrigation systems around the country. He treated his subjects as equals regardless of their religion, politics or caste.

This period marks the first spread of Buddhism beyond India. According to the plates and pillars left by Ashoka (the Edicts of Ashoka), emissaries were sent to various countries in order to spread Buddhism, as far as the Greek kingdoms in the West, in particular the neighbouring Greco-Bactrian Kingdom, and possibly even farther to the Mediterranean.

3rd Buddhist Council (c.250 BCE)

King Ashoka convened the third Buddhist council around 250 BCE at Pataliputra (today's Patna). It was held by the monk Moggaliputta. The objective of the council was to reconcile the different schools of Buddhism, to purify the Buddhist movement, particularly from opportunistic factions which had been attracted by the royal patronage, and to organize the dispatch of Buddhist missionaries throughout the known world.

The Pali canon (Tipitaka, or Tripitaka in Sanskrit, literally the "Three Baskets"), which comprises the texts of reference of traditional Buddhism and is considered to be directly transmitted from the Buddha, was formalized at that time. It consists of the doctrine (the Sutra Pitaka), the monastic discipline (Vinaya Pitaka) and an additional new body of subtle philosophy (the Abhidharma Pitaka).

The efforts of Ashoka to purify the Buddhist faith also had the effect of segregating against other emerging movements. In particular, after 250 BCE, the Sarvastivadin (who had been rejected by the 3rd council, according to the Theravada tradition) and the Dharmaguptaka schools became quite influential in northwestern India and Central Asia, up to the time of the Kushan Empire in the first centuries of the common era. The Dharmaguptakas were characterized by a belief that Buddha was separate, and above, the rest of the Buddhist community. The Sarvastivadin believed that past, present, and future are all simultaneous.

Hellenistic World

Some of the Edicts of Ashoka inscriptions describe the efforts made by Ashoka to propagate the Buddhist faith throughout the Hellenistic world, which at that time formed an uninterrupted continuum from the borders of India to Greece. The Edicts indicate a clear understanding of the political organization in Hellenistic territories: the names and location of the main Greek monarchs of the time are identified, and they are claimed as recipients of Buddhist proselytism: Antiochus II Theos of the Seleucid Kingdom (261–246 BCE), Ptolemy II Philadelphos of Egypt (285–247 BCE), Antigonus Gonatas of Macedonia (276–239 BCE), Magas of Cyrene (288–258 BCE), and Alexander II of Epirus (272–255 BCE).

"The conquest by Dharma has been won here, on the borders, and even six hundred yojanas (5,400-9,600 km) away, where the Greek king Antiochos rules, beyond there where the four kings named Ptolemy, Antigonos, Magas and Alexander rule, likewise in the south among the Cholas, the Pandyas, and as far as Tamraparni (Sri Lanka)." (Edicts of Ashoka, 13th Rock Edict, S. Dhammika).

Furthermore, according to Pali sources, some of Ashoka's emissaries were Greek Buddhist monks, indicating close religious exchanges between the two cultures:

"When the thera (elder) Moggaliputta, the illuminator of the religion of the Conqueror (Ashoka), had brought the (third) council to an end (...) he sent forth theras, one here and one there: (...) and to Aparantaka (the "Western countries" corresponding to Gujarat and Sindh) he sent the Greek (Yona) named Dhammarakkhita". (Mahavamsa XII).

Ashoka also issued Edicts in the Greek language as well as in Aramaic. One of them, found in Kandahar, advocates the adoption of "Piety" (using the Greek term Eusebeia for Dharma) to the Greek community:

"Ten years (of reign) having been completed, King Piodasses (Ashoka) made known (the doctrine of) Piety to men; and from this moment he has made men more pious, and everything thrives throughout the whole world."

It is not clear how much these interactions may have been influential, but some authors have commented that some level of syncretism between Hellenist thought and Buddhism may have started in Hellenic lands at that time.

They have pointed to the presence of Buddhist communities in the Hellenistic world around that period, in particular in Alexandria (mentioned by Clement of Alexandria), and to the pre-Christian monastic order of the Therapeutae (possibly a deformation of the Pali word "Theravada"), who may have "almost entirely drawn (its) inspiration from the teaching and practices of Buddhist asceticism" (Robert Lissen).

Buddhist gravestones from the Ptolemaic period have also been found in Alexandria, decorated with depictions of the Dharma wheel (Tarn, "The Greeks in Bactria and India"). Commenting on the presence of Buddhists in Alexandria, some scholars have even pointed out that "It was later in this very place that some of the most active centres of Christianity were established" (Robert Linssen "Zen living").

In the 2nd century CE, the Christian dogmatist Clement of Alexandria recognized Bactrian Buddhists (Sramanas) and Indian Gymnosophists for their influence on Greek thought:

"Thus philosophy, a thing of the highest utility, flourished in antiquity among the barbarians, shedding its light over the nations. And afterwards it came to Greece. First in its ranks were the prophets of the Egyptians; and the Chaldeans among the Assyrians; and the Druids among the Gauls; and the Sramanas among the Bactrians; and the philosophers of

the Celts; and the Magi of the Persians, who foretold the Saviour's birth, and came into the land of Judaea guided by a star. The Indian gymnosophists are also in the number, and the other barbarian philosophers. And of these there are two classes, some of them called Sramanas, and others Brahmins." Clement of Alexandria "The Stromata, or Miscellanies"

The Two Fourth Councils

A Fourth Council is said to have been convened in the reign of the Kushan emperor Kanishka, around 100 CE at Jalandhar or in Kashmir. Because Therevada believes the The Fourth Council of Kashmir introduced unauthentic sutras as authentic, and it was itself not present at this Fourth Council to prevent this, Theravada Buddhism does not recognize the authenticity of this council, and sometimes they call it the "council of heretical monks". Theravada Buddhism had its own Fourth Council in Sri Lanka. Therefore there are two Fourth Councils: one in Sri Lanka (Theravada), and one in Kashmir (Sarvastivadin).

It is said that for the Fourth Council of Kashmir, Kanishka gathered 500 monks headed by Vasumitra, partly, it seems, to compile extensive commentaries on the Abhidharma, although it is possible that some editorial work was carried out upon the existing canon itself. The main fruit of this Council was the redaction of Agamas and complilation of the vast commentary known as the Maha-Vibhasha ("Great Exegesis"), an extensive compendium and reference work on a portion of the Sarvastivadin Abhidharma.

Scholars believe that it was also around this time that a significant change was made in the language of the Sarvastivadin canon, by converting an earlier Prakrit version into Sanskrit. Although this change was probably effected without significant loss of integrity to the canon, this event was of particular significance since Sanskrit was the official holy language of Hinduism in India, and was also being used by other thinkers (regardless of their specific religious or philosophical allegiance), thus enabling a far wider audience to gain access to Buddhist ideas and practices. For this reason, all major (Mahayana) Buddhist scholars in India thereafter wrote their commentaries and treatises in Sanskrit. Theravada however never switched to Sanskrit, partly because Buddha explicitly forbade translation of his discourses into Sanskrit because it was an elitist religious language (like Latin was in Europe before). He wanted his monks to use a local language instead; a language which could be understood by all. Over time however, the language of the Theravadin scriptures (Pali) became a scholarly or elitist language as well.

Asian Expansion

In the areas east of the Indian subcontinent (today's Burma), Indian culture strongly influenced the Mons. The Mons are said to have been converted to Buddhism around 200 BCE under the proselytizing of the Indian king Ashoka, before the fission between Mahayana and Hinayana Buddhism. Early Mon Buddhist temples, such as Peikthano in central Burma, have been dated between the 1st and the 5th century CE.

The Buddhist art of the Mons was especially influenced by the Indian art of the Gupta and post-Gupta periods, and their mannerist style spread widely in South-East Asia following the expansion of the Mon kingdom between the 5th and 8th centuries. The Theravada faith expanded in the northern parts of Southeast Asia under Mon influence, until it was progressively displaced by Mahayana Buddhism from around the 6th century CE.

Sri Lanka was allegedly proselytized by Ashoka's son Mahinda and six companions during the 2nd century BCE. They converted the king Devanampiya Tissa and many of the nobility. This is when the Mahavihara monastery, a centre of Sinhalese orthodoxy, was built.

The Pali Canon was put in writing in Sri Lanka during the reign of king Vittagamani (r. 29–17 BCE), and the Theravada tradition flourished there, harbouring some great commentators such as Buddhaghosa (4th–5th century). Although Mahayana Buddhism gained some influence at that time, Theravada ultimately prevailed, and Sri Lanka turned out to be the last stronghold of Theravada Buddhism, from where it would expand again to South-East Asia from the 11th century. There is also a legend, not directly validated by the edicts, that Ashoka sent a missionary to the north, through the Himalayas, to Khotan in the Tarim Basin, then the land of the Tocharians, speakers of an Indo-European language.

Greco-Buddhist Interaction (2nd c. BCE–1st c. CE)

In the areas west of the Indian subcontinent, neighbouring Greek kingdoms had been in place in Bactria (today's northern Afghanistan) since the time of the conquests of Alexander the Great around 326 BCE: first the Seleucids from around 323 BCE, then the Greco-Bactrian kingdom from around 250 BCE.

The Greco-Bactrian king Demetrius I invaded India in 180 BCE as far as Pataliputra, establishing an Indo-Greek kingdom that was to last in various part of northern India until the end of the 1st century BCE. Buddhism flourished under the Indo-Greek kings, and it has been suggested that their invasion of India was intended to show their support for the Mauryan empire, and to protect the Buddhist faith from the alleged religious persecutions of the Sungas (185–73 BCE), accounts which are disputed by historians.

One of the most famous Indo-Greek kings is Menander (reigned c. 160–135 BCE). He apparently converted to Buddhism and is presented in the Mahayana tradition as one of the great benefactors of the faith, on a par with king Ashoka or the later Kushan king Kanishka. Menander's coins bear the mention "Saviour king" in Greek, and sometimes designs of the eight-spoked wheel. Direct cultural exchange is also suggested by the dialogue of the Milinda Panha between Menander and the monk Nagasena around 160 BCE. Upon his death, the honour of sharing his remains was claimed by the cities under his rule, and they were enshrined in stupas, in a parallel with the historic Buddha. Several of Menander's Indo-Greek successors inscribed the mention "Follower of the Dharma" in the Kharoshthi script on their coins, and depicted themselves or their divinities forming the *vitarka* mudra.

The interaction between Greek and Buddhist cultures may have had some influence on the evolution of Mahayana, as the faith developed its sophisticated philosophical approach and a man-god treatment of the Buddha somewhat reminiscent of Hellenic gods. It is also around that time that the first anthropomorphic representations of the Buddha are found, often in realistic Greco-Buddhist style: "One might regard the classical influence as including the general idea of representing a man-god in this purely human form, which was of course well familiar in the West, and it is very likely that the example of westerner's treatment of their gods was indeed an important factor in the innovation" (Boardman, "The Diffusion of Classical Art in Antiquity").

Rise of Mahayana (1st c.BCE–2nd c.CE)

The rise of Mahayana Buddhism from the 1st century BCE was accompanied by complex political changes in northwestern India. The Indo-Greek kingdoms were gradually overwhelmed, and their culture assimilated by the Indo-Scythians, and then the Yuezhi, who founded the Kushan Empire from around 12 BCE.

The Kushans were supportive of Buddhism, and a fourth Buddhist council was convened by the Kushan emperor Kanishka, around 100 CE at Jalandhar or in Kashmir, and is usually associated with the formal rise of Mahayana Buddhism and its secession from Theravada Buddhism. Theravada Buddhism does not recognize the authenticity of this council, and it is sometimes called the "council of heretical monks".

It is said that Kanishka gathered 500 bhikkhus in Kashmir, headed by Vasumitra, to edit the Tripitaka and make references and remarks. Allegedly, during the council there were all together three hundred thousand verses and over nine million statements compiled, and it took twelve years to complete. This council did not rely on the original Pali canon (the Tipitaka). Instead, a set of new scriptures was approved, as well as fundamental principles of Mahayana doctrine. The new scriptures, usually in the Gandhari vernacular and the Kharosthi script, were rewritten in the classical language of Sanskrit, to many scholars a turning point in the propagation of Buddhist thought. The new form of Buddhism was characterized by an almost God-like treatment of the Buddha, by the idea that all beings have a Buddha-nature and should aspire to Buddhahood, and by a syncretism due to the various cultural influences within northwestern India and the Kushan Empire.

Mahayana Expansion (1st c.CE–10th c.CE)

From that point on, and in the space of a few centuries, Mahayana was to flourish and spread in the East from India to South-East Asia, and towards the north to Central Asia, China, Korea, and finally to Japan in 538 CE.

India

After the end of the Kushans, Buddhism flourished in India during the dynasty of the Guptas (4th-6th century). Mahayana centres of learning were established, especially at Nalanda in northeastern India; which was to become the largest and most influential Buddhist university for many centuries, with famous teachers such as Nagàrjuna. The Gupta style of Buddhist art became very influential from South-East Asia to China as the faith was spreading there.

Indian Buddhism had weakened in the 6th century following the White Hun invasions and Mihirkulas persecution.

Xuanzang reports in his travels across India during the 7th century of Buddhism being popular in Andhra, Dhanyakataka, and Dravida which today rougly correspond to the modern day Indian states of Andhra Pradesh and Tamil Nadu.

While reporting many deserted stupas in the area around modern day Nepal and the persecution of buddhists by Ssanka in the Kingdom of Gouda. (In modern day West Bengal.) Xuanzang compliments the patronage of Harshavardana during the same period. After Harshavardanas kingdom, the rise of many small kingdoms that lead to the rise of the Rajputs across the gangetic plains and marked the end of Buddhist ruling clans along with a sharp decline in royal patronage until a revival under the Pala Empire in the Bengal region. Here Mahayana Buddhism flourished and spread to Bhutan and Sikkim between the 8th and the 12th century before the Palas collapsed under the assault of the Hindu Sena dynasty. The Palas created many temples and a distinctive school of Buddhist art. Xuanzang noted in his travels that in various regions Buddhism was giving way to Jainism and Hinduism. By the 10th century Buddhism had experienced a sharp decline beyond the Pala realms in Bengal under a resurgent

Hinduism and the incorporation in Vaishnavite Hinduism of Buddha as the 9th incarnation of Vishnu.

A milestone in the decline of Indian Buddhism in the North occurred in 1193 when Turkic Islamic raiders under Muhammad Khilji burnt Nalanda. By the end of the 12th century, following the Islamic conquest of the Buddhist strongholds in Bihar, and the loss of political support coupled with social and caste pressures, the practice of Buddhism retreated to the Himalayan foothills in the North and Sri Lanka in the south. Additionally, the influence of Buddhism also waned due to Hinduism's revival movements such as Advaita, the rise of the bhakti movement and the missionary work of Sufis.

CENTRAL AND NORTHERN ASIA

Central Asia

Central Asia had been influenced by Buddhism probably almost since the time of the Buddha. According to a legend preserved in Pali, the language of the Theravada canon, two merchant brothers from Bactria, named Tapassu and Bhallika, visited the Buddha and became his disciples. They then returned to Bactria and built temples to the Buddha (Foltz).

Central Asia long played the role of a meeting place between China, India and Persia. During the 2nd century BCE, the expansion of the Former Han to the west brought them into contact with the Hellenistic civilizations of Asia, especially the Greco-Bactrian Kingdoms. Thereafter, the expansion of Buddhism to the north led to the formation of Buddhist communities and even Buddhist kingdoms in the oases of Central Asia. Some Silk Road cities consisted almost entirely of Buddhist stupas and monasteries, and it seems that one of their main objectives was to welcome and service travellers between east and west.

The Hinayana traditions first spread among the Turkic tribes before combining with the Mahayana forms during the 2nd and 3rd centuries BCE to cover modern-day Pakistan, Kashmir, Afghanistan, eastern and coastal Iran, Uzbekistan, Turkmenistan and Tajikistan. These were the ancient states of Gandhara, Bactria,

Parthia and Sogdia from where it spread to China. Among the first of these Turkic tribes to adopt Buddhism was the Turki-Shahi who adopted Buddhism as early as the 3rd century BCE. It was not, however, the exclusive faith of this region. There were also Zoroastrians, Hindus, Nestorian Christians, Jews, Manichaeans, and followers of shamanism, Tengrism, and other indigenous, nonorganized systems of belief.

Various Nikaya schools persisted in Central Asia and China until around the 7th century CE. Mahayana started to become dominant during the period, but since the faith had not developed a Nikaya approach, Sarvastivadin and Dharmaguptakas remained the Vinayas of choice in Central Asian monasteries.

Various Buddhism kingdoms rose and prospered in both the Central Asian region and downwards into the Indian sub-continent such as Kushan Empire prior to the White Hun invasion in the 5th century where under the King Mihirkula they were heavily persecuted.

Buddhism in Central Asia started to decline with the expansion of Islam and the destruction of many stupas in war from the 7th century. The Muslims accorded them the status of dhimmis as "people of the Book", such as Christianity or Judaism and Al-Biruni wrote of Buddha as prophet "burxan". Buddhism saw a surge during the reign of Mongols following the invasion of Genghis Khan and the establishment of the Il Khanate and the Chagatai Khanate who brought their Buddhist influence with them during the 13th century, however within a 100 years the Mongols would convert to Islam and spread Islam across all the regions across central asia.

Parthia

Buddhism expanded westward into Arsacid Parthia, at least to the area of Merv, in ancient Margiana, today's territory of Turkmenistan. Soviet archeological teams have excavated in Giaur Kala, near Merv, a Buddhist chapel, a gigantic Buddha statue, as well as a monastery.

Parthians were directly involved in the propagation of Buddhism: An Shigao (c. 148 CE), a Parthian prince, went to

China, and is the first known translator of Buddhist scriptures into Chinese.

Tarim Basin

The eastern part of central Asia (Chinese Turkestan, Tarim Basin, Xinjiang) has revealed extremely rich Buddhist works of art (wall paintings and reliefs in numerous caves, portable paintings on canvas, sculpture, ritual objects), displaying multiple influences from Indian and Hellenistic cultures. Serindian art is highly reminiscent of the Gandharan style, and scriptures in the Gandhari script Kharosthi have been found.

Central Asians seem to have played a key role in the transmission of Buddhism to the East. The first translators of Buddhists scriptures into Chinese were either Parthian like An Shigao (c. 148 CE) or An Hsuan, Kushan of Yuezhi ethnicity like Lokaksema (c. 178 CE), Zhi Qian and Zhi Yao, or Sogdians like Kang Sengkai. Thirty-seven early translators of Buddhist texts are known, and the majority of them have been identified as Central Asians.

Central Asian and East Asian Buddhist monks appear to have maintained strong exchanges until around the 10th century, as shown by frescoes from the Tarim Basin.

These influences were rapidly absorbed however by the vigorous Chinese culture, and a strongly Chinese particularism develops from that point.

China

Buddhism probably arrived in China around the 1st century CE from Central Asia (although there are some traditions about a monk visiting China during Asoka's reign), and through to the 8th century it became an extremely active centre of Buddhism.

The year 67 CE saw Buddhism's official introduction to China with the coming of the two monks Moton and Chufarlan. In 68 CE, under imperial patronage, they established the White Horse Temple, which still exists today, close to the imperial capital at Luoyang. By the end of the second century, a prosperous community had been settled at Pengcheng (modern Xuzhou,

Jiangsu). The first known Mahayana scriptural texts are translations made into Chinese by the Kushan monk Lokaksema in Luoyang, between 178 and 189 CE. Some of the earliest known Buddhist artifacts found in China are small statues on "money trees", dated circa 200 CE, in typical Gandharan style (drawing): "That the imported images accompanying the newly arrived doctrine came from Gandhara is strongly suggested by such early Gandhara characteristics on this "money tree" Buddha as the high ushnisha, vertical arrangement of the hair, moustache, symmetrically looped robe and parallel incisions for the folds of the arms." ("Crossroads of Asia")

Buddhism flourished during the beginning of the Tang Dynasty (618–907). The dynasty was initially characterized by a strong openness to foreign influences, and renewed exchanges with Indian culture due to the numerous travels of Chinese Buddhist monks to India from the 4th to the 11th century. The Tang capital of Chang'an (today's Xi'an) became an important centre for Buddhist thought. From there Buddhism spread to Korea, and Japanese embassies of Kentoshi helped gain footholds in Japan.

However foreign influences came to be negatively perceived towards the end of the Tang Dynasty. In the year 845, the Tang emperor Wu-Tsung outlawed all "foreign" religions (including Christian Nestorianism, Zoroastrianism, and Buddhism) in order to support the indigenous Taoism. Throughout his territory, he confiscated Buddhist possessions, destroyed monasteries and temples, and executed Buddhist monks, ending Buddhism's cultural and intellectual dominance.

Pure Land and Chan Buddhism, however, continued to prosper for some centuries, the latter giving rise to Japanese Zen. In China, Chan flourished particularly under the Song dynasty (1127–1279), when its monasteries were great centres of culture and learning.

Today, China boasts one of the richest collections of Buddhist arts and heritages in the world. UNESCO World Heritage Sites such as the Mogao Caves near Dunhuang in Gansu province, the Longmen Grottoes near Luoyang in Henan province, the Yungang Grottoes near Datong in Shanxi province, and the Dazu Rock Carvings near Chongqing are among the most important and renowned Buddhist sculptural sites. The Leshan Giant Buddha, carved out of a hillside in the 8th century during Tang Dynasty and looking down on the confluence of three rivers, is still the largest stone Buddha statue in the world.

Korea

Buddhism was introduced around 372 CE, when Chinese ambassadors visited the Korean kingdom of Goguryeo, bringing scriptures and images. Buddhism prospered in Korea, and in particular Seon (Zen) Buddhism from the 7th century onward. However, with the beginning of the Confucean Yi Dynasty of the Joseon period in 1392, Buddhism was strongly discriminated against until it was almost completely eradicated, except for a remaining Seon movement.

Japan

Japan discovered Buddhism in the 6th century when Korean monks travelled to the islands together with numerous scriptures and works of art. The Buddhist religion was adopted by the state in the following century.

Being geographically at the end of the Silk Road, Japan was able to preserve many aspects of Buddhism at the very time it was disappearing in India, and being suppressed in Central Asia and China.

From 710 CE numerous temples and monasteries were built in the capital city of Nara, such as the five-story pagoda and Golden Hall of the Horyuji, or the Kofuku-ji temple. Countless paintings and sculptures were made, often under governmental sponsorship. The creation of Japanese Buddhist art was especially rich between the 8th and 13th century during the periods of Nara, Heian, and Kamakura.

From the 12th and 13th, a further development was Zen art, following the introduction of the faith by Dogen and Eisai upon their return from China. Zen art is mainly characterized by original paintings (such as sumi-e and the Enso) and poetry (especially haikus), striving to express the true essence of the world through impressionistic and unadorned "non-dualistic" representations.

The search for enlightenment "in the moment" also led to the development of other important derivative arts such as the Chanoyu tea ceremony or the Ikebana art of flower arrangement. This evolution went as far as considering almost any human activity as an art with a strong spiritual and aesthetic content, first and foremost in those activities related to combat techniques (martial arts). Buddhism remains very active in Japan to this day. Around 80,000 Buddhist temples are preserved and regularly restored.

South-East Asia

During the 1st century CE, the trade on the overland Silk Road tended to be restricted by the rise in the Middle-East of the Parthian empire, an unvanquished enemy of Rome, just as Romans were becoming extremely wealthy and their demand for Asian luxury was rising. This demand revived the sea connections between the Mediterranean and China, with India as the intermediary of choice. From that time, through trade connection, commercial settlements, and even political interventions, India started to strongly influence Southeast Asian countries. Trade routes linked India with southern Burma, central and southern Siam, lower Cambodia and southern Vietnam, and numerous urbanized coastal settlements were established there.

For more than a thousand years, Indian influence was therefore the major factor that brought a certain level of cultural unity to the various countries of the region. The Pali and Sanskrit languages and the Indian script, together with Theravada and Mahayana Buddhism, Brahmanism, and Hinduism, were transmitted from direct contact and through sacred texts and Indian literature such as the Ramayana and the Mahabharata.

From the 5th to the 13th century, South-East Asia had very powerful empires and became extremely active in Buddhist architectural and artistic creation. The main Buddhist influence now came directly by sea from the Indian subcontinent, so that these empires essentially followed the Mahayana faith. The Sri Vijaya Empire to the south and the Khmer Empire to the north competed for influence, and their art expressed the rich Mahayana pantheon of the Bodhisattvas.

VIETNAM

Srivijayan Empire (5th–15th Century)

Srivijaya, a maritime empire centred at Palembang on the island of Sumatra in Indonesia, adopted Mahayana and Vajrayana Buddhism under a line of rulers named the Sailendras. Yijing described Palembang as a great centre of Buddhist learning where the emperor supported over a thousand monks at his court. Atisha studied there before travelling to Tibet as a missionary.

Srivijaya spread Buddhist art during its expansion in Southeast Asia. Numerous statues of Bodhisattvas from this period are characterized by a very strong refinement and technical sophistication, and are found throughout the region. Extremely rich architectural remains are visible at the temple of Borobudur (the largest Buddhist structure in the world, built from around 780 CE), in Java, which has 505 images of the seated Buddha. Srivijaya declined due to conflicts with the Chola rulers of India, before being destabilized by the Islamic expansion from the 13th century.

Khmer Empire (9th–13th Century)

Later, from the 9th to the 13th century, the Mahayana Buddhist and Hindu Khmer Empire dominated much of the South-East Asian peninsula. Under the Khmer, more than 900 temples were built in Cambodia and in neighbouring Thailand. Angkor was at the centre of this development, with a temple complex and urban organization able to support around one million urban dwellers. One of the greatest Khmer kings, Jayavarman VII (1181–1219), built large Mahayana Buddhist structures at Bayon and Angkor Thom.

Following the destruction of Buddhism in mainland India during the 11th century, Mahayana Buddhism declined in Southeast Asia, to be replaced by the introduction of Theravada Buddhism from Sri Lanka.

Emergence of the Vajrayana (5th Century)

Vajrayana Buddhism, also called Tantric Buddhism, first emerged in eastern India between the 5th and 7th centuries CE.

It is sometimes considered a sub-school of Mahayana and sometimes a third major "vehicle" (*Yana*) of Buddhism in its own right. The Vajrayana is an extension of Mahayana Buddhism in that it does not offer new philosophical perspectives, but rather introduces additional techniques (upaya, or'skilful means'), including the use of visualizations and other yogic practices. Many of the practices of Tantric Buddhism are also derived from Hinduism (the usage of mantras, yoga, or the burning of sacrificial offerings). This school of thought was founded by the Brahmin Padmasambhava.

Early Vajrayana practitioners were forest-dwelling mahasiddas who lived on the margins of society, but by the 9th century Vajrayana had won acceptance at major Mahayana monastic universities such as Nalanda and Vikramshila. Along with much of the rest of Indian Buddhism, the Vajrayana was eclipsed in the wake of the late 12th century Muslim invasions. It has persisted in Tibet, where it was wholly transplanted from the 7th to 12th centuries and became the dominant form of Buddhism to the present day, and on a limited basis in Japan as well where it evolved into Shingon Buddhism.

Theravada Renaissance (11th Century CE)

From the 11th century, the destruction of Buddhism in the Indian mainland by Islamic invasions led to the decline of the Mahayana faith in South-East Asia. Continental routes through the Indian subcontinent being compromised, direct sea routes between the Middle-East through Sri Lanka and to China developed, leading to the adoption of the Theravada Buddhism of the Pali canon, introduced to the region around the 11th century CE from Sri Lanka.

King Anawrahta (1044–1077); the historical founder of the Burmese empire, unified the country and adopted the Theravada Buddhist faith. This initiated the creation of thousands of Buddhist temples at Pagan, the capital, between the 11th and 13th century. Around 2,000 of them are still standing. The power of the Burmese waned with the rise of the Thai, and with the seizure of the capital Pagan by the Mongols in 1287, but Theravada Buddhism remained the main Burmese faith to this day. The Theravada faith was also adopted by the newly founded ethnic Thai kingdom of Sukhothai around 1260. Theravada Buddhism was further reinforced during the Ayutthaya period (14th–18th century), becoming an integral part of the Thai society.

In the continental areas, Theravada Buddhism continued to expand into Laos and Cambodia in the 13th century. However, from the 14th century, on the coastal fringes and in the islands of South-East Asia, the influence of Islam proved stronger, expanding into Malaysia, Indonesia, and most of the islands as far as the southern Philippines.

However, since 1966 with Soeharto's rise of power in the aftermath of the bloody events after the so called "September 30th, 1965 murders", allegedly executed by the Communists Party, there has been a remarkable renaissance of Buddhism in Indonesia. This is partly due to the Soeharto's New Order's requirements for the people of Indonesia to adopt one of the five official religions: Islam, Protestantism, Catholicism, Hinduism or Buddhism. Today it is estimated there are some 10 millions Buddhists in Indonesia. A large part of them are people of Chinese ancestry.

Expansion of Buddhism to the West

After the Classical encounters between Buddhism and the West recorded in Greco-Buddhist art, information and legends about Buddhism seem to have reached the West sporadically. During the 8th century, Buddhist Jataka stories were translated into Syriac and Arabic as Kalilag and Damnag. An account of Buddha's life was translated in to Greek by John of Damascus, and widely circulated to Christians as the story of Barlaam and Josaphat. By the 1300s this story of Josaphat had become so popular that he was made a Catholic saint.

The next direct encounter between Europeans and Buddhism happened in Medieval times when the Franciscan friar William of Rubruck was sent on an embassy to the Mongol court of Mongke by the French king Saint Louis in 1253. The contact happened in Cailac (today's Qayaliq in Kazakhstan), and William originally thought they were wayward Christians (Foltz, "Religions of the

Silk Road"). Major interest for Buddhism emerged during colonial times, when Western powers were in a position to witness the faith and its artistic manifestations in detail. European philosophy was strongly influenced by the study of oriental religions during that period. The opening of Japan in 1853 also created a considerable interest for the arts and culture of Japan, and provided access to one of the most thriving Buddhist cultures in the world.

Buddhism started to enjoy a strong interest from the general population in the West during the 20th century, following the perceived failure of social utopias, from Fascism to Marxism. After the Second World War, the focus of progress tended to shift to personal self-realization, on the material as well as spiritual plane.

In this context, Buddhism has been displaying a strong power of attraction, due to its tolerance, its lack of deist authority and determinism, and its focus on understanding reality through self inquiry. According to the latest census it is now the fastest growing religion in Britain.

2

Buddhism Religions in Asia

HINDU PHILOSOPHIES

Hinduism is a religious category including many beliefs and traditions. Since Hinduism was the way of expressed meaningful living for quite a long time immemorial, when there was no need for naming this as a separate religion, Hindu doctrines are supplementary and complementary in nature, generally non-exclusive, suggestive and tolerant in content. Most believe that the atman (spirit, soul)—the person's true *self*—is eternal. In part, this stems from Hindu beliefs that spiritual development occurs across many lifetimes, and goals should match the state of development of the individual. There are four possible aims to human life, known as the *purusharthas* (ordered from least to greatest): *Kama* (wish, desire, love and sensual pleasure), *Artha* (wealth, prosperity, glory), *Dharma* (righteousness, duty, morality, virtue, ethics, encompassing notions such as *ahimsa* (non-violence) and satya (truth)) and *Moksha* (liberation, i.e. liberation from Samsara, the cycle of reincarnation).

In all schools of Hinduism, the meaning of life is tied up in the concepts of karma (causal action), sansara (the cycle of birth and rebirth), and moksha (liberation). Existence is conceived as the progression of the atman (similar to the western concept of a soul) across numerous lifetimes, and its ultimate progression towards liberation from karma. Particular goals for life are generally subsumed under broader yogas (practices) or dharma (correct living) which are intended to create more favourable reincarnations, though they are generally positive acts in this life as well. Traditional schools of Hinduism often worship Devas which are manifestations of Ishvara (a personal or chosen God); these Devas are taken as ideal forms to be identified with, as a form of spiritual improvement.

Advaita and Dvaita Hinduism

Later schools reinterpreted the vedas to focus on Brahman, "The One Without a Second", as a central God-like figure.

In monist Advaita Vedanta, atman is ultimately indistinguishable from Brahman, and the goal of life is to know or realize that one's atman (soul) is identical to Brahman. To the Upanishads, whoever becomes fully aware of the atman, as one's core of self, realizes identity with Brahman, and, thereby, achieves Moksha (liberation, freedom).

Dualist Dvaita Vedanta and other bhakti schools have a dualist interpretation. Brahman is seen as a supreme being with a personality and manifest qualities. The atman depends upon Brahman for its existence; the meaning of life is achieving Moksha through love of God and upon His grace.

Vaishnavism

Another branch of Hinduism is Vaishnavism, where Vishnu is the principal deity. Not all schools of Vaishnavism teach a meaning to life, but Gaudiya Vaishnavism, for example, teaches Achintya Bheda Abheda meaning worship of a separate and single true God, Krishna, while all the living entities are eternal parts and parcels of the Supreme Personality of the Godhead Krishna. The constitutional position of a living entity is to serve the Lord with love and devotion. Uninterrupted, unmotivated voluntary service to Krishna and His devotees is the purpose of life in the liberated as well as conditioned state of life.

We were in the spiritual world serving Krishna blissfully in full knowledge as we are the eternal spirit souls. Because of our aversion to Krishna and due to the desire to enjoy separation from Krishna we are in this material world undergoing the repeated cyle of birth, disease, old age and death in the acquired bodies of 8.4 million species of life, transmigrating from one body to another according to our karma and desire. The purpose of human life especially is to think beyond the animalistic way of eating, sleeping, mating and defending and engage the higher intelligence to revive the lost relationship with Krishna, our eternal Father, from whom everything came, who is the sustainer and annihilator. The revealed scriptures like Bhagavad-Gita and Srimad Bhagavatam teach the Sambandha ("Who am I? Who is God? What is my relationship with God?"), Abhideya (the process of re-establishing that lost connection with the Lord through the 9 processes of Bhakti, or "Devotional Service") and Prayojana (the result, attaining the love of the Godhead). The simplest process is to chant the maha mantra "Hare Krishna Hare Krishna Krishna Krishna Hare Hare-Hare Rama Hare Rama Rama Rama Hare Hare" in the association of Lord's devotees. While the purpose of life is to revive the lost relationship with the all-loving Lord, the purpose of material creation is to utilize the resources to go back home to Godhead, the eternal spiritual world Goloka Vrindavana, the kingdom of Godhead.

Jainism

Jainism is a religion originating in ancient India, its ethical system promotes self-discipline above all else. Through following the ascetic teachings of Jina, a human achieves enlightenment (perfect knowledge). Jainism divides the universe into living and non-living beings. Only when the non-living become attached to the living does suffering result. Therefore, happiness is the result of self-conquest and freedom from external objects. The meaning of life may then be said to be to use the physical body to achieve self-realization and bliss.

Jains believe that every human is responsible for his or her actions and all living beings have an eternal soul, *jiva*. Jains believe all souls are equal because they all possess the potential of being liberated and attaining Moksha. The Jain view of karma is that every action, every word, every thought produces, besides its visible, an invisible, transcendental effect on the soul.

Jainism includes strict adherence to ahimsa (or *ahinsa*), a form of nonviolence that goes far beyond vegetarianism. Jains refuse food obtained with unnecessary cruelty. Many practice a lifestyle similar to veganism due to the violence of modern dairy farms, and others exclude root vegetables from their diets in order to preserve the lives of the plants from which they eat.

Buddhism

Early Buddhism: Buddhism is a nondual doctrine, in which subject, object, and action are all seen as illusory. Buddhists believe that life is inherent with suffering or frustration. This does not mean that there is no pleasure in life, but the pleasure does not cause everlasting happiness. The suffering is caused by attachment to objects material or non-material which in turn causes one to be born again and again in the cycle of existence. The Buddhist sutras and tantras do not speak about "the meaning of life" or "the purpose of life", but about the potential of human life to end suffering through detaching oneself from cravings and conceptual attachments. Suffering can be overcome through human activity, simply by removing the cause of suffering. Attaining and perfecting dispassion is a process of many levels that ultimately results in the state of Nirvana. Nirvana means freedom from both suffering and rebirth.

Theravada Buddhism is generally considered to be close to the early Buddhist practice. It promotes the concept of Vibhajjavada (Pali), literally "Teaching of Analysis", which says that insight must come from the aspirant's experience, critical investigation, and reasoning instead of by blind faith. However, the Theravadin tradition also emphasizes heeding the advice of the wise, considering such advice and evaluation of one's own experiences to be the two tests by which practices should be judged. The Theravadin goal is liberation (or freedom) from suffering, according to the Four Noble Truths. This is attained in the achievement of Nirvana, or Unbinding which also ends the repeated cycle of birth, old age, sickness and death.

Mahayana Buddhism

Mahayana Buddhist schools de-emphasize the traditional view (still practiced in Theravada) of the release from individual Suffering (Dukkha) and attainment of Awakening (Nirvana). In

Mahayana, the Buddha is seen as an eternal, immutable, inconceivable, omnipresent being. The fundamental principles of Mahayana doctrine are based on the possibility of universal liberation from suffering for all beings, and the existence of the transcendent Buddha-nature, which is the eternal Buddha essence present, but hidden and unrecognised, in all living beings.

Philosophical schools of Mahayana Buddhism, such as Chan/ Zen and the vajrayana Tibetan and Shingon schools, explicitly teach that boddhisattvas should refrain from full liberation, allowing themselves to be reincarnated into the world until all beings achieve enlightenment. Devotional schools such as Pure Land Buddhism seek the aid of celestial Buddhas—individuals who have spent lifetimes accumulating positive karma, and use that accumulation to aid all.

Sikhism

The monotheistic Sikh religion was founded by Guru Nanak Dev, the term "sikh" means student, which denotes that followers will lead their lives forever learning. This system of religious philosophy and expression has been traditionally known as the Gurmat (literally "the counsel of the gurus") or the Sikh Dharma. The followers of Sikhism are ordained to follow the teachings of the ten Sikh Gurus, or enlightened leaders, as well as the holy scripture entitled the *Guru Granth Sahib,* which includes selected works of many philosophers from diverse socio-economic and religious backgrounds.

The Sikh Gurus tell us that salvation can be obtained by following various spiritual paths, so Sikhs do not have a monopoly on salvation: "The Lord dwells in every heart, and every heart has its own way to reach Him." Sikhs believe that all people are equally important before God. Sikhs balance their moral and spiritual values with the quest for knowledge, and they aim to promote a life of peace and equality but also of positive action.

A key distinctive feature of Sikhism is a non-anthropomorphic concept of God, to the extent that one can interpret God as the Universe itself (pantheism). Sikhism thus sees life as an opportunity to understand this God as well as to discover the divinity which lies in each individual. While a full understanding of God is beyond human beings, Nanak described God as not wholly unknowable, and stressed that God must be seen from "the inward eye", or the "heart", of a human being: devotees must meditate to progress towards enlightenment. Nanak emphasized the revelation through meditation, as its rigorous application permits the existence of communication between God and human beings.

EAST ASIAN RELIGIONS

Shinto

Shinto is the native religion of Japan. Shinto means "the path of the kami", but more specifically, it can be taken to mean "the divine crossroad where the kami chooses his way". The "divine" crossroad signifies that all the universe is divine spirit. This foundation of free will, choosing one's way, means that life is a creative process.

Shinto wants life to live, not to die. Shinto sees death as pollution and regards life as the realm where the divine spirit seeks to purify itself by rightful self-development. Shinto wants individual human life to be prolonged forever on earth as a victory of the divine spirit in preserving its objective personality in its highest forms. The presence of evil in the world, as conceived by Shinto, does not stultify the divine nature by imposing on divinity responsibility for being able to relieve human suffering while refusing to do so. The sufferings of life are the sufferings of the divine spirit in search of progress in the objective world.

TAOISM

Taoist cosmogony emphasizes the need for all sentient beings and all man to return to the *primordial* or to rejoin with the *Oneness* of the Universe by way of self cultivation and self realization. All adherents should understand and be in tune with the ultimate truth.

Taoists believe all things were originally from Taiji and Tao, and the meaning in life for the adherents is to realize the temporal nature of the existence. "Only introspection can then help us to find our innermost reasons for living... the simple answer is here within ourselves."

Confucianism

Confucianism recognizes human nature in accordance with the need for discipline and education. Because mankind is driven by both positive and negative influences, Confucianists see a goal in achieving the good nature through strong relationships and reasoning as well as minimizing the negative energy. This emphasis on normal living is seen in the Confucianist scholar Tu Wei-Ming's quote, "we can realize the ultimate meaning of life in ordinary human existence."

NEW RELIGIONS

There are many new religious movements in East Asia, and some with millions of followers: Chondogyo, Tenrikyo, Cao Đai, and Seicho-No-Ie. New religions typically have unique explanations for the meaning of life. For example, in Tenrikyo, one is expected to live a Joyous Life by participating in practices that create happiness for oneself and others.

God in Buddhism

The refutation of the notion of a supreme God or a prime mover is seen as a key distinction between Buddhism and other views. Hence, Buddhism is often aptly described as a "spiritual philosophy" whose sole aim is the complete alleviation of stress in samsara, called nirvana. The Buddha explicitly rejects a creator, denies endorsing any views on creation and states that questions on the origin of the world are worthless. Some theists beginning Buddhist meditation believe that the notion of divinity is not incompatible with Buddhism, but belief in a Supreme God is eminently considered to pose a hindrance to the attainment of nirvana, the highest goal of Buddhist practice.

Despite this nontheism, Buddhists consider veneration of the Noble ones very important although the two main schools of Buddhism differ mildly in their reverential attitudes. While Theravada Buddhists view the Buddha as a human being who attained nirvana or arahanthood, through human efforts, some Mahayana Buddhists consider him an embodiment of the *Dharmakaya,* who was born for the benefit of others, and not merely a human being. In addition, some Mahayana Buddhists worship their chief Bodhisattva, Avalokiteshvara and hope to embody him.

Buddhists accept the existence of beings in higher realms, known as *devas,* but they, like humans, are said to be suffering in samsara, and not particularly wiser than us. In fact the Buddha is often portrayed as a teacher of the gods, and superior to them.

God in Early Buddhism

As scholar Richard Hayes describes, "the attitude of the Buddha as portrayed in the Nikayas is more anti-speculative than specifically atheistic," although "Gautama regarded the belief in God as unhealthy."

As Hayes describes it, "In the Nikaya literature, the question of the existence of God is treated primarily from either an epistemological point of view or a moral point of view. As a problem of epistemology, the question of God's existence amounts to a discussion of whether or not a religious seeker can be certain that there is a greatest good and that therefore his efforts to realize a greatest good will not be a pointless struggle towards an unrealistic goal. And as a problem in morality, the question amounts to a discussion of whether man himself is ultimately responsible for all the displeasure that he feels or whether there exists a superior being who inflicts displeasure upon man whether he deserves it or not...the Buddha Gautama is portrayed not as an atheist who claims to be able to prove God's nonexistence, but rather as a skeptic with respect to other teachers' claims to be able to lead their disciples to the highest good." Citing the *Devadaha Sutta,* the one hundred first discourse in the *Majjhima Nikaya,* Hayes remarks "while the reader is left to conclude that it is attachment rather than God, actions in past lives, fate, type of birth or efforts in this life that is responsible for our experiences of sorrow, no systematic argument is given in an attempt to disprove the existence of God."

Brahma in the Pali Canon

Brahma is among the common gods found in the Pali Canon. Brahma (in common with all other devas) is subject to change, final decline and death, just as are all other sentient beings in samsara (the plane of continual reincarnation and suffering). In fact there are several different Brahma worlds and several kinds of Brahmas in Buddhism, all of which however are just beings stuck in samsara for a long while. Sir Charles Eliot describes attitudes towards Brahma in early Buddhism as follows:

"There comes a time when this world system passes away and then certain beings are reborn in the "World of Radiance" and remain there a long time. Sooner or later, the world system begins to evolve again and the palace of Brahma appears, but it is empty. Then some being whose time is up falls from the "World of Radiance" and comes to life in the palace and remains there alone. At last he wishes for company, and it so happens that other beings whose time is up fall from the "World of Radiance" and join him. And the first being thinks that he is Great Brahma, the Creator, because when he felt lonely and wished for companions other beings appeared. And the other beings accept this view. And at last one of Brahma's retinue falls from that state and is born in the human world and, if he can remember his previous birth, he reflects that he is transitory but that Brahma still remains and from this he draws the erroneous conclusion that Brahma is eternal."

Other Common Gods Referred to in the Canon

Many of the other gods in the Pali Canon find a common mythological role in Hindu literature. Some common gods and goddesses are Indra, Aapo (Varuna), Vayo (Vayu), Tejo (Agni), Surya, Pajapati (Prajapati), Soma, Yasa, Venhu (Visnu), Mahadeva (Siva), Vijja (Saraswati), Usha, Pathavi (Prithvi) Sri (Lakshmi) Kuvera (Kubera), several yakkhas (Yakshas), gandhabbas (Gandharvas), Nanas, garula (Garuda), sons of Bali, Veroca, etc. While in Hindu texts some of these gods and goddesses are considered embodiments of the Supreme Being. The Buddhist view was that all gods and goddesses were bound to samsara. The world of gods according to the Buddha presents a being with too many pleasures and distractions.

Abhidharma and Yogacara Analysis

The Theravada Abhidhamma tradition did not tend to elaborate argumentation against the existence of god, but in the *Abhidharmakoœa* of the Sarvastivada, Vasubandhu does actively argue against the existence of a creator god.

The Chinese monk Xuanzang studied Buddhism in India during the 7th century CE, staying at Nalanda University. There, he studied the Consciousness Only teachings passed down from Asanga and Vasubandhu, and taught to him by the abbot Silabhadra. In his comprehensive work *Cheng Weishi Lun* (Skt. *Vijnaptimatratasiddhi Uastra*), Xuanzang refutes the Indian philosophical doctrine of a "Great Lord" (Ishvara) or a Great Brahma, a self-existent and omnipotent creator deity who is ruler of all existence.

> *"According to one doctrine, there is a great, self-existent deity whose substance is real and who is all-pervading, eternal, and the producer of all phenomena. This doctrine is unreasonable. If something produces something, it is not eternal, the non-eternal is not all-pervading, and what is not all-pervading is not real. If the deity's substance is all-pervading and eternal, it must contain all powers and be able to produce all phenomena everywhere, at all times, and simultaneously. If he produces phenomena when a desire arises, or according to conditions, this contradicts the doctrine of a single cause. Or else, desires and conditions would arise spontaneously since the cause is eternal. Other doctrines claim that there is a great Brahma, a Time, a Space, a Starting Point, a Nature, an Ether, a Self, etc., that is eternal and really exists, is endowed with all powers, and is able to produce all phenomena. We refute all these in the same way we did the concept of the Great Lord."*

Mahayana and Vajrayana Doctrines

In the pramana tradition, Dharmakirti advances a number of arguments against the existence of a creator god in his

Pramanavarttikakarika, following in the footsteps of Vasubandhu. Later Mahayana scholars such as Uantarakcita and Kamalauila continued this tradition.

Tathagatagarbha and God

Mahayana Buddhism, unlike Theravada, talks of the mind using terms such as "the womb of the Thus-come One". Such positive statements arose as a correction of the common misunderstanding that emptiness is the same as nothingness – a nihilistic view.

The affirmation of emptiness by positive terminology is radically different from the early Buddhist doctrines of Anatta and refusal to personify or objectify any Supreme Reality. Mahayana Buddhism includes a sphere of devotion, where the Buddha is taken as the Supreme Reality – a kind of God who assumed human form in order to benefit all humanity:

> *"Mahayana Buddhism is not only intellectual, but it is also devotional... in Mahayana, Buddha was taken as God, as Supreme Reality itself that descended on the earth in human form for the good of mankind. The concept of Buddha (as equal to God in theistic systems) was never as a creator but as Divine Love that out of compassion (*karuna*) embodied itself in human form to uplift suffering humanity. He was worshipped with fervent devotion... He represents the Absolute (*paramartha satya*), devoid of all plurality (*sarva-prapancanta-vinirmukta*) and has no beginning, middle and end... Buddha... is eternal, immutable... As such He represents Dharmakaya."*

According to the Tathagatagarbha sutras, the Buddha taught the existence of a spiritual essence called the tathagagatagarbha or Buddha-nature, which is present in all beings and phenomena.

Dr. B. Alan Wallace writes of this doctrine:

> *"the essential nature of the whole of samsara and nirvana is the absolute space (*dhatu*) of the* tathagatagarbha*, but this space is not to be confused with a mere absence of matter. Rather, this absolute space is imbued with all the infinite knowledge, compassion, power, and enlightened activities of the Buddha. Moreover, this luminous space is that which causes the phenom-*

enal world to appear, and it is none other than the nature of one's own mind, which by nature is clear light."

Vajrayana Views

In some Mahayana traditions, the Buddha is indeed worshipped as a virtual divinity who is possessed of supernatural qualities and powers. Dr. Guang Xing writes: "The Buddha worshipped by Mahayanist followers is an omnipotent divinity endowed with numerous supernatural attributes and qualities...[He] is described almost as an omnipotent and almighty godhead."

Buddhist scholar, Dr. B. Alan Wallace, has also indicated that saying that Buddhism as a whole is 'non-theistic' may be an over-simplification. Wallace discerns similarities between some forms of Vajrayana Buddhism and notions of a divine 'ground of being' and creation.

He writes: "a careful analysis of Vajrayana Buddhist cosmogony, specifically as presented in the Atiyoga tradition of Indo-Tibetan Buddhism, which presents itself as the culmination of all Buddhist teachings, reveals a theory of a transcendent ground of being and a process of creation that bear remarkable similarities with views presented in Vedanta and Neoplatonic Western Christian theories of creation." In fact, Wallace sees these views as so similar that they seem almost to be different manifestations of the same theory. He further comments: "Vajrayana Buddhism, Vedanta, and Neoplatonic Christianity have so much in common that they could almost be regarded as varying interpretations of a single theory."

Yogacara and the Absolute

Another scholar sees a Buddhist Absolute in Consciousness. Writing on the Yogacara school of Buddhism, Dr. A. K. Chatterjee remarks: "The Absolute is a non-dual consciousness. The duality of the subject and object does not pertain to it. It is said to be void (*sunya*), devoid of duality; in itself it is perfectly real, in fact the only reality...There is no consciousness *of* the Absolute; Consciousness *is* the Absolute."

While this is a traditional Tibetan interpretation of Yogacara views, it has been rejected by modern Western scholarship, namely by Kochumuttom, Anacker, Kalupahana, Dunne, Lusthaus, Powers, and Wayman.. Scholar Dan Lusthaus writes: "They [Yogacarins] did not focus on consciousness to assert it as ultimately real (Yogacara claims consciousness is only conventionally real since it arises from moment to moment due to fluctuating causes and conditions), but rather because it is the cause of the karmic problem they are seeking to eliminate."

Zen and the Absolute

A further name for the irreducible, time-and-space-transcending mysterious Truth or Essence of Buddhic Reality spoken of in some Mahayana and tantric texts is the Dharmakaya (Body of Truth). Of this the Zen Buddhist master Sokei-An, says:

> ... dharmakaya *[is] the equivalent of God... The Buddha also speaks of no time and no space, where if I make a sound there is in that single moment a million years. It is spaceless like radio waves, like electric space-intrinsic. The Buddha said that there is a mirror that reflects consciousness. In this electric space a million miles and a pinpoint-a million years and a moment-are exactly the same. It is pure essence... We call it 'original consciousness'-'original* akasha'*-perhaps God in the Christian sense. I am afraid of speaking about anything that is not familiar to me. No one can know what IT is...*

The same Zen adept, Sokei-An, further comments: The creative power of the universe is not a human being; it is Buddha. The one who sees, and the one who hears, is not this eye or ear, but the one who is *this* consciousness. *This One* is Buddha. *This One* appears in every mind. *This One* is common to all sentient beings, and is God.

The Rinzai Zen Buddhist master, Soyen Shaku, speaking to Americans at the beginning of the 20th century, discusses how in essence the idea of God is not absent from Buddhism, when understood as ultimate, true Reality:

At the outset, let me state that Buddhism is not atheistic as the term is ordinarily understood. It has certainly a God, the highest reality and truth, through which and in which this universe exists. However, the followers of Buddhism usually avoid the term God, for it savors so much of Christianity, whose spirit is not always exactly in accord with the Buddhist interpretation of religious experience... To define more exactly the Buddhist notion of the highest being, it may be convenient to borrow the term very happily coined by a modern German scholar, 'panentheism', according to which God is... all and one and more than the totality of existence.... As I mentioned before, Buddhists do not make use of the term God, which characteristically belongs to Christian terminology. An equivalent most commonly used is Dharmakaya... When the Dharmakaya is most concretely conceived it becomes the Buddha, or Tathagata...

Primordial Buddhas

Theories regarding a self-existent "ground of being" were common in India prior to the Buddha, and were rejected by him: "The Buddha, however, refusing to admit any metaphysical principle as a common thread holding the moments of encountered phenomena together, rejects the Upanishadic notion of an immutable substance or principle underlying the world and the person and producing phenomena out of its inherent power, be it 'being', atman, brahman, or 'god.'"

In later Mahayana literature, however, the idea of an eternal, all-pervading, all-knowing, immaculate, uncreated and deathless Ground of Being (the *dharmadhatu*, inherently linked to the *sattvadhatu*, the realm of beings), which is the Awakened Mind (*bodhicitta*) or Dharmakaya ("body of Truth") of the Buddha himself, is attributed to the Buddha in a number of Mahayana sutras, and is found in various tantras as well. In some Mahayana texts, such a principle is occasionally presented as manifesting in a more personalised form as a primordial Buddha, such as Samantabhadra, Vajradhara, Vairochana, and Adi-Buddha, among others.

In some Buddhist tantric and Dzogchen scriptures, too, this immanent and transcendent Dharmakaya (the ultimate essence of the Buddha's being) is portrayed as the primordial Buddha, Samantabhadra, worshipped as the primordial lord. In a study of

Dzogchen, Dr. Sam van Schaik mentions how Samantabhadra Buddha is indeed seen as 'the heart essence of all Buddhas, the Primordial Lord, the noble Victorious One, Samantabhadra'. Dr. Schaik indicates that Samantabhadra is not to be viewed as some kind of separate *mindstream*, apart from the mindstreams of sentient beings, but should be known as a universal nirvanic principle termed the Awakened Mind (*bodhi-citta*) and present in all. Dr. Schaik quotes from the tantric texts, *Experiencing the Enlightened Mind of Samantabhadra* and *The Subsequent Tantra of Great Perfection Instruction* to portray Samantabhadra as an uncreated, reflexive, radiant, pure and vital Knowing (gnosis) which is present in all things: 'The essence of all phenomena is the awakened mind; the mind of all Buddhas is the awakened mind; and the life-force of all sentient beings is the awakened mind, too ... This unfabricated gnosis of the present moment is the reflexive luminosity, naked and stainless, the Primordial Lord himself.'

The Shingon Buddhist monk, Dohan, regarded the two great Buddhas, Amida and Vairocana, as one and the same Dharmakaya Buddha and as the true nature at the core of all beings and phenomena.

There are several realisations that can accrue to the Shingon practitioner of which Dohan speaks in this connection, as Dr. James Sanford points out: there is the realisation that Amida is the Dharmakaya Buddha, Vairocana; then there is the realisation that Amida as Vairocana is eternally manifest within this universe of time and space; and finally there is the innermost realisation that Amida is the true nature, material and spiritual, of all beings, that he is 'the omnivalent wisdom-body, that he is the unborn, unmanifest, unchanging reality that rests quietly at the core of all phenomena'.

Similar God-like descriptions are encountered in the *All-Creating King Tantra* (Kunjed Gyalpo Tantra), where the universal Mind of Awakening (in its mode as "Samantabhadra Buddha") declares of itself: I am the core of all that exists. I am the seed of all that exists. I am the cause of all that exists. I am the trunk of all that exists. I am the foundation of all that exists. I am the root of existence. I am "the core" because I contain all phenomena. I am "the seed" because I give birth to everything. I am "the cause" because all comes from me. I am "the trunk" because the ramifications of every event sprout from me. I am "the foundation" because all abides in me. I am called "the root" because I am everything.

The Karandavyuha Sutra presents the great bodhisattva, Avalokitesvara, as a kind of supreme lord of the cosmos. A striking feature of Avalokitesvara in this sutra is his creative power, as he is said to be the progenitor of various heavenly bodies and divinities. Dr. Alexander Studholme, in his monograph on the sutra, writes: 'The sun and moon are said to be born from the bodhisattva's eyes, Mahesvara [Siva] from his brow, Brahma from his shoulders, Narayana [Vishnu] from his heart, Sarasvati from his teeth, the winds from his mouth, the earth from his feet and the sky from his stomach.'

Avalokitesvara himself is linked in the versified version of the sutra to the first Buddha, the Adi Buddha, who is 'svayambhu' (self-existent, not born from anything or anyone).

Dr. Studholme comments: "Avalokitesvara himself, the verse sutra adds, is an emanation of the *Adibuddha*, or 'primordial Buddha', a term that is explicitly said to be synoymous with *Svayambhu* and *Adinatha*, 'primordial lord'."

THE ETERNAL BUDDHA OF SHIN BUDDHISM

In Shin Buddhism, Amida Buddha is viewed as the eternal Buddha who manifested as Shakyamuni in India and who is the personification of Nirvana itself. The Shin Buddhist priest, John Paraskevopoulos, in his monograph on Shin Buddhism, writes:

> *'In Shin Buddhism, Nirvana or Ultimate Reality (also known as the "Dharma-Body" or* Dharmakaya *in the original Sanskrit) has assumed a more concrete form as (a) the Buddha of Infinite Light* (Amitabha) *and Infinite Life* (Amitayus) *and (b) the "Pure Land" or "Land of Utmost Bliss"* (Sukhavati)*, the realm over which this Buddha is said to preside... Amida is the Eternal Buddha who is said to have taken form as Shakyamuni and his teachings in order to become known to us in ways we can readily comprehend.'*

John Paraskevopoulos elucidates the notion of Nirvana, of which Amida is an embodiment, in the following terms:

> '... *[Nirvana's] more positive connotation is that of a higher state of being, the dispelling of illusion and the corresponding joy of liberation. An early Buddhist scripture describes Nirvana as:... the far shore, the subtle, the very difficult to see, the undisintegrating, the unmanifest, the peaceful, the deathless, the sublime, the auspicious, the secure, the destruction of craving, the wonderful, the amazing, the unailing, the unafflicted, dispassion, purity, freedom, the island, the shelter, the asylum, the refuge...* (Samyutta Nikaya)'

This Nirvana is seen as eternal and of one nature, indeed as the essence of all things. Paraskevopoulos tells of how the *Mahaparinirvana Sutra* speaks of Nirvana as eternal, pure, blissful and true self:

> '*In Mahayana Buddhism it is taught that there is fundamentally one reality which, in its highest and purest dimension, is experienced as Nirvana. It is also known, as we have seen, as the Dharma-Body (considered as the ultimate form of Being) or "Suchness"* (Tathata *in Sanskrit) when viewed as the essence of all things... "The Dharma-Body is eternity, bliss, true self and purity. It is forever free of all birth, ageing, sickness and death"* (Nirvana Sutra)'

To attain this Self, however, it is needful to transcend the 'small self' and its pettiness with the help of an 'external' agency, Amida Buddha. This is the view promulgated by the Jodo Shinshu founding Buddhist master, Shinran Shonin. John Paraskevopoulos comments on this:

> '*Shinran's great insight was that we cannot conquer the self by the self. Some kind of external agency is required: (a) to help us to shed light on our ego as it really is in all its petty and baneful guises; and (b) to enable us to subdue the small 'self' with a view to realising the Great Self by awakening to Amida's light.*'

When that Great Self of Amida's light is realised, Shin Buddhism is able to see the Infinite which transcends the care-worn mundane. John Paraskevopoulos concludes his monograph on Shin Buddhism thus: 'It is time we discarded the tired view of Buddhism as a dry and forensic rationalism, lacking in warmth and devotion... By hearing the call of Amida Buddha we become awakened to true reality and its unfathomable working... to live a life that dances jubilantly in the resplendent light of the Infinite.'

Devas and the Supernatural in Buddhism

While Buddhist traditions do not deny the existence of supernatural beings (e.g., the *devas*, of which many are discussed in Buddhist scripture), it does not ascribe powers, in the typical Western sense, for creation, salvation or judgement, to the "gods". They are regarded as having the power to affect worldly events in much the same way as humans and animals have the power to do so. Just as humans can affect the world more than animals, *devas* can affect the world more than humans. While gods may be more powerful than humans, none of them are absolute (unsurpassed).

Most importantly, gods, like humans, are also suffering in samsara, the ongoing cycle of death and subsequent rebirth. Gods have not attained nirvana, and are still subject to emotions, including jealousy, anger, delusion, sorrow, etc. Thus, since a Buddha shows the way to nirvana, a Buddha is called "the teacher of the gods and humans". According to the Pali Canon the gods have powers to affect only so far as their realm of influence or control allows them. In this sense therefore, they are no closer to nirvana than humans and no wiser in the ultimate sense. A dialogue between the king Pasenadi Kosala, his general Vidudabha and the historical Buddha reveals a lot about the relatively weaker position of gods in Buddhism.

Though not believing in a creator God, Buddhists inherited the Indian cosmology of the time which includes various types of 'god' realms such as the Heaven of the Thirty-Three, the Four Great Kings, and so on. Deva-realms are part of the various possible types of existence in the Buddhist cosmology. Rebirth as a deva is attributed to virtuous actions performed in previous lives. Beings that had meditated are thought to be reborn in more and more subtle realms with increasingly vast life spans, in accord with their meditative ability. In particular, the highest deva realms are pointed out as false paths in meditation that the meditator should be aware of. Like any existence within the cycle of rebirth (samsara), a life as a deva is only temporary. At the time of death, a large part of the former deva's good karma has been expended, leaving mostly negative karma and a likely rebirth in one of the three lower realms. Therefore, Buddhists make a special effort not to be reborn in deva realms.

It is also noteworthy that devas in Buddhism have no role to play in liberation. Sir Charles Eliot describes God in early Buddhism as follows:

> *The attitude of early Buddhism to the spirit world — the hosts of deities and demons who people this and other spheres. Their existence is assumed, but the truths of religion are not dependent on them, and attempts to use their influence by sacrifices and oracles are deprecated as vulgar practices similar to juggling.*

The systems of philosophy then in vogue were mostly not theistic, and, strange as the words may sound, religion had little to do with the gods. If this be thought to rest on a mistranslation, it is certainly true that the dhamma had very little to do with devas.

Often as the Devas figure in early Buddhist stories, the significance of their appearance nearly always lies in their relations with the Buddha or his disciples. Of mere mythology, such as the dealings of Brahma and Indra with other gods, there is little. In fact the gods, though freely invoked as accessories, are not taken seriously, and there are some extremely curious passages in which Gautama seems to laugh at them, much as the sceptics of the 18th century laughed at Jehovah. Thus in the [Pali Canon] Kevaddha Sutta he relates how a monk who was puzzled by a metaphysical problem applied to various gods and finally accosted Brahma himself in the presence of all his retinue. After hearing the question, which was "Where do the elements cease and leave no trace behind?" Brahma replies, "I am the Great Brahma, the Supreme, the Mighty, the All-seeing, the Ruler, the Lord of all, the Controller, the Creator, the Chief of all, appointing to each his place, the

Ancient of days, the Father of all that are and are to be." "But," said the monk, "I did not ask you, friend, whether you were indeed all you now say, but I ask you where the four elements cease and leave no trace." Then the Great Brahma took him by the arm and led him aside and said, "These gods think I know and understand everything. Therefore I gave no answer in their presence. But I do not know the answer to your question and you had better go and ask the Buddha."

The Pali Canon also attributes supernatural powers to enlightened beings (Buddhas), that even gods may not have. In a dialogue between king Ajatasattu and the Buddha, enlightened beings are ascribed supranormal powers (like human flight, walking on water etc.), clairaudience, mind reading, recollection of past lives of oneself and others. Yet, according to the Buddha, an enlightened person realizes the futility of these powers and instead unbinds himself completely from *samsara* through discernment.

BUDDHISM AND OTHER RELIGIONS

The Buddha-Dhamma, or Buddhism, can be related to other religions in many ways. Here, only a few main points of comparison will be sketched.

Buddhism is a graduated system of moral and mental training with Nibbana, the highest happiness, as its goal. It is founded upon the principle of causality, the law of cause and effect in the moral domain, that is, in the field of human behavior. Above all, it is a path to liberation from suffering, a goal to be won by cultivating the Noble Eightfold Path in its three stages of morality, concentration, and wisdom *(sila, samadhi, pañña).*

Religion lays down the general lines of conduct by which a person will live his daily life; it lays down rules in such matters as respect for the lives of others, intoxicating liquors, marriage, divorce, and means of livelihood. For the believer it thus colors his or her whole attitude towards matters like birth, sex, family limitation, death, and the afterlife. Transgression of the religious code entails feelings of guilt, so the religion that one follows has a profound influence, shaping one's entire outlook on life as well as one's attitudes, whether in wholesome ways or in unwholesome ways.

Against this background, we can now see how the Buddha-Dhamma is related to other religions.

As stated earlier, the Buddhist way to Nibbana is the Noble Eightfold Path. The question then arises as to whether arahantship — perfect holiness — or Nibbana is possible outside this path. The Buddha's answer to Subhadda's question, just before he passed away, clarifies our problem: "In whatever teaching, O Subhadda, there exists the Noble Eightfold Path, there is the first saint *(sotapanna)*, there is the second saint *(sakadagami)*, there is the third saint *(anagami)*, there is the fourth saint *(arahant)*. An arahant is a perfect saint. Elsewhere there are mere semblances of saints." As the Noble Eightfold Path is found only in Buddhism, in the Buddha's own words "the other teachings are empty of true saints."

They therefore err who say that all spiritual paths lead to the same summit and that the view from the top is identical for all. The reason is simple: the Buddha saw the true nature of things clearly and completely with his own independent supramundane insight — his perfect enlightenment — and so his teaching is an exact reflection of reality, while other religious teachers had only an imperfect view of reality, with eyes dimmed by various forms and degrees of ignorance *(avijja)*.

This, however, does not imply that Buddhism is intolerant of other religions. Neither the Buddha nor his followers ever imposed his system of thought or his way of life on anyone who would not accept it of his or her own volition. Acceptance was a purely voluntary matter. Even if accepted, how much of it one should practice is one's own responsibility. But regardless of one's personal inclinations, the universal moral laws operate objectively — action being followed by due reaction, deeds by their fruits. The Buddha merely reveals the laws of life, and the more faithfully we follow them, the better it is for us, for then we act according to the Dhamma.

This peaceful policy of non-compulsion and tolerance, characteristic of the Master's teaching, is born partly of compassion and partly of understanding human nature and the nature of truth. If the vision of some is dimmed as to the merits of the teaching it is one's duty to help them to see. But one must stop there: one should not coerce others or persecute those who refuse to accept one's own beliefs. Wisdom, the ability to see things as they truly are, cannot be imposed on others from the outside. It must grow from within the individual, out of the developing sensitivity and refinement of human nature. This takes time. At any given period only few will be capable of genuinely appreciating, understanding, and realizing the Buddha's teaching, as human beings vary widely in their intellectual, moral, and spiritual capabilities. Unethical conversions are therefore unheard of in Buddhism.

Buddhist tolerance, however, should not mean apathy and indifference. That would be a misinterpretation of the term. When erroneous statements about Buddhism were made by people in the Buddha's time, the Master kindly corrected them. He even expelled his cousin Devadatta from the Sangha when occasion demanded it to preserve the purity of the Doctrine and the unity of the Sangha. Yet the Buddha was the perfect example of tolerance and compassion. Likewise monk and laity should be always watchful and should emulate the Buddha. Otherwise their case would go by default, for which they alone are to be blamed. Today various proposals are being made to create an all-embracing system of religion, the idea being simply to absorb all other religions into one's own. However, a universal religious consciousness can never be created because: (1) the various religions have fundamentally different conceptions of reality; (2) the concept and content of the good life vary between different religions — the good means one thing to a Buddhist, and another to a Christian, and yet another to a Muslim; and (3) no adherent of a religion wants his religion to be absorbed by another body. Is it not deeply rooted in human nature to believe that no other religion in the world compares with one's own?

Taking Buddhism specifically — and in detail — it is unique, a thing apart from all other religions in the world. It teaches the formula of conditioned arising *(paticca-samuppada)* and its reversal by human effort; craving as the creator of life instead of a creator

God; a becoming *(bhava)* without a self *(atta)*; personal evolution according to the quality of one's own deeds *(kamma)*; an impersonal moral order *(kamma-niyama)* with moral values and moral responsibility; free will, within limits, and therewith the possibility of a good life; survival after death by the continuity of the individual life-flux without transmigration of an individual, immutable, immortal soul; and a transcendental reality (Nibbana), realizable here and now solely by one's own effort. As such, there are major and unbridgeable differences between Buddhism and the other world religions and spiritual philosophies. The attempt to find a common denominator in the uncommon, or to adapt the Dhamma so that it does not differ from the other religions, must necessarily fail. It will only end in the debasement of the Buddha-Dhamma or in its total extinction by painless absorption.

The idea of a universal religion is both unrealistic and impracticable, a mere mirage and an idle delusion. In contrast, over 2500 years ago, the Buddha offered another way of relating religions to each other based on mutual respect yet maintaining the separate identity of each religion. To practice this method one need not become a Buddhist. It is also very practical, effective, and does no violence or offense to anyone. It is simply to cultivate regularly four basic social and ethical attitudes: (1) *metta* — a friendly feeling of loving-kindness to all beings in every situation regardless of race, creed, or caste; (2) *karuna*— compassion for all who suffer, and to take practical steps whenever possible to eliminate or alleviate those sufferings; (3) *mudita* — altruistic joy, to be happy in others' happiness, in their prosperity and success, thereby counteracting feelings of jealousy and unhealthy rivalry between individuals and groups; and (4) *upekkha* — equanimity, the maintenance of an even mind when faced with the ups and downs inherent in life. By practicing these virtues daily, a Christian becomes a better Christian, a Hindu a better Hindu, a Muslim a better Muslim. All of these qualities convey a universal message that make the practitioners universal human beings. Surely, this is universalism in religion par excellence.

This is the most satisfactory way of living harmoniously with one's fellow men and women of all faiths, fostering inter-religious goodwill and avoiding religious conflicts. By pursuing this policy for over 2500 years, there have been no religious wars in Buddhism. It is also the best method of relating the Buddha's Teaching to other religions.

Buddhism, to repeat, is unique — a thing apart from all other religions in the world. While at all times maintaining its separate identity, it should peacefully coexist with other religions, following a policy of live-and-let-live. Such a policy has paid rich dividends in the past and will continue to do so in the future. Monks and laypersons in Sri Lanka should remember this, for the good of the Sasana and the well-being of the country.

In addition, every Buddhist should:

1. live his daily life in accordance with the Master's Teaching by observing the Five Precepts, thereby showing to all that the Buddha-Dhamma yet lives and daily rules his life;
2. support only genuine bhikkhus who observe the rules of discipline (Vinaya) to ensure the purity of the Sangha;
3. give with discrimination to Buddhist causes and to humanitarian projects, as cautioned by the Buddha — to the most deserving the things most needed, as funds are limited;
4. help make known abroad his message of wisdom and compassion.

3

Buddhism in India

Buddhism arose in India and flourished for a long time. It eventually declined and disappeared from most regions of India around 13th century, but not without leaving a significant impact. In Himalayan areas like Ladakh, Arunachal Pradesh and Sikkim, Buddhist practice was continued. It has reemerged as a major faith in India in the past century.

CHARACTERISTICS

Nikaya

- Theravada is the single remaining representative of the eighteen (or twenty) Nikaya schools of Indian Buddhism, which are sometimes referred to by the controversial term Hinayana. Theravada is now practiced mainly in Sri Lanka, Myanmar, Thailand, Cambodia, and Laos.
- Another prominent Nikaya school was the Sarvastivada, much of the doctrine of which was incorporated into Tibetan Buddhism. It included one of the main branches of Indian Abhidharma that was instrumental in the creation of Yogacara doctrine. Its system of monastic rules Vinaya is still used in Tibetan Buddhism and is also somewhat influential in monastic Chinese Buddhism.

Mahayana

For a full discussion of Mahayana Buddhism:

- Madhyamaka (Middle Way), of which the most significant thinker is Nagarjuna

- Yogacara founded by Asanga and Vasubandhu. Also known as Cittamatra, Vijnanavada (Mind Only, Consciousness-Mind Only).
- Tathagatagarbha A tenet of Indian and East Asian Buddhist thought based on the third turning of the wheel of dharma and central to Yogacara.

Vajrayana

A form of Indian Buddhism that emerged in roughly the 7th century AD and later became widespread in Tibet, and also found in Japan.

History

For a full account of the spread of Buddhism in India and beyond, see the History of Buddhism and the Decline of Buddhism in India.

Modern Revival

At the beginning of the 20th century, Buddhism was almost non-existent in India (Buddhists represented under 5% of the total population of India at the time), the land of its origin. Certain tribal groups in Bengal continued to follow Buddhism, as did peoples in Ladakh and Sikkim where Tibetan culture was influential, but these groups were on the margins of Indian society.

Anagarika Dharmapala and his Followers

The original objective of the Maha Bodhi Society was to restore the glory of the Mahabodhi Temple at Bodh Gaya. But later, the scope of the its activities expanded to involve the promotion of Buddhism in India. In June 1892, a meeting of Buddhists was organized at Darjeeling. Dharmapala spoke to the Tibetian Buddhists and presented a relic of the Buddha to be sent to the Dalai Lama.

After decline of Buddhism in India, the Mahabodhi Temple was under the control of a Hindu *mahant* (abbott). Dharmapala started a campaign to return control of the temple to Buddhists. A long legal battle ensued, which Dharmapala lost in 1906.

Dharmapala built many viharas and temples in India, including the one at Sarnath, the place of Buddha's first sermon. He died in 1933, the same year he was ordained a bhikkhu. After India gained independence, the control passed from the Hindu *mahant* to the Bihar State Government of Bihar, which established a temple management committee. The first monk under the management committee was Anagarika Munindra, a member of the Maha Bodhi Society.

Dharmapala considered Buddhism an Aryan religion and stated that the next Buddha will be born in the Brahmin caste, in the city of Benares, which will then be called *Ketumati*. He also said that the Vedic Brahmanism, Zorastrianism, Muhammedanism, Judaism, Christianity, Confucianism and Saiva Vedantism were "destructive religions". He considered *Buddhagama* (Buddhism), Jainism and Vaishnavism as the only non-destructive religions. He considered Buddhism as the oldest religion and the "only religion that stands by itself":

"Christianity and Islam are alien to the people in spirit; Brahmanism is only for the high castes; and the only religion that can help the teeming millions of India is the religion of Compassion of the Buddha, the Aryan prince of the solar line of Ikshvaku."

The Maha Bodhi Society mainly attracted upper-caste people.

DALIT BUDDHIST MOVEMENT

A Buddhist revivalist movement among Dalit Indians was initiated in 1890s by Dalit leaders such as Iyothee Thass, Brahmananda Reddy, and Dharmananda Kosambi. Sri Lankan Buddhist monks played big role for Dalit Buddhist movement in India.. In, 1956 B. R. Ambedkar converted to Buddhism along with followers, giving a major impetus to the Dalit Buddhist movement in India.

Others

Dharmananda Damodar Kosambi, a Goan, was another important Buddhist thinker of India.

S. N. Goenka, a meditation teacher trained in Burma is an active Buddhist leader in India. Goenka plans to build a stupa. The most significant part of this structure is that it will be more than twice as large as the presently largest dome structure in the world, namely the Gol Gumbaz at Bijapur in India. The stones are to be placed to form a load bearing dome structure without supporting pillars inside the hall.

British Involvement

British Buddhists have played a role in revival of Buddhism in India through the work of the Karuna Trust, a London-based Buddhist charity set up by members of the Western Buddhist Order and part of the FWBO.

The Karuna Trust's work is inspired by Dr. Ambedkar and seeks to work towards his vision of liberty, equality, fraternity and justice. Karuna's work is also inspired by Sangharakshita, the founder of the Western Buddhist Order, who met Dr. Ambedkar in India. Sangharakshita deeply moved by the situation facing Dalit people, and addressed followers of Dr. Ambedkar at mass public meetings after the latter's death.

The Karuna Trust was set up in 1980 by some of Sangharakshita's disciples to address the great material suffering and poverty experienced by millions of Dalit people across India. Through educational and training projects in India and Bangladesh, Karuna supports and enable of some of the world's most disadvantaged people, who are marginalised.

Friends of the Western Buddhist Order (FWBO) is a Buddhist movement that was founded in the UK by Sangharakshita (formerly Dennis Lingwood) in 1967, followed by the Western Buddhist Order in 1968. In 1978 Indian wing of the FWBO founded, known as the Trailokya Bauddha Mahasangha Sahayaka Gana.

Japanese Involvement

A Japanese organization called the Ogawa Trust maintains Nagarjuna Hospital at Mansar, an English language school for poor students, an orphanage, cooperative home industries for women, and various other kinds of aid. The Ogawa Trust has also helped in the building of an ornate Buddhist temple at Kampti, a town near Nagpur.

An emerging religious organization called Soka Gakkai International has a chapter in India called Bharat Soka Gakkai. The group was first recognized by the Indian Government in 1986. However, the world-wide organization has been often been called a cult by it's critics; It's current leader, Daisaku Ikeda, has also been called a cult figure.

Taiwanese Involvement

Taiwanese Buddhists have contributed to the growth of Buddhism in India in multiple ways, one of which is in the ordination of Theravadin nuns. Taiwan, with one of the most active groups of nuns in the world, has begun to facilitate the ordination of women in India. In February 1998 a full ordination ceremony was held at Bodh Gaya by Taiwan's Fo Guang Shan Monastery. 132 applicants arrived to receive ordination as nuns and undertook a nine day period of training and questioning. Of these candidates 66 were from South Asia, and of these at least twenty-eight were from Maharashtra.

HISTORY OF BUDDHISM IN INDIA

Buddhism is a Dharmic religion originating in ancient India. A brief history of major events regarding the history of Buddhism in India is given below.

Siddhartha Gautama

Siddhartha Gautama was the historical founder of Buddhism. Siddhartha Gautama was born as a Kshatriya prince in ancient India.

After asceticism and meditation, Siddhartha Gautama discovered the Buddhist Middle Way—a path of moderation away from the extremes of self-indulgence and self-mortification.

Siddhartha Gautama attained enlightenment sitting under a pipal tree, now known as the Bodhi tree in Bodh Gaya. Gautama, from then on, was known as "The Perfectly Self-Awakened One", the Samyaksambuddha.

Buddha found patronage in the ruler of Magadha, emperor Bimbisara. The emperor accepted Buddhism as personal faith and allowed the establishment of many Buddhist "Viharas". This eventually led to the renaming of the entire reigon as Bihar. At the Deer Park near Varanasi in northern India, Buddha set in motion the Wheel of Dharma by delivering his first sermon to the group of five companions with whom he had previously sought enlightenment. They, together with the Buddha, formed the first saegha, the company of Buddhist monks, and hence, the first formation of Triple Gem (Buddha, Dharma and Sangha) was completed.

Buddhist Movements

Many movements emerged during the next 400 years following Buddha's passing: first the schools of Nikaya Buddhism, of which only Theravada remains today, and then the formation of Mahayana, a pan-Buddhist movement based on the acceptance of new scriptures.

Ashoka

Emperor Ashoka the Great (304 BC–232 BC) was the ruler of the Maurya Empire in present-day eastern India from 273 BC to 232 BC. Ashoka reigned over most of India after a series of military campaigns. Emperor Ashoka's kingdom streched from South Asia and beyond, from present-day Afghanistan and parts of Persia in the west, to Bengal and Assam in the east, and as far south as Mysore.

According to legend, emperor Ashoka was overwhelmed by guilt after the conquest of Kalinga, following which he accepted Buddhism as personal faith with the help of his Brahmin mentors Radhasvami and Manjushri. Ashoka established monuments marking several significant sites in the life of Shakyamuni Buddha, and according to Buddhist tradition was closely involved in the preservation and transmission of Buddhism. He used his position to propagate the relatively new philosophy to new heights, as far as ancient Rome and Egypt.

Dharma Masters

Indian shramanas propogated Buddhism in reigons, including China, Vietnam and Central Asia.

The Indian dhyana master Buddhabhadra was the founding abbot and patriarch of the Shaolin Temple. Buddhist monk and esoteric master from North India (6th Century CE), Bodhiruci is regarded as the patriarch of the Ti-Lun school. Bodhidharma (c. 6th century CE) was the Buddhist monk traditionally credited as the founder of Chan (Zen) Buddhism in China.

In 580, an Indian monk named Vinitaruci travelled to Vietnam after completing his studies with Sengcan, the third patriarch of Chinese Zen. This, then, would be the first appearance of Vietnamese Zen, or Thien Buddhism.

The Yogacara texts were composed in the period of Buddhism known to practitioners as The Third Turning of the Wheel. The Yogacara studies texts form a survey of all of The Three Turnings of the Wheel of Dharma.

Originating around a set of scriptures and treatises composed by such early Indian masters as the brothers Vasubandhu and Asanga (who was said to be inspired by the legendary Maitreya-natha), this school held a prominent position in the Indian scholastic tradition for several centuries. It was also transmitted to Tibet by Dharmarakshita who intiated Atisha into the Yogachara lineage, where its teachings became an integral part of much of Tibetan Buddhism up to modern times, and to East Asia, where it was studied with intensity for several centuries.

Padmasambhava, in Sanskrit meaning *"lotus-born"*, is said to have brought Tantric Buddhism to Tibet in the 8th century. In Bhutan and Tibet he is better known as "Guru Rinpoche" ("Precious Master") where followers of the Nyingma school regard him as the second Buddha.

Decline of Buddhism in India

Buddhism declined in India following the loss of patronage due to the fall of sympathetic kingdoms such as Magadha, Kosala, Guptas, Palas, Harshavardhana and the Kushan Empire. Foreign invasions such as the White Huns and Timur further contributed to the decline of Buddhism.

Hinduism traditionally does not evangelize. Buddhism suffered immensely during the Muslim conquest in the Indian subcontinent with muslim rulers such as Muhammad bin Qasim, Muhammad of Ghor, Qutb-ud-Din and Aurangzeb destroying temples and shrines and seeking conversion of Buddhists to Islam.

Hinduism is also known to have competed ideologically with Buddhism, notably under Adi Shankaracharya and the Bhakti movement.

Anagarika Dharmapala and his Followers

Buddhist revival began in India in 1891, when the Sri Lankan Buddhist leader Anagarika Dharmapala founded the Maha Bodhi Society. Its activities expanded to involve the promotion of Buddhism in India. In June 1892, a meeting of Buddhists was organized at Darjeeling. Dharmapala spoke to the Tibetian Buddhists and presented a relic of the Buddha to be sent to the Dalai Lama.

Dharmapala built many viharas and temples in India, including the one at Sarnath, the place of Buddha's first sermon. He died in 1933, the same year he was ordained a bhikkhu..

Tibetian Buddhism

Following Dalai Lama's departure from Tibet, Indian Prime Minister Jawaharlal Nehru offered to permit him and his followers to establish a "government-in-exile" in Dharamsala.

Tibetan exiles have settled in the town, numbering several thousand. Most of these exiles live in Upper Dharamsala, or McLeod Ganj, where they established monasteries, temples and schools. The town is sometimes known as "Little Lhasa", after the Tibetan capital city, and has become one of the centres of Buddhism in the world.

Lama Gyatso is also known to express solidarity with Hinduism, another Dharmic faith with origins in India. Lama Gyatso has also appeared in Hindu religious ocassions such as the Kumbh.

DECLINE OF BUDDHISM IN INDIA

The Decline of Buddhism in India, in the land of its birth occurred for a variety of reasons, and happened even as it continued to flourish beyond the frontiers of India. Buddhism was established in the area of ancient Magadha and Kosala by Gautama Buddha in the 6th century BCE, in what is now modern Uttar Pradesh and Bihar. Buddhism, over the next Over 1500 years became the region's dominant belief system, spreading across Indian sub-continent. After the death of Gautama Buddha, Buddhism saw rapid expanzion in its first century, especially in northern and central India.

The Mauryan Emperor Ashoka (304-232 BCE) and later monarchs encouraged the expansion of Buddhism into Asia through religious ambassadors. Chinese scholars traveling through the region between the 5th and 8th centuries CE, such as Faxian, Xuanzang, I-ching, Hui-sheng, and Sung-Yun, began to speak of a decline of the Buddhist *sangha,* especially in the wake of the White Hun invasion. A continuing decline occured after the fall of the Pala dynasty in the 12th century CE, continuiung with the later destruction of monasteries by Muslim conquerors. Buddhism was virtually extinct by the end of the 19th century. In recent times, Buddhism has seen a revival in India due to the influence of Anagarika Dharmapala, Dr. B. R. Ambedkar and Tenzin Gyatso.

BUDDHISM UNDER VARIOUS GOVERNMENTS

The Sungas

Following the Mauryans, Pusyamitra Sunga is linked in legend with the persecution of Buddhists and a resurgence of a Hinduism that forced Buddhism outwards to Kashmir, Gandhara and Bactria.. There is some doubt as to whether he did or did not persecute Buddhists actively.

A Buddhist tradition holds him as having taken taking steps to check the spread of Buddhism as "the number one enemy of the sons of the Sakya's and a most cruel persecutor of the religion". The *Divyavadana* ascribes to him the razing of *stupas* and *viharas* built by Ashoka, the placing of a bounty of 100 dinaras upon the heads of Buddhist monks (*Shramanas*) and describes him as one who wanted to undo the work of Ashoka. This account has however been described as "exaggerated".

Historian Romila Thapar writes that the Asokavadana legend is, in all probability, a "Buddhist version of Pusyamitra's attack of the Mauryas", and reflects the fact that, with the declining influence of Buddhism in the Imperial court, Buddhist monuments and institutions would receive less attention.

Some historians have rejected the accuracy of the Buddhist texts that record Pushyamitra's persecution of Buddhists. The first accounts appear two centuries after Pushyamitra's reign in *Asokavadana* and the *Divyavadana*. Koenraad Elst posits that historical facts confirm that Pushyamitra allowed and patronized the construction of monasteries and Buddhist universities in his domains, as well as the still-existent stupa of Sanchi.

While Sir John Marshall states that it is possible that the original brick stupa built by Ashoka was destroyed by Pusyamitra and then restored by his successor Agnimitra. Arhaelogical evidence is scarce and uncertain.Following Ashoka's sponsorship of Buddhism, it is possible that Buddhist institutions fell on harder times under the Sungas but no evidence of active persecution has been noted. Etienne Lamotte observes: *"To judge from the documents, Pushyamitra must be acquitted through lack of proof."*

The Sungas were patrons of Hinduism and their lack of royal patronage was also a setback to Buddhism, resulting in the splintering of Buddhism into many forces. Some of them were: the *Saravastivadins*, *Mahasargikas*, *Sthaviravadha*, and *Yogacara*. This resulted in a diversity of opinions and interpretations that led to a conflict between warring schools shortly after the fall of the Mauryans. Later Sunga kings were seen as more amenable to Buddhism and as having contributed to the building of the stupa at Bharhut.

Hinduism traditionally does not evangelize. Hinduism competed in spirtual and political realm with Buddhism. Buddhism also flourished in the realms of the Bactrian kings.

Guptas

Buddhism and saw a brief revival under the Guptas. By the 4th to 5th century Buddhism was already in decline in northern India, even as it was achieving multiple successes in Central Asia and along the Silk Road as far as China. It continued to prosper in Gandhara under the Shahi kingdom.

White Huns

Central Asian and North Western Indian Buddhism weakened in the 6th century following the White Hun invasion who followed their own religions such as Tengri, Nestorian Christianity, and Manichean. Their King Mihirakula who ruled from 515 BC suppressed Buddhism destroying monasteries as far as modern-day Allahabad before his son reversed the policy.

Harsha

In the North and west the collapse of Harshavardana's kingdom gave rise to many small kingdoms. This led to the rise of the martial Rajputs clans across the gangetic plains and marked the end of Buddhist ruling clans along with a sharp decline in royal patronage until a revival under the Pala Empire in the Bengal region. Subsequently the replacement of Buddhist royal lines with Hindu royals and the rise of martial Rajput dynasties further pressured Buddhism.

Muhammad Bin Qasim

In AD 711, Muhammad bin Quasim attacked the southern shores of Sindh. Muhammad Bin Quasim is linked with Islamic persecution of Buddhists. Quasim destroyed a Buddhist holy site and built a mosque in it's place.

It was claimed that the Buddhists helped bin Qasim in conquering parts of India. Al-Baladhuri recorded that two "Samanis" went to Qasim to negiotiate for peace, however he also recorded that it was the inhabitants of Nirum who sent the priests to Qasim. Muhammad bin Qasim also demolished temples and monasteries, e.g. he built at Nirun a mosque on the site of the temple of Budh.

Mahmud of Ghazni

By the 10th century Mahmud of Ghazni defeated the Hindu-Shahis effectively removing Hindu influence and ending Buddhist self-governance across Central Asia and the Punjab region. He demolished both stupas and temples during his numerous campaigns across north-western India but left those within his domains and Afghanistan alone even as al-Biruni recorded Buddha as the prophet "Burxan".

Mahmud of Ghazni is said to have been an iconoclast. Hindu and Buddhist statues, shrines and temples were looted and destroyed and many Buddhists had to take refuge in Tibet.

Pala's

In the east under the Palas in Bengal, Mahayana Buddhism flourished and spread to Bhutan and Sikkim. The Palas created many temples and a distinctive school of Buddhist art. Mahayana Buddhism flourished under the Palas, between the 8th and the 12th century before it collapsed at the hands of the attacking Sena dynasty.

Muhammad of Ghor

Muhammad attacked the north-western regions of the Indian subcontinent many times. Gujarat later fell to Muhammad of Ghor's armies in 1197. Muhammad of Ghor's armies destroyed many Buddhist structures, including the great Buddhist university of Nalanda.

In 1200 Muhammad Khilji, one of Qutb-ud-Din's generals destroyed monasteries fortified by the Sena armies, such as the one at Vikramshila. Many monuments of ancient Indian civilization were destroyed by the invading armies, including Buddhist sanctuaries near Benares. Buddhist monks who escaped the massacre fled to Nepal, Tibet and South India.

The Mongols

In 1215 Genghis Khan conquered Afghanistan and devastated the Muslim world. In 1227 after his death his conquest was divided and Chagatai established the Chagatai Khanate where his son Arghun made Buddhism the state religion during which time he came down harshly on Islam and demolished mosques to build many stupas. He was succeeded by his brother, and then his son Ghazan who converted to Islam and in 1295 who changed the state religion and after his reign and the splitting of the Chagatai Khanate little mention of Buddhism or the stupas built by the Mongols can be found in Afghanistan and Central Asia can be found in Afghanistan and central Asia.

Timur (Tamarlane)

Timur was a 14th-century warlord of Turco-Mongol descent, conqueror of much of Western and central Asia, and founder of the Timurid Empire.

Timur destroyed Buddhist establishments and raided areas in which Buddhism had flourished.

Mughals

Mughal rule also contributed to the decline of Buddhism. They are reported to have destroyed many Hindu temples and Buddhist shrines alike or converted many sacred Hindu places into Muslim shrines and mosques. Mughal rulers like Aurangzeb destroyed Buddhist temples and monasteries and replaced them with Islamic mosques.

IDEOLOGICAL AND FINANCIAL CAUSES

Financial Reasons

Buddhist monasteries were well-funded and life within was relatively easy. To avoid unwanted members, many monasteries became selective about whom they admitted, in some cases based on social class. This further cut off the sangha from Indian society.

Xuanzang's Report

Xuanzang reports in his travels across India during the 7th century that Buddhism was popular in Andhra, Dhanyakataka, and Dravida which today roughly correspond to the modern day Indian states of Andhra Pradesh and Tamil Nadu. He also reports numerous ruined and deserted stupas in the conquered Buddhist regions such as by the regions around modern day Nepal, as well as the persecution of Buddhists by Ssanka in the Kingdom of Gouda.

Xuanzang compliments the patronage of Harshavardana during this same period while noting in his travels that in various regions Buddhism was giving way to Jainism and Hinduism.

Philosophical Divergence with Adi Shankara

In 9th century A.D. the Buddhist philosophers started to lose ground with the Hindu Saint Adi Shankara. Shankaracharya debated with Buddhist monks and raised issues with Buddhist philosophy.

The rejection of the notion of Atman and yet the endorsement of rebirth, could not be explained by the Buddhists. The resurgence of Hinduism with the ideas of Shankaracharya led to reduction of royal patronage of the Buddhist monks. As political patronage failed it came under increasing pressure by Hinduism and the revival movements of Adi Shankara. Shakyamuni Buddha eventually came to be venerated as a manifestation of the Hindu god Vishnu.

Sufis and the Bhakti Movement

When Islam arrived in India, it sought conversion from, not assimilation to or integration with, the already present religions. Under Sufi influence, the pressures of caste and with no political support structure left in place to resist social mores many converted to Islam in the Bengal region.

After the Mongol invasions of Islamic lands across Central Asia, many Sufis also found themselves fleeing towards India and around the environs of Bengal. Here their influence, caste attitudes towards Buddhists, previous familiarity with converting Buddhists, a lack of Buddhist political power, Hinduism's resurgence through movements such as the Advaita and the bhakti movement, all contributed to a significant realignment of beliefs relegating Buddhism in India to the peripheries.

Islam

Hinduism traditionally does not evangelize. Hinduism does not allow conversion of non believers to the faith; it then tolerates the existence of other beliefs. When conquered, Islamic rulers have been known to force coversion or flee the land under Islamic rule; otherwise punishable by enslavement or even execution.

Buddhism suffered immensely during the Muslim conquest in the Indian subcontinent with muslim rulers such as Muhammad bin Qasim, Muhammad of Ghor, Qutb-ud-Din and Aurangzeb destroying temples and shrines and seeking conversion of Buddhists to Islam.

According to Dr. B. R. Ambedkar, "there can be no doubt that the fall of Buddhism was due to the invasions of the Muslims." He wrote: "Thus the origin of the word ["but", Persian for "idol"] indicates that in the Muslim mind idol worship had come to be identified with the religion of Buddha. To the Muslims they were one and the same thing.

The mission to break idols thus became the mission to destroy Buddhism. Islam destroyed Buddhism not only in India but wherever it went. Bactria, Parthia, Afghanistan, Gandhara and Chinese Turkestan (...) in all these countries Islam destroyed Buddhism."

The Arabic invaders described Indian Pagans as But-parast, and idol-breakers as but-shikan. The word "but" is derived from Buddhism, but the Arabs used it for "Indian paganism" in general. Therefore in Arabic chronicles it is not always evident if Buddhists, Hindus or other Indian religions are meant.

Survival of Buddhism in India

At the beginning of the modern era, Buddhism was very nearly extinct in mainstream Indian society. Some tribal peoples living in the territory of modern India did continue to practice Buddhism. In Bengal, the Bauls still practice a syncretic form of Hinduism that was strongly influenced by Buddhism. There is also evidence of small communities of Indian Theravada Buddhists existing continuously in Bengal in the area of Chittagong up to the present.

Buddhist institutions flourished in eastern India right until the Islamic invasion. Buddhism still survives among the Barua, a community of Bengali/Magadh descent that migrated to Chittagong region. Indian Buddhism also survives among Newars of Nepal.

In Orissa, Mahima Dharma, a derivative of Buddhism, survived until 18th century.

The Hindu Kayasthas, a community of scribes in North India, had been a supporter of Buddhism since the early period. They continued to support Buddhism until about 12th-13th century in some regions.

Buddhism survived in Kashmir valley until 13-14th century, perhaps slightly longer in the nearby Swat Valley. In Ladakh region, adjacent to Kashmir valley, Tibetan Buddhism survives. Tibetan Buddhism must have been popular in Kashmir at one time, as we learn from Rajatarangini of Kalhana.

In Tamilnadu and Kerala, Buddhism survived until 15-16th century. At Nagapattinam, in Tamil Nadu, Buddhist idols were cast and inscribed until this time, and the ruins of the Chudamani Vihara stood until they were destroyed by the Jesuits in 1867. In south in some pockets, it may have survived even longer.

BUDDHISM IN KASHMIR

Kashmir has been one of the most important centres for the spread and development of Buddhism. Buddhism was an important part of the classical Kashmiri culture, as is reflected in the Nilamata Purana and the Kalhana's Rajatarangini. Buddhism is generally believed to have become dominant in Kashmir in the time of Emperor Ashoka, although it was widespread there long before his time. It enjoyed the patronage not only of the Buddhist rulers but of Hindu and early Muslim rulers too. From Kashmir, it spread to the neighbouring Laddakh.

Surrendra

The first known ruler of Kashmir, Gonanda (mentioned by Kalhana in his Rajatarangini), was related to Jarasandha, who ruled Magadha during the time of the Kurukshetra war. Surrendra is perhaps the fist Buddhist ruler of Kashmir. He erected the first viharas in Kashmir. One of these, known as Narendrabhavana, was in the city of Sauraka (Suru, beyond the Zoji La.) The other viḥara was at Saurasa, corresponding to the village Sowur on the shore of Anchar Lanke to the north of Srinagar.

Mauryan Period

Ashoka

Kalhana claims that though it was situated far from the Mauryan capital (Pataliputra), Kashmir enjoyed all the benefits of Ashoka's benign rule.

The provincial capital Shrinagari (Srinagar) was 'resplendent with prosperity and wealth.'

According to some Buddhist writers including Taranatha, the Buddhist preacher Madhyantika introduced saffron cultivation into Kashmir. Buddhism and Shaivism flourished side by side in Kashmir during Ashoka's time and received the Emperor's patronage in equal measure. Kalhana notes that Ashoka built two Shiva temples at Vijayeshvara (Bijbihara), and ordered several others renovated. In Vitastatra (Vethavutur) and at Shuskaletra (Hukhalitar) he built a number of viharas and stupas. He deputed Madhyantika for the propagation of Buddhism in Kashmir and Gandhara.

Ashoka's Successors

Buddhism suffered a temporary eclipse during the reign of Ashoka's successors Jalauka and Damodara. Kalhana describes how a large number of Buddhist scholars were vanquished in debates with Jalauka's guru Avadhuta, and hence traditional observances were slowly revived. Later,. however, Jalauka created a big vihara, the Krityashramavihara, in the vicinity of Varahamula (Baramulla), which was still existed as late as the 11th century. The history of Kashmir after Damodara is not certain until the time of the Kushanas.

Kushana Period

The Kushana period saw a great resurgence of Buddhism in Kashmir, especially during the reign of Kanishka. The fourth Buddhist Council was held in Kashmir, under the presidency of Katyayaniputra, in Kanishka's time. The south Indian Buddhist philosopher Nagarjuna lived in Kashmir during the Kushana period.

Post-Kushana Reaction

During the reign of Abhimanyu, which in Kalhana's chronicle follows that of Kanishka, Buddhist scholars under the guidance of Nagarjuna defeated the Shaivite clergy in debates, encouraging people to choose Buddhism. However, during the time of Chandradeva, revival of knowledge of the works of Patanjali, like the Mahabhashya which had become rare, led to a resurgence of Shaivism. By the time of Gonanda, the old philosophy was completely revived. Nothing is known about the religious affiliations of Pratapaditya, a scion of the Gupta dynasty and his successors, except that they are stated to have ruled well, and fullest liberty of faith was accorded. Buddhism is stated by Kalhana and Hiuen Tsang to have suffered severe setbacks under the Huns, especially under Mihirakula, whom Hiuen Tsang describes as a great persecutor of the Buddhists.

Meghavahana

Upon Mihirakula's death, Kashmir was ruled by Meghavahana, who belonged to the old ruling dynasty of Kashmir. Meghavahana was a staunch Buddhist, who issued a proclamation against killing of all animals at the very time of his coronation, and built numerous stupas.

Buddhist Influence in Kashmir

In Kalhana's time, and before, there was no apparently no distinction between "Hindus" and Buddhists in Kashmir. Kalhana himself used Buddhist terms and expressions as a Buddhist would.

Nilamata Purana was the text of the worshippers of Nila Naga, the Naga worship was common in Kashmir. It mentions the prevalence of Buddhist worship as a common practice in Kashmir.

Here are some quotes from Nilamat Purana from Kashmir (trans. by Dr. Ved Kumari). It correctly represents the religious spirit of ancient India.

709-710a : O Brahman, the god Visnu, the lord of the world, shall be (born as) the preceptor of the world, Buddha by name, at the time when the Pusya is joined with the moon, in the month of Vaisaksha, in twenty eighth Kali Age.

710b-12 : Listen from as to how his worship should be performed in the bright-half, from that period onwards, in uture. The image of Buddha should be bathed (with water rendered holy) with all medicinal herbs, all jewels and all scents, in accordance with the sayings of the Sakyas. The dwellings of the Sakyas (i.e. Viharas) should be whitewashed with care.

713 : Here and there, the Caityas-the abodes of the god-should be provided with paintings. The festival, swarming with the actors and the dancers, should be celebrated.

714 : The Sakyas should be honoured with Civara (the dress of a Buddhist mendicant), food and books. All this should be done till the advent of Magha.

715 : *O twice-born, eatable offerings should be made for three days. Worship with flowers, clothes etc. and charity for the poor (should continue for three days).*

Kalhana's Rajatarangini mentions that a monumental metallic image of Buddha once stood in Srinagar, which was eventually destroyed by Sikandar Butshikan. A significant number of beautifully crafted Buddhist bronzes have survived. In Kashmir valley, a Buddhist Bhikshu was present in Baramula in 13th century. The Kashmiri Pandits still worship the triratna symbol.

HARSHA OF KASHMIR

Harsha (ruled AD 1089-1111) was a king of Kashmir who is frequently mentioned because of his unusual conduct. William Dalrymple in a review of *The Buddha and the Sahibs* by Charles Allen published in *The Guardian* writes:

"It was because of this persecution, several centuries before the arrival of Islam, that the philosophy of the Buddha, once a serious rival to Hinduism, virtually disappeared from India: Harsha Deva, a single Kashmiri raja, for example boasted that he had destroyed no less than 4,000 Buddhist shrines."

This would seem to support the view that Buddhism and Hinduism were enemies in ancient India. This is however not supported by available evidence. Harsha's conduct has recently been a subject of some discussion.

Harsha started out as a capable and noble king, then ran into financial trouble because of his spending habits. For the gold, he started raiding temples and destroying statues.

From Contemporary Text: Rajatarangini

Kalhana's *Rajatarangi* gives an interesting account of Harsha. Note that Kalhana's father Champaka was a minister of Harsha. Harsha wrote during the time of Jayasimha (AD 1127-59).

He destroyed both Hindu and Buddhist temples, and is credited with creating an office of "*devotpaatana-nayaka*", destroyer of gods. In Kalhana's time, Buddhism was flourishing in Kashmir, and was not considered a distinct religion from "Hinduism". He refers to Buddhists' idols just like Brahmnaical ones. Kalhana was very familiar with Buddhism, and mentions Buddhist concepts accurately. Buddhism appears to have survived in Kashmir for a long time. It has been suggested that somewhere at Baramulla a Buddhist monk was present until 14th century. Abul-Fazl, author of *Ain-e-Akabari* was able to locate Buddhists in Kashmir.

King Harsha appears to have become insane. From Taranaga VII (Stein's translation):

1128: Other parasites plundered him by showing an old woman and saying "There, we have brought your mother Bappika from heaven.

1129: Others brought slave girls before him and said they were goddesses. He worshipped them, and abandaning his exalted position and wealth was laughted at by people.

1148: He had carnal intercourse with his sisters, and angered by a harsh word he punished and violated Naga, the daughter of his father's sister."

It has been suggested that he had been influenced by Turushkas:

1149: While continually supporting the Turushka captains-of-hundreds with money, this perverse-minded [king] ate domesticated pigs until his death.

Here Kalhana appears be to stating that Harsha did not even follow the religion of the people he was favoring. He however does call Harsha "that Turushka":

1095: There was not one temple in a village, town or in the city which was not despoiled of its images by that turushka, king Harsha.

1096: Only two chief divine images were respected by him, the illustrious Ranaswamin in the City, and Martanda [among the images] in townships.

1097-97: Among colossal images, two statues of Buddha were saved through requests addressed by chance to the king at a time when he was free with his favours, namely the one a Parihasapura by the singer Kanaka, who was born there and other in the City by Sramana (monk) Kusalsri."

The statue at Parihaspura was built by Lalitadity-Muktapida.

1203:.. he made the glorious [statue of] the Great Buddha which reached up to the sky.

Abul-fazl mentions that the temples of Parihasapura were finally destroyed by Sikandar "Butshikast" (1389-1413).

There was a great fire in Srinagar during the reign of Sussala. All the buildings were burnt except the colossal Buddha:

1184: In the City, which was reduced to a heap of earth, there remained visible and aloft only the great Buddha, which blackened by smoke, and without its abode, resembled a burned tree."

That reminds one of the Great Buddha of Kamakura, the wooden temple of which was destroyed by a tidal wave. The temple of the Great Buddha of Nara was similarly destroyed by fire, but was later rebuilt. A colossal copper image of Buddha once stood in Nalanda, said by Hsuan-Tsang to have been 80 feet (24.6 m) tall. The great Buddhas of Kashmir may have been similar.

DYNASTIES OF ANCIENT KASHMIR

Rajatarangini of Kalhana is a rare chronicle that gives us a fairly direct insight into how things happened in pre-Islamic India. It gives a long account of kings of Kashmir.

- Gonanda I: The first king of Kashmir Gonanda I was a relative (bandhu) of Jarasasamdha of Magadh (Rajatarangini I 59). We can take that to mean that he belonged to the same family.

- Lost and Unknown kings: Skipping over "lost kings" we come to Lava of an unknown family. After his family, Godhara of another family (anya-kulodbhavah) ruled (I 95).
- Mauryas and Kushanas: We now come to Asoka who built many stupas, and his son Jalauka, presumably Mauryas. Then after a Damodara ("of Asoka's kula or another"), we have Hushka, Jushka and Kanisha, obviously the Kushanas.
- Gonandiya: After an Abhimanyu, we come to the main Gonandiya dynasty, founded by Gonanda III. He was (I 191) the first (aadyah) of his race, ("like Raghu was for the Raghus"). Nothing is known about his origin. His family ruled for many generations.
- Some others: Eventually a Pratapaditya, a relative of Vikrmaditya (not the Shakari; II 6) became king. After a couple of generations a Vijaya (from another family: anya kulajo II 62). His son Jayendra was followed by Sandhimat-Aryaraja who had the soul of Jayendra's minister Sandhimati.
- Gonandiya again: After him, Meghavahana of the Gonandiya family was brought back from Gandhara. His family ruled for a few generations. Meghavahana was a devout Buddhist and he prohibited animal slaughter in his domain.
- Huns: Placed within the two periods of Gonandiya rule are Mihirakul and Toramana, we know that they were Huns, but that is not noted by Kalhana. There is some confusion about timing here.
- Karkota dynasty: we are on firmer ground here. Gonandiya Baladitya made his ashva-ghasa-kayastha named Durlabhavardhana (officer in charge of fodder: III 489) his son-in-law because he was handsome. Now Durlabhavardhana was really son of a Naga (a divine being) Karkota (III 490) who had cohabited with urlabhavardhana's mother while she took her bath. Lalitaditya-Mukipada, the great conqueror was born in this noble family.

- Utpala: In the Karkota family, Lalitapida had a concubine, a daughter of a Kalyapala (IV 678). Her some was Chippatajayapida. The young Chippatajayapida was advised by his maternal uncle Utpalaka or Utpala (IV 679). Eventually Karkota dynasty ended and a grandson of Utpala became king.
- Kutumbi: After the Utpala dynasty, a Yashaskara became king. (V 469). He was a great-grandson of a Viradeva, a Kutumbi (V 469). Here I think Kutumbi = kunabi (as in kurmis of UP and Kunbi of Gujarat/Maharastra). He was the son of a treasurer of Karkota Shamkaravarman.
- Divira and Lohara: After a young son of Yashaskara, Pravaragupta, a Divira (clerk), became king. His son Kshemagupta married Didda, daughter of Simharaja of Lohara. After ruling indirectly and indirectly, Didda placed Samgramaraja, son of her brother on the throne, starting the Lohara dynasty. The Lohara family was founded by a Nara of Darvabhisara (IV 712). He was a vyavahari (perhaps merchant) who along with others who owned villages like him had set up little kingdoms during the last days of Karkotas. The Loharas ruled for many generations. The author Kalhana was a son of a minister of Harsha of this family.
- Damar and others: After Loharas, a Damara family ruled. Then a general Ramchandra became king. His daughter Kota Rani married Tibetan Rinchan, who became Muslim.

Thus we have these, with a guess about their origin:

1. Kshatriya
2. Maurya
3. Kushan
4. Gonandiya
5. Huna
6. Karkota: an ashva-ghasha-kayastha, a son of a Naga divinity
7. Kalyapal (liquor vender)
8. Kutumbi (farmer ?)
9. Divira (clerk)

10. Lohara: Vyavahari (merchant)
11. Unknown.

Only one dynasty can be directly linked with an ancient Kshatriya clan, and that too belonging to a somewhat pre-historical period. Note that there were quite a few Brahmins in Kashmir, in fact they formed a powerful lobby. Occasionally some of then refused to accept agraharas from some rulers, but they do not seem to have objected otherwise. The concept of four distinct varnas must have become obsolete even by then.

THE GOD IDEA IN EARLY BUDDHISM

The Buddha of the Pali suttas (scriptures) dismisses as "foolish talk", as "ridiculous, mere words, a vain and empty thing" (Digha-Nikaya No. 13, Tevijja Sutta) the notion that Brahmins (the priestly caste), who according to the Buddha have not in fact seen Brahma face to face, can teach others how to achieve union with what they themselves have never beheld.

This is not a denial of the existence of Brahma, however, but merely intended (by the Buddha) to indicate the folly of those religious teachers who would lead others to what they themselves do not personally know.

Yet Brahma himself, for example, while not denied by the Buddha, is in no way viewed by him as a sovereign, all-knowing, all-powerful Creator God. Brahma (in common with all other devas) is subject to change, final decline and death, just as are all other sentient beings in samsara (the plane of continual reincarnation and suffering).

Instead of belief in such a would-be Creator God as Brahma (a benign heavenly being who is in reality not yet free from self-delusion and the processes of rebirth), the wise are encouraged to practise the Dharma (spiritual truth) of the Buddha, in which right vision, right thinking, right speaking, right acting, right living, right effort, right attentive awareness, and right meditative absorption are paramount and are said to bring spiritual Liberation. The "God idea" forms no part of Theravada Buddhism's doctrine of release from suffering-although some see in the "deathless realm of Nirvana" a hint of an impersonal, transcendental Absolute.

Sir Charles Elliot in his *Hinduism and Buddhism: An Historical Sketch* correctly describes God in early Buddhism as: The attitude of early Buddhism to the spirit world—the hosts of deities and demons who people this and other spheres.

Their existence is assumed, but the truths of religion are not dependent on them, and attempts to use their influence by sacrifices and oracles are deprecated as vulgar practices similar to juggling.

The systems of philosophy then in vogue were mostly not theistic, and, strange as the words may sound, religion had little to do with the gods. If this be thought to rest on a mistranslation, it is certainly true that the dhamma had very little to do with devas.

Often as the Devas figure in early Buddhist stories, the significance of their appearance nearly always lies in their relations with the Buddha or his disciples.

Of mere mythology, such as the dealings of Brahma and Indra with other gods, there is little. In fact the gods, though freely invoked as accessories, are not taken seriously, and there are some extremely curious passages in which Gautama seems to laugh at them, much as the sceptics of the 18th century laughed at Jehovah.

Thus in the [Pali Canon] Kevaddha Sutta he relates how a monk who was puzzled by a metaphysical problem applied to various gods and finally accosted Brahma himself in the presence of all his retinue. After hearing the question, which was "Where do the elements cease and leave no trace behind?"

Brahma replies, "I am the Great Brahma, the Supreme, the Mighty, the All-seeing, the Ruler, the Lord of all, the Controller, the Creator, the Chief of all, appointing to each his place, the Ancient of days, the Father of all that are and are to be." "But," said the monk, "I did not ask you, friend, whether you were indeed all you now say, but I ask you where the four elements cease and leave no trace."

Then the Great Brahma took him by the arm and led him aside and said, "These gods think I know and understand everything.

Therefore I gave no answer in their presence. But I do not know the answer to your question and you had better go and ask the Buddha."

Even more curiously ironic is the account given of the origin of Brahma. There comes a time when this world system passes away and then certain beings are reborn in the "World of Radiance" and remain there a long time.

Sooner or later, the world system begins to evolve again and the palace of Brahma appears, but it is empty. Then some being whose time is up falls from the "World of Radiance" and comes to life in the palace and remains there alone.

At last he wishes for company, and it so happens that other beings whose time is up fall from the "World of Radiance" and join him. And the first being thinks that he is Great Brahma, the Creator, because when he felt lonely and wished for companions other beings appeared.

And the other beings accept this view. And at last one of Brahma's retinue falls from that state and is born in the human world and, if he can remember his previous birth, he reflects that he is transitory but that Brahma still remains and from this he draws the erroneous conclusion that Brahma is eternal.

He who dared to represent Brahma (for which name we might substitute Allah or Jehovah) as a pompous deluded individual worried by the difficulty of keeping up his position had more than the usual share of scepticism and irony. The compilers of such discourses regarded the gods as mere embellishments, as gargoyles and quaint figures in the cathedral porch, not as saints above the altar.

Mahayana and Tantric Mystical Doctrines

Although there are countless Buddhas, their essence is one-that of "Tathata" ("suchness" or "that-ness")-, and it is in this sense that the Buddha proclaims himself as "Tathagata" and exalts himself in theistic terms beyond all other "gods" when he declares: "I am the god above the gods, superior to all the gods; no god is like me-how could there be a higher?" (*Lalitavistara Sutra*).

There are also many examples in the Pali Canon, where the Buddha shows his magical superiority over the Brahma class of gods. So this was already present in the Pali scriptures/agamas.

His realm ("dhatu"), of which he is the "Holy King" (*Nirvana Sutra*), is further said to be inherent in all beings. This indwelling, indestructible, incomprehensible, divine sphere or essence is called the "Buddha-dhatu" (Buddha-sphere, Buddha-nature, Buddha-realm) or "Tathagatagarbha" in such sutras as the "Mahaparinirvana Sutra" and the "Anunatva-Apurnatva-Nirdesa". Further, the idea of an eternal, all-pervading, all-knowing, immaculate, uncreated and deathless Ground of Being (the *dharmadhatu*, inherently linked to the *sattvadhatu*, the realm of beings), which is the Awakened Mind (*bodhicitta*) or Dharmakaya ("body of Truth") of the Buddha himself, is promulgated in such texts. This essence of nature is seen as Shunyata, the true reality. This is the seed from which Buddhahood arises. In the Mahavairocana Sutra, this essence of the one ultimate Buddha, named Vairocana, is symbolised by the letter "A", which is said to reside in the hearts of all beings and of which Buddha Vairocana declares:

> *"[the mystic letter 'A'] is placed in the heart location: it is Lord and Master of all, and it pervades entirely all the animate and inanimate. 'A' is the highest life-energy ..." (The Maha-Vairocana-Abhisambodhi Tantra).*

This great Vairocana Buddha is called: "the Bhagavat [= Blessed One-a term traditionally linked in Indian discourse with "the Divine"], Master of the Dharma, the Sage who is completely perfect, who is all-pervasive, who encompasses all world systems, who is All-Knowing, the Lord Vairocana".

The Tantric text, *The Sarva-Tathagata-Tattva-Samgraha*, eulogises the supreme Buddha Vairocana in the following theistic paeons:

> *"He is universal Goodness, beneficial, destroyer [of suffering], the great Lord of Happiness, sky womb, Great Luminosity ... the great All-perceiving Lord ... He is without beginning or end ... [He is] Vishnu [God] ... Protector of the world, the sky, the earth ... The elements, the good benefactor of beings, All things ... the Blessed Rest, Eternal ... The Self of all the Buddhas ... Pre-eminent over all, and master of the world."*

Similar God-like descriptions are encountered in the *All-Creating King Tantra* (Kunjed Gyalpo Tantra), where the universal Mind of Awakening (personified as "Samantabhadra Buddha"- the "All-Good") declares of himself:

"I am the core of all that exists. I am the seed of all that exists. I am the cause of all that exists. I am the trunk of all that exists. I am the foundation of all that exists. I am the root of existence. I am 'the core' because I contain all phenomena. I am 'the seed' because I give birth to everything. I am 'the cause' because all comes from me. I am 'the trunk' because the ramifications of every event sprout from me. I am 'the foundation' because all abides in me. I am called 'the root' because I am everything." (The Supreme Source).

There is also in Mahayana Buddhism, the concept of an Adibuddha (Adi-Buddha). This being is the primordial, self-existent, self-created Buddha who is the personification of Shunyata or emptiness; that all phenomena lack true existence yet still appear, this basis that is found in all phenomena. However, all these so called God-like figures, i.e Samantabhadra, Vairochana, Vajradhara etc. are traditionally understood to be personifications of emptiness, the true nature of all phenomena. Some Buddhists see the above Samantabhadra Buddha quote as radically subjective psychology, while still others will insist that the words mean what they say and do communicate the sense of an actual sustaining Buddhic force or spiritual essence behind and within all phenomena.

GOD AS MANIFESTATION OF MIND

One of the more important Mahayana Sutras, the Lankavatara Sutra, states that the notions of a sovereign God, Atman are figments of the imagination or manifestations of the mind and can also be an impediment to perfection as this leads to attachment to the concept of "God": All such notions as causation, succession, atoms, primary elements, that make up personality, personal soul, Supreme Spirit, Sovereign God, Creator, are all figments of the imagination and manifestations of mind.

No, Mahamati, the Tathagata's doctrine of the Womb of Tathagata-hood is not the same as the philosopher's Atman.

However, the same sutra also sees the Buddha reveal that he is the One who is actually being addressed when beings project from their unawakened minds notions of Divinity and address themselves to "God". The many names for such ultimate Being or Truth are in fact said by the Buddha to be unwitting appellations of the Buddha himself. He states: The same can be said of myself as I appear in this world of patience before ignorant people and where I am known by uncounted trillions of names.

They address me by different names not realizing that they are all names of the one Tathagata.

Some recognize me as Sun, as Moon; some as a reincarnation of the ancient sages; some as one of "ten powers"; some as Rama, some as Indra, and some as Varuna. Still there are others who speak of me as The Un-born, as Emptiness, as "Suchness," as Truth, as Reality, as Ultimate Principle; still there are others who see me as Dharmakaya, as Nirvana, as the Eternal; some speak of me as sameness, as non-duality, as un-dying, as formless; some think of me as the doctrine of Buddha-causation, or of Emancipation, or of the Noble Path; and some think of me as Divine Mind and Noble Wisdom.

Thus in this world and in other worlds am I known by these uncounted names, but they all see me as the moon is seen in the water.

Though they all honour, praise and esteem me, they do not fully understand the meaning and significance of the words they use; not having their own self-realization of Truth they cling to the words of their canonical books, or to what has been told to them, or to what they have imagined, and fail to see that the name they are using is only one of the many names of the Tathagata.

In their studies they follow the mere words of the text vainly trying to gain the true meaning, instead of having confidence in the one "text" where self-confirming Truth is revealed, that is, having confidence in the self-realization of noble Wisdom.

In the "Sagathakam" section of the sutra, one also reads of the reality of the pure Self (atman), which (while not identical to the atman of the Hindus) is equated with the Tathagatagarbha (Buddha-

Essence): "The *atma* [Self] characterised with purity is the state of self-realisation; this is the Tathagatagarbha, which does not belong to the realm of the theorisers.".

This Tathagatagarbha is in the *Lankavatara Sutra* identified with the root or all-containing Consciousness of all beings, the Alaya-vijnana. This Tathagatagarbha-Alayavijnana is stated not to belong to the realm of speculation, but can be understood directly by:

> *"those Bodhisatva-Mahasattvas [great Bodhisattvas] who like you [Mahamati] are endowed with subtle, fine, penetrative thought-power and whose understanding is in accordance with the meaning...".*

4

Teachings of the Buddha

These are the basic teachings and concepts in Buddhism.

Karma: Actions have consequences; so our lives are conditioned by our past actions.

Rebirth: Consciousness continues after death, and finds expression in a future life.

Liberation from Karma: By following the Buddha's path one escapes the cycle of craving and suffering.

The Four Noble Truths: These are the essentials of Buddhism.

Enlightenment: The highest goal of life is to reach Enlightenment; a state of being that goes beyond suffering.

Dharma: The teachings and hence the way to nirvana.

The Core of Buddhist Teaching: At the heart of the Buddha's teaching lie The Four Noble Truths and The Eightfold Path which lead the Buddhist towards the path of Enlightenment.

Facing the Truth: The Buddha taught that the human tendency is to avoid the difficult truths of life and this in turn leads to suffering. By enabling the mind to be at peace through meditation a human being can confront reality and overcome hatred and craving.

THE BUDDHA'S LIFE

According to traditional accounts, Siddhartha was born in 563BC. His father was Shuddhodana, a leader of the Shakya peoples, who ruled from Kapilavastu, near the border between India and

Nepal. At his conception, his mother, Maya, dreamt that a great white king elephant touched her with a lotus blossom. As the time of his birth neared, she set out for her native village of Devadaha, but when she reached a grove at Lumbini, she gave birth, Siddhartha appearing from her side. She died only seven days after his birth. The Mauryan Emperor Ashoka (r. 273-36] erected a pillar to mark the place, which was rediscovered in 1898.

The circumstances of his conception and manner of his birth made it evident that he was no ordinary child. This was confirmed when a sage named Asita came down from the Himalayas to see the child, and, after inspecting his features, declared that he would either be a world conqueror or become the enlightened one (Buddha).

To those who are lost in the desert tracks of Samsara, he shall proclaim a way which shall lead to liberations;...creatures scorched by the fire go greed fueled by sense objects, he will refresh with the rain of the Law (dharma).

Lamenting that he would not live to hear his teachings, he directed his disciple Nalaka to follow the new teacher.

The King, naturally pleased that his son might become a world-conqueror and equally alarmed at the prospect he might become a religious teacher, resolved that his son would know only the pleasures of the princely life and never encounter anything which might tempt him toward religion.

Prince Siddhartha accordingly grew up amid the luxury and pleasures of the palace, became adept at archery, and excelled in other princely accomplishments. A princely education included the Vedas, together with phonetics, ritual, grammar, etymology, metrics, and astronomy, which made it possible to better understand their meaning. Yet even though kept away from the sorrows of the world, the boy evinced an unusual sensitivity that presaged his future.

Once when his father was performing a ritual plowing ceremony, the boy, effortlessly and without any training, became absorbed in a deep meditative concentration, which would later be called the First Meditation (dhyana). On another occasion, he observed birds pulling worms from the earth, and reflected on how every living thing harms other things as a consequence merely of living.

MARRIAGE, AWAKENING, AND THE GREAT RENUNCIATION (547-533)

Despite these awakenings of his meditative nature, at 16 he married Yasodhara and continues to live a life of ease and luxury, having three palaces-one for the hot season, one for the cold, and one for the rainy season. Later he is said to have recalled: I was delicate, excessively delicate. In my father's house were three lotus ponds made expressly for me, one with blue lotuses, one with red and another with white. I used no sandalwood except that of Kashi and my turban, tunic, dress, and cloak were all from Kashi. A white umbrella was held over me night and day so that I would be untouched by heat or cold, dust, leaves or dew.

But when he ventured out of the palace, he encountered human misery. Four episodes are counted as his awakening. When he saw an old man, Prince Siddhartha reflected that though old age is unwelcomed it is inevitable. Later he saw a cripple and reflected that though people try to avoid contact with sick people, illness is unavoidable. And when he saw a corpse, he realized that though people hate death it is the inevitable end of all. Finally when he saw an ascetic, he reflected that it was possible to renounce worldly things and be free of the entanglements of things and he came to realize that the pleasures of the palace were a hindrance to his development. A life in a household is cramped and confined, a den of dust, but the life of the homeless wanderer is as the open air of heaven! About this time his son was born and named Rahula because his father said "an impediment (rahu) has been born; a fetter has been created." Against his parents' wishes, and in the middle of the night on his birthday at 29, he awoke to see the dancing girls from the party sleeping:

Some with their bodies wet with trickling phlegm and spittle; some grinding their teeth, and muttering and talking in their sleep; some with their mouth agape; some with their clothing dishelved displaying their nakedness.

The scene awakened in the Prince an aversion to sensual pleasures, showing him such pleasures concealed loathsomeness of material things. So Siddhartha secretly left the palace on his favourite horse with his charioteer to seek the good (kusala). When he reached the Anoma river, he shaved his head, put on the robes of an ascetic, giving his charioteer his princely clothes to return to the palace. He then continued southward toward Rajagriha, the capital of Magadha.

The Intellectual Milieu

In India there was an ancient tradition of meditation and asceticism, dating to the Indus Valley civilization about 2500BC. A great body of literature, called the Upanishads, had developed which summarized the teachings of ascetics. There were two patterns of asceticism: that of the brahmans (priests) and that of the wandering ascetics, called sramanas, "those who strive." The Brahmans followed the Four Stages of life: studying under a teacher when young; returning home to marry and raise a family; turning over daily affairs to a son and taking up meditative practices; and, finally, leaving home to live in the forest, there to die.

The Sramanas take up the life of wandering as youths, discipline themselves through austerities, and practice a "discipline" or yoga. The goal of all their efforts was Liberation, which was defined differently by different thinkers. But a common thread was disdain for the gods and practices of the Vedas and a ferment of ideas, ranging from atheism to personal devotion to a personal god (bhakti). We know from Buddhist and Jain texts that more than twenty different sects, today mostly known only by name, flourished at that time.

The Six Teachers

- At the time Siddhartha began his life as a wandering ascetic, there were in northern India six famous ascetics who led groups of disciplines: Purana Kassapa who argued that the person is unaffected by the goodness or badness of his actions. Morality did not exist; murder and theft were acceptable as those acts did not harm those who performed them.

- Makkhali Gosala who contended that a person's success or failure was due to fate and that an individual's actions could not influence the course of his life. His followers were knows as the Ajivakas, which probably refers to their practice of extreme austerities, love of solitude, and disdain for any kind of comfort. So difficult a practice never had many followers, yet the school continued to exist until the 14th century AD.
- Ajita Keshakambala, who was materialist, held that everything was composed of four elements (earth, water, fire, and wind), and that moral acts were meaningless. This position was later maintained by the Lokayata or Charvaka tradition.
- Pakudha Kacchayana who held that there were seven elements, the four recognized by Ajita plus pain, pleasure, and life. The elements are unchanging and are the only reality. Thus if a person is stabbed with a knife, the knife does nothing but pass through the spaces between the elements, thus is of no consequence, even if the person dies. This position is later represented in the Vaisesika school.
- Sanjaya Bellatthiputta who refused to answer any question directly, being a skeptic because of doubts about the nature of knowledge and investigations of logic, and who, through his students, exercised an important influence on Buddhism.
- Mahavira, one of the founding figures of Jainism. Mahavira belonged to the nirgrantha ascetics, those who freed themselves from all fetters through the practice of austerities until they conquered (jain) ignorance. Jainism belongs with Buddhism as one of the great heterodox schools of Indian thought.

THE ATHEISM OF BUDDHA

The Christian critics of Buddhism call Buddha an atheist, nominally because he said nothing about God, really because his conception of God differs from their own.

I have already attempted to show that the silence of Buddha about God—the Supreme Reality—was quite compatible with a sublimely spiritual conception of God and a deeply spiritual faith in him. I have shown that such a conception and such a faith were in the air that Buddha breathed, and that, if he had accepted them and made them his own, the very reverence which they would have generated would have bound him to silence in the presence of his audience,—the rank and file of mankind. I have shown that his own ethical teaching was the practical exposition of this unformulated theology,—the revelation of it, not as a theology but as a scheme of life, to those who would have been bewildered by it, and who would therefore have misunderstood and misapplied it, had any attempt been made to expound it to them in words, I have inferred from this that Buddha did believe in God, not as the West believes in him, but as the Far East, at the highest level of its imaginative thinking, has ever believed in him,—as the Supreme Reality which is at the heart of the Universe, and which is at once the life and soul of Nature and the true self of Man.

But the fact remains that Buddha, though he preached the gospel of deliverance, said nothing about God. To us, with the Jehovah-virus in our veins, to us who for many centuries have been content to believe that the Universe is under the direct rule of that national deity whose sayings and doings are recorded in the Hebrew Scriptures, it seems the height of impiety to keep silence about God. It is well for us to remind ourselves that in the Far East, in the days of India's spiritual greatness, it was deemed the height of impiety to talk freely about God. We call the silence of the East atheistic.

The sages of India, though they would have thought it discourteous to say so, would have regarded our loquacity as profane. To unveil to the mind of the average man ideas which are in the nature of things so large, so deep, and so subtle that, without mental power of a very high order, it is impossible to grasp their initial—let alone their final—meaning, is to expose the most sacred of all truths to the risk (the certainty, one might almost say) of being misinterpreted and misused. From such a risk the sages of India shrank as from blasphemy against the Divine. It may be difficult for us to enter into this feeling, but it is well that we should know that it did (and does) exist.

The silence of the Far East has another aspect, and one which is equally repugnant to the "orthodox" thought of the West. In itself, in the eloquence of its dumbness, it is an abiding protest, not merely against the profane loquacity of Western dogmatism, but also against its deadly despotism. To tell men that they must, under pain of eternal damnation, believe such and such things about God—or rather accept as divinely true such and such theological formulae, whether they see any meaning in them or not—is to quench in their breasts that spark of spiritual freedom which is also the germ of spiritual life.

It is true that the symbolical presentation of religious truth, which official Brahmanism adopted in preference to the doctrinal, may develop, as it certainly did in India, into a ceremonial despotism as oppressive as any that the creeds of the West have ever exerted. But Buddha's own silence was agnostic, in the deeper sense of the word, to the very core. We could imagine him saying to his disciples: "I have given you my reasons for urging you to enter the Path. If those reasons commend themselves to you, enter the Path and see to what goal it will lead you.

But do not ask me to explain my own explanation. Do not ask me for deeper reasons than those which I have given you. Do not ask me to tell you what I, for one, believe about the greatest of all great matters. The words that make sense to me would ring as nonsense in your ears.

The thoughts that bring light to me would dazzle you to the verge of blindness. And I should but deepen your perplexity if I tried to give you the guidance that you seek. But the Path itself will enlighten you if you will trust yourself to it; and when you have followed it far enough you will be wise with a wisdom beyond that of the wisest sage." The idea which underlies the whole of Buddha's teaching—underlying what he said and also what he left unsaid—the idea that knowledge of divine truth must be evolved from within, instead of being imposed from without, is the direct negation of that idea of a supernatural revelation, which underlies all the creeds of the West.

After all, it is not so much the silence of Buddha that the West regards as atheistic, as the creed which that silence hints at and seems, in a sense, to shadow forth,—a creed which seals the lips of those who see deepest into the heart of its hidden truth. The orthodox Christian, who believes that to give assent to a series of formulae is to enter into possession of divine truth, and who therefore regards intolerance as a virtue and self-assertion as a sacred duty, feels instinctively that a creed which will not suffer itself to be formulated, and which therefore makes no attempt to impose its yoke upon human thought, is the hereditary enemy of his faith. His instinct has not misled him. Between the "Higher Pantheism" of India and the Supernaturalism of the Western World there is, in the region of ideas, a truceless war. Had Buddha tried to expound the creed of his heart, it would assuredly have been branded as atheistic by those who now apply that epithet to his silence.

"Such divinity," said the late Canon Liddon, "as Pantheism can ascribe to Christ is, in point of fact, no divinity at all. God is Nature, and Nature is God; everything indeed is Divine, but also nothing is Divine; and Christ shares this phantom divinity with the universe,—nay with the agencies of moral evil itself. In truth, our God does not exist in the apprehension of Pantheistic thinkers; since, when such truths as creation and personality are denied, the very idea of God is fundamentally sapped, and... the broad practical result is in reality neither more nor less than Atheism." The writer of this passage proves nothing by his arguments but his fundamental inability to understand a creed which belongs to a plane of thought on which his mind has never learned to move: and, having misrepresented that creed beyond recognition, he brands it with a title which he regards as in the highest degree opprobrious and offensive.

"Men become personal," says Dr. Newman, "when logic fails; it is their mode of appealing to their own primary elements of thought and their own illative sense, against the principles and the judgment of another." When A calls B an atheist, he does not necessarily mean that B denies the existence of God. What he does mean is that B's conception of God differs fundamentally from his own, and that he cannot by any effort of thought place himself at B's point of view.

On the whole, then, I incline to the opinion that Christianity calls the teaching of Buddha atheistic, chiefly because it suspects that behind his scheme of life and at the heart of his silence dwells a rival conception of God. If this is so, Christianity has misplaced its censure; for if trust is of the essence of faith, there is no conception of God to which the term atheistic is so strangely inappropriate as to that which sealed the lips of Buddha. Curiosity and doubt are the foster-mothers of theology; but he who has once convinced himself, as Buddha must have done, that light and love are at the heart of the Universe, ceases to be curious about God. In the glow of his radiant and all-embracing optimism the petty theories by which man seeks to justify to himself the ways of God and his own timid faith in God, are seen to be worthless and vain. The sceptics who pride themselves on their "orthodoxy" are startled and alarmed by his silence. But out of its depths comes forth, whenever one listens for it, a message, not of atheistic denial but of whole-hearted trust in God,—trust so full, so firmly rooted, and so sure of itself, that silence alone can measure its strength and its serenity.

"And I say to mankind, Be not curious about God,

For I who am curious about each am not curious about God,

(No array of terms can say how much I am at peace about God and about death)."

THE PESSIMISM OF BUDDHA

In each of the charges that it brings against the teaching of Buddha, the West delimits with precision the range of its own thought. When it attempts to prove that Buddha denied the Ego, what it succeeds in proving is that its own conception of the Ego is as narrow and commonplace as that of the materialists and semi-materialists of Buddha's day. For the only reason that it gives for ascribing to Buddha denial of the Ego is that he refused to identify it with any of the things—form, sensation, and the like—of which the "ignorant, unconverted man" says, "This is mine; this am I."

So, too, when the West accuses Buddha of atheism, it tells us, by implication, how crudely anthropomorphic is its own conception of God. Buddha, who refused to individualize the Ego, would have been false to his deepest convictions had he allowed himself, in any respect or degree, to individualize the Supreme Reality. But because he kept silence about God rather than use words which might seem (however figuratively) to individualize him, he is held to have "denied the Divine." This means that if the West may not worship the Jewish Jehovah or some kindred deity, it will reject as untenable the whole idea of God.

Let us now consider the charge of pessimism which is so often brought against Buddha. In formulating this charge, the West defines with precision the limits of its own conceptions, first of happiness and then of the Universe. The true pessimist—who is also the true atheist—is he who sees darkness, and darkness only, at the heart of the Universe. Was Buddha a pessimist in this sense of the word? That he regarded the earth life as full of sorrow is undeniable. Does this convict him of pessimism? Not unless the earth-life is the only life, and the visible world the "all of being."

The impermanence of everything earthly seems to have impressed itself deeply on Indian thought. In the West we live, and are content to live, from year to year, and even from day to day; and we regard as permanent things that will last unchanged for a few generations, or even for a few years. But the far-sighted Indian mind, looking backward and forward through vast stretches of time, saw that sooner or later everything outward, however secure of life it might seem to be, must change and fade and pass away. To the Brahmanic thinkers the impermanence of things was a proof of their unreality. But Buddha, who made his appeal, first and foremost, to the "general heart of man," saw that impermanence reveals itself to the many, not as unreality but as sorrow. He saw also that the connection between impermanence and sorrow is the outcome of the widespread tendency to mistake the impermanent for the real. Men cling to shadows and lean on reeds. The shadows fail them, and so cause disappointment and disillusionment. The reeds "pierce their bosoms," "and then they bleed." Seeing that this was so and must be so, Buddha did what he could to make men realize that this life, as they conceived it, was full of suffering. But he did this, not because he despaired of Nature, but because he had unbounded trust in her.

Far from teaching men that life was intrinsically evil, he taught them that the evil in it, the suffering which seemed to be of its essence, was in large measure the result of their own ignorance—their "ignorance of the true being and the true value of the Universe"—and that those who could detach themselves from whatever was impermanent and changeable might, even while on earth, enjoy a happiness higher and purer than any that the soul of man could consciously desire. So far was he from being a pessimist, in the deeper and darker sense of the word, that at the heart of Nature he could see nothing but light. If that light dazzled his eyes and blinded him to the lesser light that plays over the surface of life, his blindness was a proof, not of the despair of his soul, but of the very excess of its optimistic faith.

There are passages in the "Imitation of Christ" which might have been written by the Sages of the Upanishads. Such are "Amor ex Deo natus est; nec potest nisi in Deo requiescere." "Fili, ego debeo esse finis tuus supremus et ultimus, si vere desideras esse beatus." "Omnia vanitas præter amare Deum et isti soli servire." If Indian idealism is pessimistic, so is the outlook on earth and on life which finds expression in these inspired aphorisms. But surely it is not pessimism but abounding optimism which makes a man pitch his standard of happiness immeasurably high, and yet believe that the resources of the Universe are more than equal to any demand that the aspiring heart may make upon them.

He who could say to his followers: "What you deem happiness is unworthy of the name. There are better things than this in store for you. There are treasures of happiness in store for you,—pure, perfect, imperishable, real. These will be given to you freely if you will but win them for yourselves":—he who could say this (or the equivalent of this) had reached the highest conceivable level of optimism. To accuse him of pessimism is to make confession of one's own lack of imagination, of insight, and of faith. Those who believe that the surface life is the only life and that its pleasures are the beginning and end of happiness, and who assume that

Buddha's faith coincided with their own, may well regard him, when they learn that he saw nothing but sorrow and suffering in the surface life and its pleasures, as the gloomiest and most uncompromising of pessimists. But the charge that they bring against him recoils upon themselves. If the surface life is the only life, and if its pleasures are the beginning and end of happiness, then indeed there is darkness—the darkness of death—at the heart of the Universe. But Buddha's conception of life, if he was true, as he believed himself to be, to "the spirit of the ancient faith," was the exact opposite of this; and what he saw at the heart of the Universe was, not the darkness of death, but the glory of Nirvana.

THE EGOISM OF BUDDHA

On this point the Western critics of Buddhism are divided. Some of them, including Dr. Rhys Davids, Dr. Paul Carus, and other enemies of the Ego, contend that Buddha's teaching was ultra-stoical, in that he bade men do right for right's sake only, the sole reward which the doer was allowed to look forward to being the enjoyment of inward peace during that twilight hour which should precede the final extinction of his life. Others, including the critics who seek to depreciate Buddhism in the supposed interest of Christianity, contend that Buddha was an egoistic hedonist, who taught each man in turn to think of himself and his own welfare only, and whose conception of happiness had so little in it of idealism or aspiration that it scarcely rose above the level of providing for humanity an early escape from sorrow and pain.

The answer to those who regard Buddha as ultra-stoical is that, as a matter of plain historical fact, what he set before men, when he bade them enter the Path, was the prospect, not of doing right for right's sake (he would probably have seen no meaning in those words) but of winning release from suffering—the suffering of those who struggle in the whirlpool of rebirth,—and of entering into bliss—the bliss of those who will return to earth no more.

In giving this answer I may seem to justify the critics who brand Buddha's scheme of life as egoistic. But no. Buddha's scheme of life was as far from being egoistic as from being ultra-stoical.

It is the word self that misleads us. With the doubtful exception of the word Nature, there is no word in which there are so many pitfalls. When we ask whether a given scheme of life is egoistic or not, our answer will entirely depend on the range of the self for which the scheme in question makes provision. To get away from self is impossible; but it may be possible to widen self till it loses its individuality and becomes wholly selfless. Long before that ideal point has been reached, long before the individual has become one with the Universal Self, the word egoistic will have lost its accepted meaning.

That Buddha's teaching was entirely free from the cant of altruism may be admitted without hesitation. Accepting as a fact, which can neither be gainsaid nor ignored, that every man naturally and instinctively seeks his own happiness, and that therefore in the last resort the desire for happiness is the only motive to which the moralist can appeal, Buddha took upon himself to teach men to distinguish the semblance of happiness from the reality, to detach themselves from the former and to win their way to the latter. "Tous les hommes," says Pascal, "recherchent d'etre heureux: cela est sans exception. Quelques differents moyens qu'ils y emploient, ils tendent tous a ce but. C'est le motif de toutes les actions de tous les hommes, jusqu'a ceux qui vont se pendre." It is impossible for me to prefer my neighbour's happiness to my own; for if I am asked why I take such pains to make him happy, I can but answer (in the last resort) that it makes me happy to do so.

Buddha's teaching is equally free from the cant of Stoicism. To bid men do right for right's sake "in the scorn of consequence," is as though a doctor should order his patients to eat the right sort of food for the sake of its rightness, and without regard to its effect on the health of the eater. What is it that constitutes rightness in food,—and in conduct? The right food (from a doctor's point of view) is presumably the food that ministers most effectively to the health of the patient; and it is in the interest of his health, and not of any abstract conception of rightness, that the patient is advised to eat it. It is the same, mutatis mutandis, with right conduct. The exhortation to do right for right's sake is saved from being meaningless only by the tacit assumption that right doing makes, on the whole and in the long run, for the happiness of the doer.

Indeed, it is because such and such courses of action make for the true happiness of him who follows them, and for no other reason, that we call them right. In other words, the epithet right, as applied to conduct, withholds its meaning from us until we define it in terms of happiness. That being so, it is surely better that the moralist should make his appeal (as Buddha openly did) to man's unquenchable desire for happiness than to a motive which would be utterly ineffective were it not that its air of sublime disinterestedness is, in the nature of things, a hollow sham.

But, while Buddha steered clear of the quick-sands of altruism and pseudo-stoicism, he took care not to wreck his scheme of life on the less dangerous, because more plainly visible, rock of egoism. It is when we begin to study the details of the scheme, that we see how little it deserves to be called egoistic. Based as it is on the conviction that the Ego—the real self—is not to be identified with "form," with "sensation," with "perception," or with anything else that is impermanent and changeable, it keeps one aim steadily in view,—to detach man, by a course of self-discipline which may last through many lives, from each of his apparent or lower selves, and to help him to find his true self.

As it is attachment to the apparent or lower self—that tendency to identify oneself with what is impermanent and changeable, which makes one say of this thing and of that, "This is mine: this am I: this is my Ego"—as it is this clinging, grasping, self-asserting frame of mind which is the root of all selfishness (to use a homelier word than egoism), it is clear that Buddha's scheme of life, far from, being egoistic or self-regarding, was in its essence a scheme for the extirpation of "self."

Buddha did not say to his disciples, what the altruist professes to say, "Thou shalt love thy neighbour better than thyself." He did not even say to them in so many words, "Thou shalt love thy neighbour as thyself." But he bade them enter a path which, if faithfully followed, would lead each man at last to love all men as himself. For if one is to escape from the impermanent, one must take refuge in the Eternal; and the Eternal and the Universal are the same fundamental reality looked at from different points of view. Every precept that Buddha gave has one positive aim in view,—to help the soul to expand its life or, in a word, to grow. But to the process of soul-growth there are no assignable limits. The soul has not attained to maturity, has not fulfilled its destiny, has not found its true self, until (according to the sublime conception which is at the heart of the "ancient faith") it has become one with the Universal Self, and in becoming one with it has become one with all men and all things. When that stage has been reached, when the Ego has become all-embracing, the last trace of "egoism" will have vanished, and the precept, "Thou shalt love thy neighbour as thyself" (the real meaning of which will not till then have been apprehended) will at last have been fulfilled. So, too, will the desire of the heart for happiness.

It is by the Christian, the professed follower of Christ, that the charge of egoism is most frequently brought against the teaching of Buddha. It is strange that such a charge should come from such a quarter. Will the Christian consent to brand as egoistic the teaching of his own Master? The conception of life which underlies Christ's searching question: "What is a man profited if he shall gain the whole world and lose his own soul?" is, according to the view that we are able to take of it, either ignobly selfish or sublimely self-forgetful. On this point opinions may differ. What is certain is that the gospel of Buddha is neither more nor less "egoistic" than the Gospel of Christ. For at the heart of each gospel is the same overmastering conviction that it is better for a man to find "his own soul"—his own true self—than to "gain the whole world."

In conclusion. The desire for unreal happiness—the Protean desire which Buddha sought to extinguish—leads us into all the highways and byways of selfishness, and into every haunt of error and delusion; and the phantom which is ever flitting before us ends by eluding our grasp. But the desire for real happiness—the desire which Buddha at once appealed to and strove to foster—is the desire (self-justifying and self-fulfilling) for oneness with the All; nor will that "egoistic" desire have found final fulfilment till it has provided an escape for the soul from the prison-house of "self" into the boundless ether of love.

BUDDHISM AND SLAVERY

Slavery would seem to be incompatible with a fundamental idea of Buddhism; that of freeing oneself of attachments:

Thus the ideal community of the selfless arahants form an ideal, or a standard on which ethical and moral judgement of lay societies are based. Thus such violations of human rights as slavery, torture, etc. could only be a movement in the opposite direction to the ideal, for these violations all result from strong attachment to the self of the violators of human rights.

Wayne R. Husted, Damien V. Keown, Charles S. Prebish, Buddhism and Human Rights, 1998

Buddhist teachings don't explicitly forbid slavery, but the eightfold path says that engaging in trade in living beings is not a right form of livelihood. This appears to ban Buddhists from engaging in the slave trade.

...a lay follower should not engage in five types of business. Which five? Business in weapons, business in living beings, business in meat, business in intoxicants, and business in poison. Eightfold path

Other texts seem incompatible with many aspects of slavery itself.

For example, this quotation requires Buddhists to ensure that their workers and servants are properly treated:

In five ways should a master minister to his servants and employees:
by assigning them work according to their ability,
by supplying them with food and with wages,
by tending them in sickness,
by sharing with them any delicacies,
by granting them leave at times.

Sigalovada Sutta

Despite these texts there's no doubt that slavery was part of some Buddhist cultures, although many of these slaves were servants, rather than slaves of the sort traded across the Atlantic.

Richard Gombrich has argued that the Buddha did not intend to do away with slavery: Though it could well be argued that the Buddha made life in the world more worth living, that surely was an unintended consequence of his teaching. To present him as a sort of socialist is a serious anachronism.

He never preached against social inequality, only declared its irrelevance to salvation. He neither tried to abolish the caste system nor to do away with slavery.

While a famous sermon, the Sumanna-phala Sutta, stresses the practical benefits for a slave in leaving his servitude and joining the Order, in fact runaway slaves were not allowed to join the Order.

Moreover, though in ancient India there was no caste or other form of social ranking within the Order itself, the Order soon came to own (lay) slaves.

Richard F. Gombrich, Theravada Buddhism: A Social History from Ancient Benares to Modern Colombo, 1988

In fact the restrictions placed on monks required them to have some form of servant in monastic communities. So for example if monks were to obey the rule barring the cooking and storing of food, they would need somebody to do it for them. Some Buddhist commentaries warn that slaves are not allowed, unless they are called "called monastery servants (aramika) or legalisers (kappiya-karaka)".

Gombrich also notes that:

at one point the Vinaya commentary says in so many words that kings gave slaves to monasteries, and that they could not be ordained unless they had first been freed. Inscriptions record that people gave money for the specific purpose of maintaining monastic slaves-and offered the resulting merit to all living beings. Richard F. Gombrich, Theravada Buddhism: A Social History from Ancient Benares to Modern Colombo, 1988

If granting endowments to maintain slaves at monasteries was considered meritorious, freeing them from slavery was considered even more meritorious. Thus the device of offering slaves to monasteries provided a two-fold way for the acquisition of merits.

Rahula, Walpola (1956), History of Buddhism in Ceylon: the Anuradhapura Period, Colombo. Quoted in Gombrich

Some kings in Ceylon offered themselves to the monastic community "as slaves and then redeemed themselves, thus combining a symbolic gesture of total humility with extreme munificence". In 9th century China Buddhist institutions are reputed to have employed 150,000 slaves, who were taken over by the Taoist Emperor Wu-tsung in 845 as part of his action against the Buddhist community.

In some parts of South East Asia Buddhist locations were a sanctuary for those fleeing more oppressive forms of slavery:

Where Buddhist monastic orders had claimed political retreats from state military power, their estates and temple complexes became sanctuaries where peasants sought the exemption from state conscription and corvee that 'slavery' to a privileged individual or institution provided. Gwyn Campbell, The Structure of Slavery in Indian Ocean Africa and Asia, 2004

Pagoda Slaves

In some Buddhist cultures a male slave would become free if their owner allowed them to become a Buddhist monk.

In Kampuchea a person could be made a 'Pagoda Slave' if they were found guilty of certain crimes-as could members of their family up to seven degrees removed. Pagoda slaves did domestic and maintenance work on temple sites. While pagoda slaves might have a relatively easy life for a slave they ranked very low on the social ladder and had an extra disadvantage:

Pagoda slaves, who were supposed to belong only to Buddha, could not be redeemed. Gwyn Campbell, The Structure of Slavery in Indian Ocean Africa and Asia, 2004

Because pagoda slaves could not be redeemed their children inherited slave status. Pagoda slaves were found mostly in what are now Burma and Thailand. Pagoda slaves weren't only 'criminals' or the descendants of slaves; people could be given to monasteries for slave use. Among Buddhist reformers of slavery was King Thibaw of Burma, a former monk. He paid 40,000 rupees in 1883 to buy the freedom of many slaves; 1,000 of those he freed are said to have become Buddhist monks and novices.

Slavery and Karma

Some writers think that slavery is justified by the doctrine of karma. They argue that people are born into slavery or become slaves because of their bad actions in a previous life. The way for a slave to progress towards salvation was to obey his or her owner, and do so willingly and without any bad feelings.

Pure Land Buddhism

Pure Land Buddhism: Pure Land Buddhism offers a way to enlightenment for people who can't handle the subtleties of meditation, endure long rituals, or just live especially good lives.

The essential practice in Pure Land Buddhism is the chanting of the name of Amitabha Buddha with total concentration, trusting that one will be reborn in the Pure Land, a place where it is much easier for a being to work towards enlightenment.

Pure Land Buddhism adds mystical elements to the basic Buddhist teachings which make those teachings easier (and more comforting) to work with.

These elements include faith and trust and a personal relationship with Amitabha Buddha, who is regarded by Pure Land Buddhists as a sort of saviour; and belief in the Pure Land, a place which provides a stepping stone towards enlightenment and liberation. Pure Land Buddhism is particularly popular in China and Japan.

History: Pure Land Buddhism as a school of Buddhist thinking began in India around the 2nd century BCE.

It spread to China where there was a strong cult of Amitabha by the 2nd century CE, and then spread to Japan around the 6th century CE. Pure Land Buddhism received a major boost to its popularity in the 12th century with the simplifications made by Honen.

A century later Shinran (1173-1262), a disciple of Honen, brought a new understanding of the Pure Land ideas, and this became the foundation of the Shin (true) sect. Pure Land Buddhism took off in Japan when the monk Honen (1133-1212) simplified the teachings and practices of the sect so that anyone could cope with them. He eliminated the intellectual difficulties and complex meditation practices used by other schools of Buddhism. Honen taught that rebirth in the Pure Land was certain for anyone who recited the name with complete trust and sincerity. Honen said that all that was needed was...

saying "Namu Amida Butsu" with a conviction that by saying it one will certainly attain birth in the Pure Land.

The result was a form of Buddhism accessible to anyone, even if they were illiterate or stupid.

Honen didn't simplify Buddhism through a patronising attitude to inferior people. He believed that most people, and he included himself, could not achieve liberation through any of their own activities. The only way to achieve Buddhahood was through the help of Amitabha.

The Shin Sect

A century after Honan, one of his disciples, Shinran (1173-1262) brought a new understanding of the Pure Land ideas. Shinran taught that what truly mattered was not the chanting of the name but faith. Chanting on its own had no value at all. Those who follow the Shin school say that liberation is the consequence of a person achieving genuine faith in Amitabha Buddha and his vow to save all beings who trusted in him.

AMITABHA

Amitabha in context: The Pure Land sect emphasises the significant role played in liberation by Amitabha (which means Immeasurable Light) who is also called Amitayus (which means Immeasurable Life).

People who sincerely call on Amitabha for help will be reborn in Sukhavati-The Pure Land or The Western Paradise-where there are no distractions and where they can continue to work towards liberation under the most favourable conditions.

The nature of Amitabha is not entirely clear. Encyclopedia Britannica describes him as "the great saviour deity worshiped principally by members of the Pure Land sect in Japan." Another writer says "Amitabha is neither a God who punishes and rewards, gives mercy or imposes tests, nor a divinity that we can petition or beg for special favours". The mystical view of Amitabha regards him as an eternal Buddha, and believes that he manifested himself in human history as Gautama, or "The Buddha". Amitabha translates as "Amito-fo" in Chinese and "Amida" in Japanese.

The Story of Amitabha

Once there was a king who was so deeply moved by the suffering of beings in the world that he gave up his throne and became a monk named Dharmakara.

Dharmakara was heavily influenced by the 81st Buddha and vowed to become a Buddha himself, with the aim of creating a Buddha-land that would be free of all limitations.

He meditated at length on other Buddha-lands and set down what he learned in 48 vows. Eventually he achieved enlightenment and became Amitabha Buddha and established his Buddha-land of Sukhavati.

His most significant vow was the 18th, which said: "If I were to become a Buddha, and people, hearing my Name, have faith and joy and recite it for even ten times, but are not born into my Pure Land, may I not gain enlightenment."

Since he did gain enlightenment, it follows that those who do have faith and joy and who recite his name will be born into the Pure Land.

Pure Land Essentials

Nembutsu: This means concentration on Buddha and his virtues, or recitation of the Buddha's name.

No special way of reciting the name is laid down. It can be done silently or aloud, alone or in a group and with or without musical accompaniment. The significant thing is to chant the name single-mindedly, while sincerely wishing to be reborn in the Pure Land.

Scripture: The Pure Land scriptures include The Infinite Life Sutra, The Contemplation Sutra and The Amitabha Sutra.

Chanting: Chanting the name of Amitabha Buddha does not do anything at all to help the person to the Pure Land. Chanting is nothing more than an expression of gratitude to Amitabha Buddha and an expression of the chanter's faith. But it's not possible to do away with the chanting: Shinran wrote "the True Faith is necessarily accompanied by the utterance of the Name".

Faith: Shin Buddhists say that faith in Amitabha Buddha is not something that the believer should take the credit for since it's not something that the believer does for themselves. Their faith is a gift from Amitabha Buddha.

And in keeping with this style of humility, Shin Buddhists don't accept the idea that beings can earn merit for themselves by their own acts; neither good deeds, nor performing rituals help. This has huge moral implications in that it implies (and Shinran quite explicitly said) that a sinner with faith will be made welcome in the Pure Land-even more welcome than a good man who has faith and pride.

Popularity: The sect's teachings brought it huge popularity in Japan, since here was a form of Buddhism that didn't require a person to be clever, or a monk, and that was open to the outcasts of society.

It remains a popular group in Buddhism-and the reasons that made it popular 700 years ago are exactly the same ones that make it popular today.

Understanding Pure Land

Is this a new understanding of Buddhism?

On the surface Pure Land Buddhism seems to have moved a very long way from the basic Buddhist ideas, and it's significant to see how it might actually fit in. The way to do this is to tackle each issue and see what's really going on.

Amitabha Buddha is treated as if he were God: On the surface, yes. But perhaps chanting Amitabha Buddha's name is not praying to an external deity, but really a way of calling out one's own essential Buddha nature. However some of Shinran's writings do speak of Amitabha Buddha in language that a westerner would regard as describing God.

The Pure Land appears to be a supernatural place: On the surface, yes. But perhaps the Pure Land is really a poetic metaphor for a higher state of consciousness. Chanting the name can then be seen as a meditative practice that enables the follower to alter their state of mind. (This argument is quite hard to sustain in the face of the importance given to chanting the name in faith at the moment of death-when some supernatural event is clearly expected by most followers.

And the chanting is not regarded solely as a meditative practice by most followers. However gaps between populist and sophisticated understanding of religious concepts are common in all faiths.) There is no reliance on the self to achieve enlightenment.

On the surface, yes. But in fact this is just a further move in the direction that Mahayana Buddhism has already taken to allow assistance in the journey to liberation. And the being still has much work to do when they arrive in the Pure Land. (Shinran however taught that arriving in the Pure Land was actually the final liberation-the Pure Land was nirvana.)

Tibetan Buddhism

Tibetan Buddhism is a religion in exile, forced from its homeland when Tibet was conquered by the Chinese. At one time it was thought that 1 in 6 Tibetan men were Buddhist monks. The best known face of Tibetan Buddhism is the Dalai Lama, who has lived in exile in India since he fled Chinese occupation of his country in 1959.

Tibetan Buddhism combines the essential teachings of Mahayana Buddhism with Tantric and Shamanic, and material from an ancient Tibetan religion called Bon. Although Tibetan Buddhism is often thought to be identical with Vajrayana Buddhism, they are not identical-Vajrayana is taught in Tibetan Buddhism together with the other vehicles.

History: Buddhism became a major presence in Tibet towards the end of the 8th century CE.

It was brought from India at the invitation of the Tibetan king, Trisong Detsen, who invited two Buddhist masters to Tibet and had significant Buddhist texts translated into Tibetan.

First to come was Shantarakshita, abbot of Nalanda in India, who built the first monastery in Tibet. He was followed by Padmasambhava, who came to use his wisdom and power to overcome "spiritual" forces that were stopping work on the new monastery.

Groups within Tibetan Buddhism

- Nyingmapa: Founded by Padmasambhava, this is oldest sect, noted in the West for the teachings of the Tibetan Book of the Dead.
- Kagyupa: Founded by Tilopa [988-1069), the Kagyupa tradition is headed by the Karmapa Lama. Significant Kagyupa teachers include Naropa, Marpa, and Milarepa.
- Sakyapa: Created by Gonchok Gyelpo (1034-1102) and his son Gunga Nyingpo (1092-1158).
- Gelugpa: (The Virtuous School) Founded by Tsong Khapa Lobsang Drakpa (also called Je Rinpoche) (1357-1419), this tradition is headed by the Dalai Lama.

Special Features of Tibetan Buddhism

- the status of the teacher or "Lama"
- preoccupation with the relationship between life and death
- significant role of rituals and initiations
- rich visual symbolism
- elements of earlier Tibetan faiths
- mantras and meditation practice.

Tibetan Buddhist practice features a number of rituals, and spiritual practices such as the use of mantras and yogic techniques.

Supernatural beings are prominent in Tibetan Buddhism. Buddhas and bodhisattvas abound, gods and spirits taken from earlier Tibetan religions continue to be taken seriously. Bodhisattvas are portrayed as both benevolent godlike figures and wrathful deities. This metaphysical context has allowed Tibetan Buddhism to develop a strong artistic tradition, and paintings and other graphics are used as aids to understanding at all levels of society.

Visual aids to understanding are very common in Tibetan Buddhism-pictures, structures of various sorts and public prayer wheels and flags provide an ever-present reminder of the spiritual domain in the physical world.

Tibetan Buddhism is strong in both monastic communities and among lay people.

The lay version has a strong emphasis on outwardly religious activities rather than the inner spiritual life: there is much ritual practice at temples, pilgrimage is popular-often including many prostrations, and prayers are repeated over and over-with the use of personal or public prayer wheels and flags.

There are many festivals, and funerals are very significant ceremonies.

Lay people provide physical support to the monasteries as well as relying on the monks to organise the rituals.

ASPECTS OF FAITH

Lamas

A lama is a teacher. They are often a senior member of a monastic community-a monk or a nun-but lay people and married people can also be lamas. They are very often reincarnations of previous lamas.

As well as being learned in Buddhist texts and philosophy, lamas often have particular skills in ritual.

The Dalai Lama

Dalai is a Mongol word meaning ocean, and refers to the depth of the Dalai Lama's wisdom.

The first Dalai Lama to bear the title was the 3rd Dalai Lama, Sonam Gyatso. (The two previous incarnations were named "Dalai Lama" after their deaths.)

The current Dalai Lama (2002), Tenzin Gyatso, was born in Amdo, Tibet in 1935 and is the fourteenth Dalai Lama.

The Karmapa Lama

Karmapa means "one who performs the activity of a Buddha". The current incarnation (2002) is the 17th Karmapa. Two individuals have been declared the 17th Karmapa; Orgyen Trinley Dorje is generally and officially recognised as the official 17th Karmapa, however a rival Buddhist group give their allegiance to Trinlay Thaye Dorje.

Tantra: Tibetan Buddhism was much influenced by Tantra, and this has brought in a wealth of complex rituals and symbols and techniques. Tantra originated in India and appears in both the Hindu and Buddhist traditions. It brings Tibetan Buddhism a magical element and a rich portfolio of heavenly beings. It also brings a wide variety of spiritual techniques such as mantras, mandalas, ceremonies, and many varieties of yoga.

Rituals: Rituals and simple spiritual practices such as mantras are popular with lay Tibetan Buddhists. They include prostrations, making offerings to statues of Buddhas or bodhisattvas, attending public teachings and ceremonies.

Tibetan temple ceremonies are often noisy and visually striking, with brass instruments, cymbals and gongs, and musical and impressive chanting by formally dressed monks. It takes place in strikingly designed temples and monasteries.

Advanced Practices: Tibetan Buddhism also involves many advanced rituals. These are only possible for those who have reached a sophisticated understanding of spiritual practice.

There are also advanced spiritual techniques. These include elaborate visualisations and demanding meditations. It's said that senior Tibetan yoga adepts can achieve much greater control over the body than other human beings, and are able to control their body temperature, heart rate and other normally automatic functions.

Living and Dying: Tibetan Buddhism emphasises awareness of death and impermanence. Everything is always dying-the cells of our bodies are dying even while we live, reminding us of our own impermanence. And all the living things around us are dying, too.

This awareness should not produce sadness or despair, nor should it cause a Buddhist to start a frantic pursuit of the impermanent pleasures of life. Instead, it should lead the Buddhist to see the value of every moment of existence, and be diligent in their meditation and other religious practice. Awareness of death, combined with the understanding of the impermanence of everything, leads the Buddhist to realise that only spiritual things have any lasting value.

Preparing for Death: Tibetan Buddhists use visualisation meditations and other exercises to imagine death and prepare for the bardo. They work towards a holistic understanding and acceptance of death as an inevitable part of their journey.

Another way of preparing for death is to take part in helping those who have died through their experience in the bardo. This not only aids the dead, but enables the living practitioner to gain a real experience of the bardo, before they themselves enter it.

Even those who cannot gain the spiritual awareness to have a consciousness of the bardo are helped by achieving a greater experience of the impermanence of everything.

Tibetan Book of the Dead: This is one of the great texts of Tibetan Buddhism, and a big seller in the west. The English title is not a translation of the Tibetan title-the book's true name is Great Liberation through hearing during the intermediate state, commonly known in Tibet as Liberation through hearing.

The book deals with the experiences of a person as they pass between death and rebirth.

Bardo

Bardo is the state between death and rebirth. The different schools of Tibetan Buddhism have different understandings of this state which is regarded as lasting for 49 days.

The experience of a person during bardo depends on their spiritual training during life. An untrained person is thought to be confused as to where they are, and may not realise that they have died. People are often unwilling to give up attachment to their previous life-and their negative emotions-may cause their rebirth to be less good than it would otherwise have been. In traditional Tibetan Buddhism, the dead person is helped through bardo by a lama who reads prayers and performs rituals from the Book of the Dead, advising the deceased to break free from attachment to their past life and their dead body. In some schools of Tibetan Buddhism, the lama will actively help the dead person to transfer their consciousness from their body, in preparation for rebirth.

Many Tibetan Buddhists believe that it is possible for those left behind to assist the dead person on their journey by doing spiritual work that increases the merits of the deceased and thus helps them to a better rebirth.

During the 49 day period the dead can see clearly into the minds of those left behind, which allows the living to help the dead by thinking good thoughts, meditating on Buddha and other virtuous beings, and engaging in spiritual practices.

PATH OF THE LIFE

Let us suppose that a great prophet appeared on earth, one who was in equal degrees a lover of his kind and a dreamer of spiritual dreams. Let us suppose that this prophet had drunk at the pure fountain of Indian thought, that he had accepted and assimilated the ideas which found expression in the Upanishads, the idea of the reality of the soul, of the development of the individual soul through a chain of earth-lives, of the consummation of this process of development in the union of the individual with the Universal Soul and its consequent admission into a life of unimaginable peace and bliss. Let us further suppose that, when his heart and mind had become saturated with these ideas, he became possessed with the desire to communicate them to his fellow-men. Let us imagine him looking down, from the standpoint of his exalted faith, on the toiling, suffering masses of mankind.

Let us picture to ourselves the sorrow that must have pierced his heart when he saw how profoundly ignorant were the masses of the great truth which he had made his own; how entirely they were absorbed in the pursuit of what was material, trivial, perishable, unreal; how they were living, without knowing it, in a world of shadows and illusions; how even religion, which must once have had an inward meaning, had become for them a round of ceremonies and a network of formula; how dense, in fine, and how deadly were the mists that overhung their lives, and how seldom could those mists be parted by any breath of spiritual freedom, or pierced by any ray of spiritual hope and joy.

Let us suppose that he then looked forward into the future, and saw his fellow men returning to earth again and again, and leading lives as hollow, as purposeless, and as joyless as the lives which they were leading then; the process of their soul-growth being so slow, owing to their fundamental ignorance of reality, that for a long sequence of earth-lives no appreciable progress could be made. Would not the sympathetic sorrow which the vision of the present had awaked in him, be intensified by his vision of the future; and would not the longing to help his fellow men, to enlighten them, to lead them into the path of light and life, become at last an absorbing passion which left no room in his heart for any other desire?

But how could he give men the knowledge that they needed? It was ignorance of reality that had darkened and debased their lives. It was knowledge which they were waiting for, knowledge of what was real and what was true. How could he give them this most rare and most precious of all gifts? How could he transform their sense of reality, and quicken and purify their perception of truth? Philosophical knowledge of the truth of things is, for obvious reasons, beyond the reach of the masses. The average man has no turn for metaphysical speculation, and the worse service that one can render him is to tempt him to indulge in it; for in the atmosphere of verbal controversy reality becomes an abstraction, truth becomes a formula, while love, which is the real unsealer of all spiritual secrets, inevitably withers and dies.

The intuitive apprehension of the truth of things is equally, and for equally obvious reasons, beyond the reach of the masses. The "psychical" faculties, which generate that rare but vividly real type of knowledge, though potentially present in all men, are developed in an exceedingly small minority; and the premature attempt to develop them would end in hysteria being mistaken for inspiration, and hallucination for divine truth. The emotional apprehension of the truth of things may seem to be within the reach of ordinary men. In reality it also is reserved for a chosen few; for it is only in the genuinely poetic nature that it can maintain its equable heat and pristine purity. In lower natures it burns itself away in the pitchy flames of undisciplined sentiment, and dies out at last into formalism, dogmatism, and other "bodies of death." Moreover, the teacher who appeals to the spiritual emotion of his disciples, and who thereby enters into emotional relations with them, and through them with their disciples and spiritual descendants, runs one serious risk.

The chances are that, sooner or later, those who come under his influence, without having known him in the flesh, and who are therefore free to construct imaginary pictures of his life and person, will transfer to his personality the devotion which he wished them to give to his ideas, and will end by regarding his inevitable limitations, or rather the limitations of their own imagination—for by this time the teacher will have become a legendary hero—as the very boundaries of reality.

There remains what I have elsewhere called the real apprehension of ultimate truth. This, and this alone, is within the reach of all men. The actual expansion of the soul, in response to the forces in Nature that are making for its development, will give men, little by little, the knowledge that they need; for, as the soul expands, as it increases in wisdom and stature, its consciousness will enlarge its horizon, its vision will become clearer and deeper, and its sense of proportion will be transformed. When the knowledge of reality has been finally won, the attractive forces of earth, which will then be felt to be wholly illusory, will have ceased to act, and the end of the soul's pilgrimage will be at hand. The best service, then, that a man can render to his fellow men is to persuade them to enter the path of soul-growth. Or rather—for they entered it long ago—to follow it, no longer blindly and instinctively, but deliberately and of their own free will; and, by thus consciously cooperating with the expansive forces of Nature, to shorten the path of soul-growth, and to hasten the advent of its glorious goal.

That our prophet, looking at things from the standpoint of his own higher knowledge, should desire to render this service to his fellow men, may be taken for granted. But how should he persuade men that escape from the cycle of earth-lives was intrinsically desirable, that the path of soul-growth was the path of real life, that the goal to which it would lead them was worthy of their highest aspiration and their most strenuous endeavour? If their ignorance of reality was as dense as it seemed to be, to what faculty should he appeal and on what ground of admitted truth should he take his stand?

The relation between knowledge and action, in the sphere of moral life, presents a problem which is insoluble, except on one hypothesis. Our difficulty is that for right action we need right knowledge; that for right knowledge we need inward enlightenment; that for inward enlightenment we need the transforming influence of a life of right action. There is but one way of escape from this seemingly vicious circle. Apply the law of development to the inward life of the soul; and it will become clear that the sense of reality, like every other sense and power, exists in embryo in each individual man.

It is to this embryonic sense of reality that our prophet would make his appeal. In doing so, he would provide both for the development of that sense, and for the concurrent development in the soul of his disciple of the germ of his own teaching. For the sense of reality, like every other sense and power, grows by being exercised; and if it is to be exercised, it must be appealed to and called upon to exert itself. It follows that, in appealing to a man's sense of reality, one helps it to grow; and it follows that, in helping the sense to grow, one trains it to understand and respond to the appeal that is made to it.

We may conjecture, then, that the teacher who wished to lead men to the knowledge of reality would begin by assuming that the sense of reality was latent in every heart. He would say to them, "Does this earth-life really satisfy you? Cannot you see for yourselves that in the last resort it is hollow and unreal? Do the prizes for which you strive content you when you have won them? Do they not crumble into dust as you grasp them? Everything that earth can give you—health, wealth, pleasure, power, success, fame—proves to be either transient or illusory. Health lasts a few years, and is then undermined by disease and decay. Wealth has neither meaning nor value except so far as it enables you to buy pleasure, power, success, and fame. Pleasure palls upon you, and at last ceases to please. Or, if it does continue to please, age and disease forbid you to enjoy it. Power brings with it a weight of care and responsibility. Success has its counterpart in failure, for:

'Things won are done: joy's soul lies in the doing.'

Fame is 'Enjoyed no sooner but despised straight.'

Look down the vista of the years. If you continue to desire the things of earth, you will return to earth, drawn by the influences that now attract you, again and again. Does this prospect content you? Has your experience of earth been so happy that you wish to renew it again and again? Is it not true that the earth-life brings real happiness to those only who have found inward peace?

And is it not true that inward peace, though it can transfigure earth and make it spiritual and beautiful, is won by detachment from earth, not by devotion to it? This inward peace, in enjoying which you drink the only draught of real happiness that the earth-life can offer you, is a faint foretaste of what is in store for the soul when all its wanderings are over. Beyond all earth-lives a goal awaits you—a goal which crowns and completes the process of the soul's evolution—the goal of deep, perfect, inexhaustible bliss. This reward will be yours when you have broken the last of the ties by which earth attracts you, and in doing so have escaped, once and for ever, from the 'whirlpool of rebirth.'"

If there was anything in the heart of man which could respond to this appeal, the seed of the prophet's teaching would have been safely sown. His philosophy would have taught him that his appeal would not be made in vain. The germ of divine wisdom is implicit in the germ of soul-life; and the teacher who took for granted that men could see for themselves the inner truth of things, would find that the insight with which he credited them would evolve itself, little by little, in response to his appeal.

But, be it carefully observed, he would make his appeal to the people as simple and direct as possible. He would not attempt to base it on metaphysical or theological grounds. He would not employ arguments which appeal to the intellectual faculties only, for he would know that the people have no capacity for abstract speculation, and he would infer from this that the more cogent a metaphysical or a theological argument might seem to be, when addressed to popular thought, the more certain it would be to delude and mislead. The reticence which he would thus impose upon himself might carry him very far, but he would respect all its obligations. He would make no attempt to lead the undeveloped minds of his hearers into the presence of what was ultimate, either in themselves or in the world at large. He would say nothing to them about the "Ego," nothing about God. He would put no truth before them which was not in some measure self-evident.

To say that life, as we know it, is full of pain, sorrow, and disappointment; that its pleasures are transitory and delusive; that its prizes are intrinsically worthless; that the inward peace which moral goodness generates is the only real happiness; and that to escape into a world of inward peace is, therefore, the highest imaginable bliss;—to advance such arguments as these is to appeal to an inward sense which exists potentially in all men. But to go beyond the limits of those simple yet profound conceptions, would be to lead men into a region of doubt, bewilderment, and wordy strife.

Having won from men some measure of assent to the self-evident truths which he had set before them, the teacher would proceed to draw for them the practical inferences from his premises. He would tell them that there was a path, by following which they would become gradually detached from earth and its shadows and delusions, and brought within sight of their spiritual goal; and he would then teach them how to enter that path and walk in it.

The path of deliverance is the path of soul-growth. As the soul grows, and its perceptive faculties widen and deepen, the unreality of the earth-life will become gradually apparent; and when this has been fully realized, the last chain that binds the soul to earth will snap of its own accord, and deliverance will be won. The one thing needful, then, the one thing which every man ought to do and which any man can do, is so to live as to make his soul grow. How is this to be done? We need not go far for an answer to this question. In the first place, all the influences which directly thwart the growth of the soul must be subdued and disarmed.

The lusts and passions of the animal self; the desires and ambitions, the moods and impulses, that are generated by petty egoism; the tendencies, whatever they may be, that make for the contraction of the life of the soul, for the restriction of its vital energies to the plane of the lower self,—all these must, for obvious reasons, be kept under due control. To allow the soul to identify itself with any of the lower selves which egoism seeks to magnify, would be fatal to its spiritual progress. Also, since it is of the essence of the new scheme of life to entrust to each man in turn the duty of ordering his own goings, it is clear that if any carnal or semi-carnal desire or passion were allowed to seize the helm of the will, the voyaging soul would make early shipwreck.

This is the negative side of soul-growth. The positive side is of even greater importance. If the soul is to grow, it must go out of itself into some sphere of being which seems for the moment to lie beyond its own. Now there are many avenues of escape from the ordinary self; and each of these helps, in its own way, to foster the growth of the soul. But there is one and one only which is open to all men,—the avenue of sympathy, of living or beginning to live in the lives of other persons and other things.

In teaching men to live in the lives of others, our moralist would be content to lead them on from strength to strength, and would make no attempt to initiate them, while they were still in pupilage, into the esoteric mystery of an all-embracing, all-consuming love. He would take for granted that the germ of sympathy was in every heart, and that the germ would evolve itself, under the stress of the natural forces that make for the expansion of the soul, when once the adverse influences that hindered its outgrowth had been removed or, at least, reduced to inaction. What hinders the outgrowth of sympathy is not the lust of cruelty (for that is a rare and artificial by-product of human development), but the reckless egoism which prompts the strong, in the general struggle for existence, to trample down the weak.

The impulse—half fear, half anger—which makes a man strike in self-defence; the "instinct to live" which makes him ready to sacrifice life in other beings in order that he may preserve it in himself; the desire for material comfort and well-being, which makes him reckless of the comfort and well-being of others, these tendencies are not in themselves incompatible with sympathy, though they may, if uncontrolled, develop into darker and deadlier passions, and generate an egoism more callous and more self-seeking than that from which they spring. But the scheme of life which we are considering has provided for all the animal and semi-animal passions being placed under due control; and he who had laid this teaching to heart would be ready to receive the further lesson, that he ought to refrain from wanton unkindness, first to his fellow-men, and then to all other living things.

In other words, though he would be left free to take whatever steps might prove to be necessary for the protection and preservation of his life, he would be taught that no wound was to be wantonly inflicted, no life to be recklessly destroyed; and that, speaking generally, each man in turn was to make his pilgrimage on earth as free as might be possible from harm and offence to others. Under the influence of this teaching, gentleness, kindness, and tolerance would gradually impregnate the atmosphere of man's daily life; and in that atmosphere the germ of sympathy would make strong and steady growth.

To trace the stages in the growth of that soul-expanding germ would be beside my present purpose. That the destiny of sympathy is to transform itself into the passion of spiritual love, can scarcely be doubted. It is of the essence of the individual life to seek to outgrow itself, to seek to mingle itself with other lives on its way to that Universal life which is its own true self; and when once the individual life has begun to lose itself in the lives of others, a process has been initiated, of which absorption into the Universal life—itself the highest imaginable development of love—is the natural and necessary consummation.

But one who was addressing himself to the rank and file of mankind, and was therefore taking thought for the earlier stages of soul-growth, would be careful to disabuse the minds of his disciples of the idea that there was any short cut to spiritual perfection. The critic who looks at things from the standpoint of the "enthusiasm of humanity," may possibly condemn the gospel of sympathy as a cold and pallid substitute for the gospel of love; but the moralist who had taken upon himself to lead the average man into the path of life, would not allow this criticism to deflect him from his purpose.

Knowing that in the earlier stages of soul-growth self-control was the one thing needful, and that until the self-seeking desires had been mastered the outgrowth of the soul-expanding desires was not to be looked for; and knowing further that sympathy, which has much in common with self-control, and follows naturally from it, would gradually prepare the way for the outgrowth of spiritual love and the desires that are akin to it, or rather would itself, in the natural course of things, develop into these;—knowing this, the idealistic moralist would be content that men should aim in the first instance at the skyline which was visible to them, and that the heights which this hid from view should unfold themselves, little by little, as the soul surmounted the foothills of its life. Herein he would show his practical wisdom and make good his claim to be a teacher of mankind. The premature development of the "enthusiasm of humanity" and other spiritual passions might well have fatal consequences; for experience has amply proved that the lower desires and impulses are all too ready to masquerade as the higher,—lust, for example, as love, race-hatred as patriotism, religious intolerance as spiritual devotion, egoism as self-respect, censoriousness and uncharitableness as moral zeal.

The truth is that in ordinary men the passion of love necessarily directs itself towards what is individual and quasi-concrete, whereas sympathy, just because it is a colder and paler sentiment, has an immeasurably wider and more abstract range. There are indeed exceptional natures which can sublimate personal into impersonal love; but, speaking generally, if the impersonal passion of universal love is to be our goal, the safer path to it,—at any rate in the earlier stages of man's development,—will be that of the impersonal sentiment of sympathy rather than the personal passion of love.

The master principle, that deliverance from the illusions of earth is to be won by self-control and sympathy, would be embodied in a simple "Law." It is in this form, and no other, that the new philosophy of life would have to be presented to the rank and file of mankind. It may be possible for ordinary men to see for themselves that escape from the "whirlpool of rebirth" into the calm haven of inward peace and spiritual bliss, is a desirable end; but the teacher who should try to explain to them that this end was to be compassed by the practice of self-control and the cultivation of sympathy, would find that his words had missed their mark. The average man has no turn for abstract thinking; and to ask him to trace the logical connection between this or that moral principle and the paramount end of life, is to set him a task beyond his power. What is needed for his edification is to give him a few simple moral rules, and to tell him that these, if faithfully followed, will lead him to the goal that he desires to reach.

But the rules that are given him must be simple and few. In other words, they must be the axiomata media of morality, the broad rules of life which mediate between the master principles of moral action and those meticulous details into which the mind that values rules for their own sake is so ready to descend. The force and authority of each rule must be self-evident. The teacher must be able to say to his disciples: "Cannot you see for yourselves that this course of action is better than that,—that continence (let us say) is better than incontinence, sobriety than intemperance, kindness than cruelty, gentleness than violence?"

In making this appeal to his disciples he would at once exercise and cultivate their spiritual intelligence and their power of moral choice. When we say that the force and authority of the axiomata media of morality are self-evident, we imply that they stand very near to the moral principles which are behind them, so near that, in yielding to their attractive force, the soul is brought into subconscious contact with the truth and beauty of the teacher's philosophy of life. We imply, in other words, that the simple rules of a sane morality are in themselves a source of inward illumination, and that the soul which disregards them sins, in some sort, "against light and knowledge" and misuses its power of choice.

To this proposition there are corollaries which are of profound importance. The growth of the soul, and its consequent absorption into itself of forces and influences which seem to be external to its life, are necessarily accompanied by the diminution of outward pressure and the consequent growth of freedom; and it stands to reason that, when the individual has become one with the Universal Self, so that all forces and all influences are gathered at last within the compass of its conscious life, absolute freedom will have been won.

It follows that freedom is the very counterpart of spiritual life. Now freedom is of two kinds,—freedom to know and freedom to do; and these two are in the last resort one. The teacher who would lead men into the path of life must assume at the outset that man is free, potentially if not actually,—free both to discern good from evil and to make his choice between the two; and he must so shape his teaching that this dual faculty shall be constantly exercised, and to that extent encouraged to grow.

It is because the teacher who limits himself, when framing his Law, to a few axiomata media and refuses to go further into detail, makes ample provision, first for the recognition and then for the culture of spiritual freedom,—it is for this, if for no other reason, that he must take rank as the wisest of Lawgivers.

The superiority of a simple to an elaborate Code of Law, in respect of the services that they respectively render to the cause of spiritual freedom, may be looked at from another point of view. The connection between the broader rules of conduct and the goal by which obedience to those rules is at last to be rewarded, though possibly not directly traceable by the man of average insight and intelligence, is always felt by him to be natural and real.

In an elaborate Code of Law, on the other hand, nine-tenths of the rules that men are directed to obey are so unreasonable and so unattractive that the man who obeys them can neither discern their moral significance, nor see that there is any natural connection between his obedience and his promised goal.

The consequence is that he gets to regard both the law and its reward as wholly alien from his own inward life. He is to obey such and such rules of conduct because he is told to obey them, and for no other reason; and if, and so far as, he is obedient to them, he is to reap such and such rewards, not because there is any natural connection between his conduct and its recompense, but because the irresponsible despot who framed the Code of Law chose, for reasons of his own, to attach certain prizes to obedience, and certain penalties to rebellion. When such a conception of life and duty has fully established itself, spiritual freedom has been mortally wounded, and the soul has entered the valley of the shadow of death.

Against this danger the teacher who regarded soul-growth as both the way and the end of "salvation," would be ever on his guard. Not only would he make his moral rules as few, as simple, and as broad as possible, but he would also impress upon his disciples that by obeying those rules, by following the path, which they marked out for them, they would, in the natural course of things, arrive in due season at the promised goal of inward peace and bliss;—a goal which is so vitally connected with the way of living that leads up to it, that those who seek it enjoy it in some measure before they reach it, its foreglow—"the peace which passes all understanding"—falling in ever deepening splendour on each successive stage in the path of life.

He would therefore warn his disciples against whatever scheme of conduct might tend to substitute a mechanical for a spiritual, a supernatural for a natural, conception of life and duty.

Thus he would teach them that "sacrifices and burnt offerings" could profit them nothing; that ceremonial observances had no intrinsic meaning or value; that obedience to rules, for the mere sake of obedience, far from strengthening their souls, would entangle them at last in the clinging meshes of the infinitesimal. He would teach them, further, that actions produce their natural and necessary consequences, and that the most vital of these is the reaction of what is done on the soul of the doer.

Is the soul really growing? Are the earth-ties being strengthened or weakened? These are the questions which men must learn to ask themselves, and to answer. It is by the strictly natural process of growth, and in no other way, that the soul is to be "saved alive"; and the idealistic teacher would urge his disciples to repudiate the authority of his own law, if it set any other path or any other ideal than that of soul-growth before them.

Above all—and this is perhaps "the conclusion of the whole matter"—the teacher who preached the gospel of soul-growth would impress upon his disciples that each of them must work out his salvation for himself; that he must take the conduct of his life into his own hands; that he must enlist his will-power on the side of those natural forces which are ever making for the expansion of his life; that his will-power was in fact the last and the highest of those natural forces; that its outgrowth had come, gradually and naturally, with the outgrowth of his soul; that whatever tended to arrest its growth tended also, and in an equal degree, to arrest the growth of his soul; that in this, as in other matters, the end of life must control the way, and the way foreshadow the end; that in this, as in other matters, a man must achieve his ideal by applying it to the solution of his practical problems, and giving expression to it in the daily round of his life.

5

The Ethics of Buddhism

It is well-known that Buddhism is the most ethical of "religions". An important part of the Noble Eightfold Path relates to the development of ethical conduct; for many a layperson Buddhist practice consists mainly in the "keeping of the precepts"; many Bhikkhus see in the Vinaya rules the essence of the religious life; and even many of the paramitas expected of those aspiring to Buddhahood are ethical in nature. Yet to present the teaching of the Buddha as being solely and exclusively concerned with ethics could serve as a detraction from the real objective of the Buddha-Dhamma, which is to serve as a path or vehicle leading to Enlightenment.

While conforming to the norms of Buddhist ethics is essential for this purpose this alone will not guarantee the elimination of ignorance (avijja), which is the real meaning of Enlightenment. The tendency of some exponents of the Dhamma to represent Buddhism as just another ethical system is misleading, especially when put before a newcomer to the Dhamma who may not be able to distinguish between Buddhist ethics and the precepts of other ethical teachers, and may conclude that Buddhism has nothing new to offer.

All religions inculcate some basic ethics, whether relating to individual or to social conduct. Indeed the advocacy of an ethical system does not need a religious framework, and some: of the great ethical teachers of the world (*e.g.* Socrates or Confucius) did not feel the need for one. The religion-surrogates of the modern world, like Humanism, rationalism, or Communism, have all evolved their own norms of ethics, however inadequate we may consider them to be. Wherein, then, lies the uniqueness of Buddhist ethics? This question could be answered in many ways, but here we shall look at it from the standpoint of three criteria.

First of all there are the ethical rules themselves. When we consider what actions are considered "good" and what are deemed to be "bad", it might appear that there is a great deal of agreement between the different ethical Systems. Such actions like killing, theft, sexual misconduct, and falsehood seem to be condemned universally. The differences emerge when we examine the question more closely, *e.g.* when we investigate the rationale for these rules, whether they are absolute or are relative to some other end, and so on. The rule against killing could be taken as an example. Many ethical systems proscribe only the killing of humans (*i.e.* murder), but Buddhism applies the rule to all sentient existence. Furthermore even in the case of humans, exceptions are sometimes allowed, *e.g.* for "holy" or "just" war. Buddhism admits of no such exemptions. In Buddhism the ethical quality of actions depends on the mental factors associated with their commission or even contemplation, and on the impact they have on the well-being of others.

If action is committed with greed, aversion or delusion it is unwholesome (akusala), but the degree of moral reprehensibility (and karmic consequence) depends on a whole host of factors. Even an "accidental" killing could have adverse consequences if it was caused through negligence and unmindfulness, which is a kind of "Delusion" (moha). What has been said of the rule regarding killing, may also be extended to the other ethical precepts as well. Furthermore Buddhist ethics does not stop at the Five Precepts (panchasila), which provides only the very minimum for the proper conduct of lay persons.

The second criterion that could be adduced for the evaluation of ethical Systems relates to the motivation for adhering to the ethical rules of the system, religious or secular. In Buddhism the goal of ethical conduct is self-control, self-understanding, and self-development.

It is an essential prerequisite for the training of the mind, the elimination of ignorance and the attainment of Enlightenment.

Theistic religions usually require the adherence to their ethical precepts as a means to the union with God, whether in an abstract metaphysical sense or more directly as entry into a kingdom ruled by God, or even the enjoyment of pleasures in a heavenly paradise.

In such a system the most important rule, precept or commandment is not usually an ethical one, but belief in, love of, submission and obedience to, and veneration of God. This is thus placed at the head of the Judeo-Christian decalogue, with the ethical rules coming subsequently. When we look at "secular" ethics, such as those embodied in legal systems, the objective is usually the avoidance of social conflict, the regularization of property rights, and the like.

Of course, some secular laws (*e.g.* those relating to the so-called "victimless crimes") are more directly "moral" in nature, but these too usually are indirect social objectives. The pursuit of Buddhist ethics too leads to social harmony, but this harmony is achieved through individual perfection, rather than through the compulsory observance of legalistic rules. But because of the non-compulsive nature of Buddhist ethics, they are not intended to replace the laws of society, but neither are those of other ethical systems erected on religious and philosophical foundations.

The third aspect of the question relates to the way in which "good" and "bad" conduct results in appropriate consequences. This is the question of the "policing of the rules". Here two approaches may be distinguished. One is where some kind of trial and punishment (or reward) is instituted individually for each person. The supreme judicial authority could be God to the theist; or simply the normal judicial processes of society in the case of the secularist and the materialist. The second approach relies on the workings of an impersonal law (like the Law of Karma in its Buddhist and Hindu-Jam forms).

The legal model of trial-and-punishment is best suited to the enforcement of the laws of society, such as are necessary for the preservation of the authority of the State and the well-being of society. When this model is used to evaluate personal moral conduct and behaviour, as in the theory of divine judgement, several curious features arise. One that could be mentioned is the doctrine of the "forgiveness of sins". According to this doctrine the exercise of divine grace could wipe out "sins" and negate the principle that actions bring their own reward. In such a system the ultimate factor which determines the destiny of an individual is not the scrupulous observance of the ethical rules of the system, but the element of blind faith in its dogmas.

In Buddhism the operation of the law of kamma (karma) is all-pervasive and universal. Its exact modus operandi is not detailed, and may not be immediately obvious. Unlike in some other versions of the karmic hypothesis, in Buddhism there is no mechanical equivalence between action and result (vipaka). As mentioned above the karmic quality of an act depends on a whole host of circumstances. In the accumulation of kammas, good and bad, the fruiting of some may be postponed or delayed while that of others could be immediate. What is certain is that the law of kamma makes divine authority, divine grace, etc. redundant.

Thus in spite of superficial similarities, Buddhist ethics differs from other ethical systems when analysed in detail. In the Noble Eightfold Path the elements corresponding to morality and ethics are Right Speech, Right Action and Right Livelihood. These three together constitute siila. The cultivation of siila normally proceeds alongside progress in the other two great constituents of the Path, namely mental training (bhavana) and wisdom-insight (panna). Because of the mutually supportive nature of the three components of morality, mental development and wisdom, it is difficult to argue about the relative importance of these three components. Nonetheless it has long been the generally accepted view that panna is both the threshold as well as the culmination of Buddhist practice, with the other two components of *sla* and bhavana being the chief means to the realization of this great objective.

The distinction between ends and means is very important in the understanding of the true place of ethics in Buddhism. For the ordinary person (putujjana) ethical conduct may appear to be an end in itself, but for the adept (sekha) it is a means to the realization of a greater end. Because of the Buddha's custom of proclaiming the Dhamma according the varied capacities of his listeners, there are diverse references to the importance of siila in the Buddha's discourses which at first sight might appear to be inconsistent or even contradictory. This apparent inconsistency, however, disappears when the actual context is considered. By way of illustration we can consider two places in the Pali Cannon of Buddhism which seem to attach different degrees of importance to morality (siila) in the Buddha's system.

"The first of these comes from the Brahmajala Sutra. This is the first discourse in the Sutra Pitaka (the section dealing with Buddhist doctrines), and this exalted position accorded to it reflects its importance to the early Buddhists, perhaps to the Buddha himself. This discourse was occasioned by a report brought to the Buddha of derisive commuents made on him, his Doctrine and the Sangha by a wandering teacher called Suppiya, and the equally unfounded praise bestowed on him by Brahmadatta a follower of Suppiya.

This had led to conflict between teacher and pupil, and disquiet amongst the followers of the Buddha. The Buddha commences the discourse by advising his followers to consider all statements made about him, whether favourable or unfavourable, in an objective manner, with equanimity and even-handedness, and then to reject what was wrong, whether it be unfounded blame or unfounded praise, and to point out these errors in a calm and reasoned manner.

The Buddha anticipated that much of the praise heaped on him would be for the wrong reasons: "It is in respect only of trifling things (appamattakam) or matters of little value (oramattakam), or mere morality (siilamattakam) that an unconverted man (putujjana) when praising the Buddha would speak". What is interesting from our point of view is that the Buddha considers the mere keeping of ethical rules to be a matter not worthy of any real praise. In this sutra the Buddha groups ethical rules into three categories.

The first of these (the cula siila) contains the basic ethical precepts (like the "killing of living things") which are usually included amongst the Five Precepts laid down for the guidance of lay persons. The other two categories (the majjhima and maha siilas) contain, ethical rules of lesser importance or those specially laid down for monks. As against these "moralities", none of which is deserving of real praise, the Buddha describes those things that are deserving of real praise. These are the "things profound difficult to realize, hard to understand, tranquillising, sweet, not to be grasped by mere logic, subtle, comprehensible only to the wise".

More specifically they turn out to be the realization of Right View (samma ditti), and the refutation of wrong views, in which connection the Buddha outlines the famous list of sixty-two schools of thought, ranging from theism to materialism, which then as now, were the main contenders with the Dhamma. Even though the Brahmajala was mainly concerned with what was praiseworthy in a Buddha, it does provide a clear statement of the principle that wisdom-insight (panna) ranks above siila and bhavana in the accomplishments necessary for the realization of the Buddhist goal of Nibbana. The second extract from the Dhama which we shall consider seems to paint a slightly different picture. This is probably the best known stanza in the Dhamapada, itself the best-known of the Buddhist books. This Stanza (No.183) with its usual translation is as follows:

Sabbapapassa akara.na.m, kusalassa upasamapda,
sacittapariyodapana.m eta.m Buddhana sasana.m
Not to do any evil, to do good,
To purify one's mind, this is the teaching of the Buddhas.

The ethical import of this Stanza is obvious. It seems to claim that the Buddha's teaching is threefold: avoid unethical conduct, cultivate good deeds, and train one's mind. There is no question of the ethical purport of the first two postulates. "Training the mind" could also be interpreted as an ethical postulate, especially when we consider the Buddhist view that evil thoughts generated by an unguarded mind are karmically effective.

The last phrase of this Stanza is usually taken to mean that the three ethical postulates constitute the whole (or at least the most important part) of the Dhamma. However it could be taken to mean that these ethical principles are part of the teachings of the Buddha, and not necessarily the part that constitutes the Buddha's unique discovery. In the Commentary to the Dhammapada it is stated that this and the two following Stanzas constituted the admonition (ovadagata) delivered by the previous legendary Buddhas to bhikkhus on the uposatha days.

In the explanation of the meaning of the terms in this Stanza, the Commentator says that "to do good" really means the "generation and development of skilful acts from ordination until the realization of the path of Arahat-hood", while "purifying the mind" means the elimination of the five "hindrances" which are obstacles to the realization of jhanic states during meditation. All this is in keeping with the general purpose of these stanzas, which was to serve as exhortations to Bhikkhus on the uposatha day, and not to serve as a summary of the Buddha-Dhamma.

The uniqueness of Buddhist ethics lies in its many outstanding qualities. It is all-embracing and comprehensive without being impractical or impossible to follow. It is free from taboos relating to diet, dress, behaviour etc. which very often pass as ethical principles. It serves the needs of the worldling as well as those of the recluse. It is useful to the rich and to the poor; to the powerful as well as to the powerless. To conform to Buddhist ethics one need not have to be a "Buddhist"; and it serves as a norm to measure the ethical standard of other teachings. But Buddhist ethics is only the threshold for those who wish to pursue the Buddha's path to Enlightenment and the end of all ill.

BUDDHIST ETHICS

Pai Lu-tien, a famous Chinese poet, author, and statesman who lived in the thirteenth century of the Christian era, once went to see an eminent Buddhist monk whose saintly life was known far and near, and asked him if he would instruct him in the essentials of Buddhist doctrine. The monk assented and recited the following gatha:

"Commit no wrong, but good deeds do,
And let thy heart be pure,
All Buddhas teach this truth,
Which will for aye endure."

The statesman-poet was not at all satisfied with this simple moral teaching, for he expected to have something abstruse, recondite, and highly philosophical from the mouth of such a prominent and virtuous personality. Said the poet, "Every child is familiar with this Buddhist injunction. What I wish to learn from you is the highest and most fundamental teaching of your faith." But the monk retorted, "Every child may know of this gatha, but even a silvery-haired man fails to put it into practice." Thereupon, it is said, the poet reverentially bowed and went home meditatively.

If we are requested today to state what is the most fundamental in Buddhist ethics, we have to make the same assertion. There may be and in fact are many schools and denominations in Buddhism, each claiming to have transmitted the true spirit of Buddha; but they will be unanimous in declaring that the gatha aforementioned is one of the common grounds on which they all stand.

"Sabba papassa akaranam" is heard in all Southern monasteries, and the lines "Chu wo mo tso, etc.," are seen everywhere in the Eastern lands of Buddhism.

If Buddhism were called a sort of ethical culture society on account of this simple code of morality, its followers would make no objection to it, for the recognition of a personal God, or the conception of original sin, or belief in a risen Christ is not thought indispensable to Buddhist salvation.

Let a man do what is good and avoid what is bad and have his heart as pure as he can of all egotistic impulses and desires, and he will be delivered from the clutches of ignorance and misery. What ever his dogmatic views on religion, he is one of the enlightened who are above bigotry, intolerance, vanity, conceit, pedantry, and prejudice. He must truly be said to be one whose spiritual insight has penetrated into the depths of existence.

Now, the question is: What is good? What is evil? And how is the heart to be cleansed? I am not going to discuss here these great ethical and religious problems from a mere theoretical point of view. Buddhism has nothing to do with utilitarianism or intuitionalism or hedonism or what not. Buddhism is most practical in its announcement of what constitutes goodness. It dogmatically and concretely points out good deeds one by one. First, negatively, it enumerates ten deeds of goodness (kusalam) as most fundamental in Buddhist ethics; while, positively, it considers the six paramitas (virtues of perfection) or eightfold path as the route leading to a virtuous life.

The ten deeds of goodness are: (1) Not to kill any living being; (2) Not to take anything that does not belong to oneself; (3) Not to look at the other sex with an unclean heart; (4) Not to speak falsehood; (5) Not to calumniate; (6) Not to use vile language; (7) Not to make sensational utterances; (8) Not to be greedy; (9) Not to be out of temper; and lastly, (10) Not to be confused by false doctrines. Later Buddhists, however, make ten affirmative propositions out of those just mentioned, thus: It is good (1) to save any living being, (2) to practise charity, (3) to be clean-minded, (4) to speak truth, (5) to promote friendship, (6) to talk softly and gently, (7) to be straightforward in speech, (8) to be content with one's own possessions, (9) to be meek and humble, and (10) to think clearly and rightly.

The six paramitas or virtues of perfection are: (1) Charity, which includes the giving away of worldly possessions as well as the proclamation of the Good Law, (2) The observation of the moral precepts as formulated by Buddha, (3) Meekness, (4) Strenuosity, (5) Contemplation, (6) Spiritual enlightenment.

The eightfold path is: (1) Right view, (2) Right reflection, (3) Right speech, (4) Right deed, (5) Right livelihood, (6) Right striving, (7) Right understanding, (8) Right contemplation.

In these various enumerations of Buddhist virtues, what is most unique are perhaps the virtues of strenuosity and those of contemplation and enlightenment. To be good Buddhists, we must never be indolent, whiling away our time to no purpose. Mere piety will not do, so long as there is some work to be accomplished for the sake of humanity and civilization.

Love, again, must be accompanied with enlightenment, for the affection is very frequently wasted on account of its blindness. God-fearing is recommendable, but without contemplation we fail to recognize the purport of our own position in the system of the universe. Mere passion leads to fervour and violence if not properly guided by contemplation which brings enlightenment, revealing the reason of existence and purifying the heart of ignorance.

Ignorance, according to Buddhism, is the root of all evil, and therefore it advises us in strong terms to have ignorance completely destroyed. And it is only then that the all-illuminating light of enlightenment guides us gloriously to the destination of all beings, where we gain purity of heart, and whatever flows from this eternal fountain of purity is good.

It is evident, then, that by purity of heart is meant absence of ignorance and self-will. But it is not a negative condition, for the most essential postulate of Buddhism is that in each of us there abide the indwelling reason of the universe, which, when released from the temporal bondage of ignorance and self-will, becomes the master of itself by reducing everything to subjection and restoring it to its right place. In a pure heart, therefore, the universal reason manifests itself in its full glory and works its own destiny unmolested.

What one with such a heart wills is what makes the bird sing and the flower smile, what has raised the mountain and makes the water flow. He is hungry and the universe wishes to eat; he is asleep and all the world hybernates. This sounds extraordinary, but the enlightened understand it perfectly well. We cannot make the blind see what we ourselves see. The blind may protest that we are deceiving them; but could we do otherwise, inasmuch as they are deprived of the sense we have, or they have not yet learned how to make use of it? It is declared by Buddhists, therefore, that to realize fully the sanctity of religious life one must have Buddha-wisdom awakened from its unconscious slumber in which it is indulging from time out of mind.

Analytically, purity of heart consists of sympathy and intelligence, and on this groundwork the structure of practical Buddhism is founded. Sympathy is the tremulation of the spiritual cord which unites the hearts of all sentient beings; and it is intelligence that discovers the presence of the sacred cord in every one of us and keeps it from being entangled. The cord freely responds to cries of suffering. The heart contrives to effect all the possible means to relieve sentient beings from misery and ignorance. The ten deeds of goodness, the eightfold path, the six virtues of perfection, and many other good things all flow from this one source of pure-heartedness. It is, then, of unqualified importance in the ethics of Buddhism to have one's heart perfectly cleansed and free from the dust of egotism which has been accumulating through the want of enlightenment. In this sense "blessed are the pure in heart"; they may not see God as he is superficially and superstitiously understood, but they will surely come into personal touch with the ultimate authority of conduct and also perceive that the author is not residing outside of their being but within themselves. We read in the Dharmapada:

"Manopubbangama dhamma, manosettha, manomaya;
Manasa, ce padutthana bhasati va karoti va,
Tato nam dukkham anveti, cakkara va vahato padam.
"Manopubbangama dhamma, manosettha, manomaya;
Manasa ce pasannena bhasati va karoti va,
Tato nam sukhara anveti, chaya va anapayini."

In this respect Buddhism can be said to have a decidedly idealistic tendency, since it fully recognizes the paramountcy of ideas in the moral realm. But we must not lose sight of the fact that Buddhism is not a system of metaphysics, but a religion which is practical more than anything else. What it teaches is the profound spiritual experience of every enlightened man, while the philosopher and theorist will speculate on the facts and offer whatever interpretation they may please or feel compelled to give to account adequately for them.

Buddhism is often charged with passiveness and quietism, lacking the "push" of some other religions; and the backwardness of Asiatic nations in the general march of humanity is sometimes ascribed to the influence of Buddhism. Though I am not here entering upon any lengthy polemics, a few words may not be altogether inopportune to refute such an erroneous opinion as this.

If there is anything passive in Eastern culture, which is often no more than tolerance or indifference or self-restraint, it is not due to Buddhism but to the racial idiosyncrasy of Asiatic peoples. Buddhism teaches contemplation and tranquillity and at the same time strenuosity, indefatigable energy in following truth and in destroying ignorance. We see many admirable examples among its believers who have fully illustrated these virtues in their person. The history of Buddhism, while perfectly free from bloodshed and inhumanity, evidences how far its moral teachings have been carried out. Buddhist ethics is not certainly passive or negative, unless the absence of arrogance, aggressiveness, intolerance, bigotry, and fanaticism could be called so.

Religion in its social aspect is not omnipotent, nor is it absolute, as is imagined by some. It is, like many other things created by man, a human institution; it has been discovered, shaped, developed according to the inner necessity of mankind; and as long as he is imperfect and steering his course through innumerable obstacles, religion also must share his imperfection and adapt itself to ever-changing surroundings. Instead of imposing its ideals upon man tyrannically and absolutely, religion reconciles itself to his needs, going through all the necessary modifications.

Therefore, one religion is diversely interpreted by different peoples among whom it may thrive. To suppose that religion could do anything it desires without regard to individual, national, racial peculiarities is far from the fact. The difference between Oriental and Occidental civilization is by no means due to the difference between Christianity and Buddhism.

On the other hand, the difference between the two religions is due to the difference between the two great types of Civilization. Truth, be it religious or philosophical or scientific, is universal, and as such does not allow any modification or distortion. But it suffers modification in its practical application, for it is like a mathematical formula or figure. When conceived a priori, it is formal and not subject to any concrete individualization, which latter in fact is the condition of its particular forms.

In conclusion let me say most emphatically that the ethics of Buddhism is summed up in the purification of the heart, in keeping oneself unspotted even though living in the world; and from this eternal root must sprout such things of God as love, a heart of compassion, the virtue of strenuosity, humbleness of mind, longsuffering, forbearing one another, forgiving one another, and freedom from all evils. It is said that there were eighty-four thousand virtues of perfection practised by all Bodhisattvas, but they are no more than so many leaves and branches growing from the one stem of pure-heartedness.

ECONOMIC ETHICS OF BUDDHISM

Buddhist economic ethics--that is Buddhist values with regard to wealth and economic activity, either within society or within the sangha--are often slighted in Western scholarly studies of Buddhism even though they play a significant role as a part of overall Buddhist philosophy regarding social life and even enlightenment itself. This is due perhaps partly to an implicit interpretation of Buddhism among some scholars as being a religion focused primarily upon an individualistic pursuit of enlightenment rather than also a set of practiced social, political, and economic ethics.

To an extent of course this characterization holds true, for at least a part of both the Theravada and Mahayana traditions. Yet it also ignores clearly developed Buddhist attitudes and values toward economic activities, some explicitly expressed in the various Vinaya codes for monks, others less explicitly, but still clearly enough, in various stories and sutras which lay out general principles of behaviour for lay believers.

This chapter offers an outline of the development of Buddhist economic ethics using examples from early Theravada Buddhism in India and the Mahayana tradition as it evolved in India, medieval China, and medieval and early modern Japan, in order to illustrate the pattern of continuities and transformations these ethics have undergone.

By "economic ethics" the chapter refers to four broad areas: (1) attitudes toward wealth, *i.e.*, its accumulation, use, and distribution, including the issues of economic justice and equality/inequality; (2) attitudes toward charity, *i.e.*, how and to whom wealth should be given; (3) attitudes toward human labour and secular occupations in society; and (4) actual economic activities of temples and monasteries which reflect the lived-practice of Buddhist communities' economic ethics. By "Buddhist," the chapter refers to mainline Buddhist thinking in history, as represented by the various Vinaya codes, sutras and stories, and economic activities of major sects, monasteries, and temples.

Since I will be dealing with a range of "Buddhisms" as they developed in various times and places, I have relied upon previous scholarly work to help define what the general trends of the economic ethics of these various "Buddhisms" were. This approach assumes that there was no one Buddhist economic ethic for all of these different times and places, just as there is no one "Buddhism."

Yet through an examination of the economic ethics of these different "Buddhisms," certain continuities and differences between them become clear. Moreover, the presence of these continuities would seem to allow us to make a number of tentative conclusions about what the development and nature of these various Buddhist economic ethics as a whole might share. These can be summarized as follows:

(1) Buddhist soteriologies affect Buddhist economic ethics in fundamental ways. By defining how enlightenment is achieved, what enlightenment is and what has ultimate value, Buddhist soteriologies set the parameters for what Buddhist economic ethics will be in any particular tradition or school of Buddhism.

(2) Within these soteriologies, the major Buddhist concepts of karma, anaatman, "suunyataa and pratiitya-samutpaada (dependent coorigination) each help determine the shape of the Buddhist economic ethics of any particular school. However, the impact of these conceptions ultimately is ambiguous and depends to a large extent upon the interpretation of them within the particular sociocultural and historical situation.

(3) Contrary to the common image of monk and laity ethics being two completely separate realms with little commonality, the ideal economic ethics of monks and laity share a common overall principle (that of non-attachment to wealth). Yet, they still differ in both specifics (rules regarding wealth, labour, and the like) and specificity (how explicitly they define the proper attitudes and morals regarding wealth, labour, and so on).

(4) The development and evolution of Buddhist economic ethics within Theravada and Mahayana reveal both lines of continuity between these traditions (*e.g.*, lay ethics emphasizing sharing of wealth with others) as well as clear transformations in ideas (*e.g.*, Zen attitudes toward monk labour). Transformations usually are traceable to the influence of indigenous thought or of other historical peculiarities in the way Buddhism was accepted in the new country where it entered (*e.g.*, China and Japan).

(5) Buddhist economic ethics tend not to be just the reflection of religious attitudes toward the economy but also religious attitudes toward the state (polity). This latter relationship (Buddhism and the polity) usually was characterized by interdependence and reciprocity, that is, state support for the sangha in return for the sangha's spiritual protection and legitimization of the state. The implication of this relationship for Buddhist economic ethics was that they usually (a) did not challenge or question the existing economic distribution of wealth but emphasized instead religious giving to the sangha (daana) as the ideal social action; and (b) relied upon secular authorities (the king or state) to help define the specifics of lay Buddhist economic ethics, along with guidelines given in various sutra.

(6) Buddhist economics ethics for the laity were not inherently antagonistic to the development of capitalism, but in fact supported a primitive capitalism among the merchant classes in early Buddhist India, and medieval China and Japan. This could be seen in both merchant-type lay ethics, which encouraged the accumulation of wealth along with certain restraints on consumption of this wealth, and direct economic activities by Buddhist monasteries themselves, which led to innovations in business practices and implicit support for commercial tendencies in society as a whole.

(7) Issues of economic equality and distributive justice were dealt with in Buddhist economic ethics primarily through the ideas of karma, religious giving (daana), and compassion (karuna) and focused less on changing the

overall existing distribution of wealth than on cultivating the proper ethical attitudes toward wealth and giving. At the same time, in the occasional use of Maitreya by revolutionary and other protest movements, there were the beginnings of the development of a more socially activist and transformative economic ethic focusing on ideas about economic and political justice.

In the remainder of this chapter, I will examine the above themes in more depth, beginning with evidence from early Theravada and then moving on to Mahayana in its main forms in India, China, and Japan. Given the space limitations, only the major trends of both teachings and actual economic practices will be discussed. Together however, these offer sufficient evidence to form an overall picture of Buddhist ethics as they evolved over time, as well as some tentative conclusions about the relationship between Buddhist economic ethics and such issues as the development of capitalism and concepts of economic justice.

BUDDHIST ETHICS AND SOCIAL CRITICISM

Buddhism arose in India during a period of intense intellectual and social ferment. It was a period during which the authority of the Vedas had been placed in doubt, the concept of god as a supreme being and creator was in question, the hereditary restrictions on caste mobility were under attack, and the efficacy of Brahminical rituals was being challenged.

The authors of the Upanishads had opened the door for various heterodox currents to emerge in society, and amongst the most significant of these were the Lokayatas who polemicized against religious charlatans, and the Nyayavadis whose rational epistemology created the foundation for intense philosophical debate and encouraged the investigation of the real world based on reason and logic, freed from the burden of superstition and irrational adherence to burdensome rituals. Various ideological sects competed for the attention and acceptance of the ruling elites and the public. The most important amongst these were the Jains and the Buddhists. Although each of the various sects made original and interesting contributions to philosophy, it was the early

Buddhists who attempted to provide a unified philosophical system where ethical conduct and social criticism lay at the very core of their ideological system.

Although today, Buddhism is viewed as a religion by many of its followers, the early Buddhists sects were either strongly atheistic or agnostic. The atheists believed that rather than "God having created man in his own image" it was man who had created "God" in his image. In their view, the liberation of humanity was contingent upon humanity shedding the delusion that "God" existed.

Other parables from surviving Buddhist texts indicate agnosticism. For instance, there is a suggestion that Buddhist followers ought not to waste their time on unsolvable metaphysical questions such as "does god exist". The search to identify the "one true god" or to speculate on the nature of god was seen as an exercise in futility.

But the most frequently cited argument against god by the Buddhists was that if an omnipotent and omniscient being such as "God" truly existed, and who was also all good, there could not be the kind of dukkha (suffering) that was so widespread in the real world.

These shlokas (verses) from the Bhuridatta Jataka illustrates this point:

> *If the creator of the entire world they call "God" be the lord of every being, why does he order such misfortune, and not create concord?*

If the creator of the entire world they call "God" be the lord of every being, why let prevail deceit, lies and ignorance, why create such inequity and injustice?

If the creator of the entire world they call "God" be the lord of every being, then an evil master is he, knowing what's right did let wrong prevail!

Unlike religions that ascribed earthly miseries to human sinfulness that brought upon the wrath of a vengeful god who needed to be feared, Buddhism saw the root of human suffering in ignorance that could only be ended through the acquisition of wisdom. Rather than expect some supernatural entity to end human suffering, the Buddhists argued that it was in human hands to end their sorrows through conduct and action driven by knowledge and correct understanding of human nature and the physical world. Hence, the aspiration for knowledge (jigyasa) was seen as the answer to blind faith. Although the Buddhists were not alone in developing this view, the elaboration of this point of view became pivotal to early Buddhist philosophy.

Central to Buddhist philosophy was an understanding of human nature and what caused dukkha-*i.e.* human suffering. They saw human personality as constituting five attributes, *i.e.* body, feeling, perception, disposition and consciousness, and used this framework to develop their understanding of human suffering. Citing examples of conditions that led to human suffering, such as aging, sickness and death, or association with the unpleasant, (or separation from the pleasant), or the inability to get what one wished-they concluded that suffering was a condition of stress and conflict inherent within human existence and interaction with the world.

They also connected suffering to the very impermanence of things. They observed how people lamented over the loss of a loved one, or experienced sorrow when something or someone that had once given them happiness became separated from them. They noted that even human pleasures were not immune from suffering because they didn't last forever, and the loss of pleasure inevitably left people feeling deprived. Seeing as how clinging to things (that were necessarily impermanent) was one of the primary causes of dukkha, they cautioned against excessive attachment. At the same time, they recognized a recurring and more general type of existential unease and anxiety (aniccha) that arises from the very transience of life, and our inability to control or comprehend all worldly phenomenon, which they characterized as viparinama-dukkha.

But the Buddhists did not see dukkha only emanating from the difficulties of an individual. They also saw suffering emerge on a much larger scale from hostile social conditions such as poverty, war, and social oppression which they described as dukkha-dukkha. As a formula (char-mulya) for addressing these different types of suffering, the Buddhists advocated a four-fold scheme of (a) recognizing the problem *i.e.* suffering (dukkha); (b) identifying the cause of the suffering-such as craving stemming from ignorance (samudaya); (c) establishing the goal of ending the problem (nirodha)-*i.e.* the cessation of suffering (nirvana); (d) conducting life in a manner that was consistent with the cessation of suffering-following the right path or engaging in the right practice (marga).

Followers were thus goaded into developing both a sense of personal ethics and a social conscience:

> *"He who has understanding and great wisdom does not think of harming himself or another, nor of harming both alike. He rather thinks of his own welfare, of that of others, of that of both, and of the welfare of the whole world. In that way one shows understanding and great wisdom." Anguttara Nikaya-(Gradual Sayings)*
>
> *"By protecting oneself (e.g., morally), one protects others; by protecting others, one protects oneself." Samyukta Nikaya (Kindred Sayings)*

Human actions (kamma, kaama, or karma) in the Buddhist framework were to be judged based on both the intention or motive (chetanaa) and the consequences (vipaaka) of the action. Altruistic actions which helped in the establishment and promotion of a just society were encouraged in the dharmaniyama (moral duty code).

{The discourses, or sutras in the Digha Nikaya, illustrate how there was deep concern with the creation of social conditions favourable to the cultivation of Buddhist values and the expansion of social equity and justice. These views undoubtedly influenced the creation of a "welfare state" during the reign of emperor, Ashoka (B.C. 274-236)}

In their theories of causality Buddhists challenged the view that human destiny was unaffected by the ethics or morality of human actions. They countered the doctrine of amoral causation (akriyavaada) whose adherents argued that there was no merit in doing good and no demerit for doing evil. (An extreme expression of such thinking was seen in philosophers who denied all morality and saw no crime in the killing of any person.)

Realizing that such a world-view could lead to the rejection of moral distinctions and personal responsibility for ones actions, they argued strenuously against such beliefs. They also argued against the theory of Makkali Ghosha (or Ghoshala) who believed that human fate was predetermined, and therefore denied that human actions had any bearing on the results of things (ahetuvaada) and maintained that human intention and effort were essentially powerless in changing human destiny, and therefore advocated fatalism (niyati).

They also countered philosophers from the school of "absolute skepticism" who doubted everything and never committed themselves to any specific position in doctrinal debates. Philosophers from this school such as Sanjaya Belarthaputra (who was known as a theorist of endless equivocation or an equivocationist (amraavikkhepavaadin)) were criticized in the Brahmajaala Sutra (or Sutra) as "eel-wrigglers" who were incapable of taking a definitive stance on the vital philosophical questions of the day. Such skepticism was seen as emanating from both the fear of being in error and the lack of knowledge (or inability) to provide reasonable answers to question put forward for discussion. Such all-pervading doubt coupled with a cynical skepticism (vichikicchaa) was viewed as a serious mental hindrance, a fetter in the path to wisdom.

Other theories that contradicted the notion that human actions mattered were theories of accidentalism (ahetu-apachayavaada), theistic determinism (ishvaranimmaanavaada) and past-action determinism (purvaketavaada or purvekatahetu). All of these were opposed by the Buddhists. Accidentalism was an indeterminist theory which held that whatever was experienced was uncaused and unconditioned by human intervention. Theistic determinism was a determinist theory, which held that whatever was experienced was due to God's will or by plan of a "Supreme-Being". Past-action determinism was also a determinist theory, but it held the belief that whatever was experienced, whether pleasurable or painful or indifferent was entirely due to ones past actions (from a previous life), and ones present actions had no relevance. The danger in each of these theories was highlighted in these words: "Thus for those who fall back on these three erroneous views as essential dogma, there is neither the will to do what is ought to be done, or not to do what is ought not to be done, nor necessity to do this deed or abstain from that deed. No moral improvement or intellectual culture can be expected from them."

Some of the theories in circulation at that time built on a germ of truth but generalized to the point of absurdity. For instance the accidentalists were correct only to the extent that certain things did indeed appear to happen by random chance or accident. But they failed to recognize that sometimes what may have seemed to be accidental was more due to inadequate understanding or improper or incomplete perception, and that other activities had a clearly discernible cause. To deal with the extreme generalizations of such theorists, they introduced a middle standpoint for their epistemology and ethics.

They thus rejected the theory admitting that everything exists (sabba atthii ti) and in permanence-*i.e.* the extreme of eternalism (sassatavaada), and its opposite which advocated that nothing actually exists (sabba natthii ti) *i.e.* nihilism (the denial of all reality in real-world phenomenon) or the extreme of annihilationalism (ucchedavaada). Related to their critique of the eternalist and nihilist philosophies was their rejection of both hedonism and self-mortification (attakilamathaanuyoga) which they viewed as painful, fruitless, unprofitable and ignoble.

Buddhist texts also expressed suspicion about claims by heretical teachers of being constantly "all-knowing" and "all-seeing" and in possession of "all-embracing knowledge-and-vision." Such claims were countered with arguments relating to the actual behaviour of such charlatans in different situations. For instance, they wondered why such "all-knowing" and "all-seeing" spiritual teachers lost their way in an unfamiliar place or why they were unable to escape from trouble while countering a fierce animal such as dog, elephant, horse or bull. Moreover, if they were really omniscient, they wouldn't need to ask for people's names, clans, or the name of a village or market town or make enquiries about anything. That they did such things indicated that their knowledge was evidently limited just like that of any average worldly person (puthujjana).

Unlike religions that were based on revealed truth or the sanctity of every word in a holy textbook, the Buddhist belief system prescribed reasoning based on investigation as the means of determining ones dhamma, (or dharma as in Hindu practise). In a parable in the Kaalaama Sutra, followers of Budhism are advised not to accept any moral codes on the following ten grounds: (1) Vedic authority (anussava), (2) tradition (paramparaa), (3) hearsay or report (itikiraa), (4) textual authority (pittakasampadaa), (5) apparent agreebility of the view (sama o no garu), (6) authority of the holder of the view (takkahetu), (7) apparent logicality of the view (nayahetu), (8) the fact that the view is an accepted standpoint (aakaaraparivitakka), (9) inadequate reflection on reasons (bhabbaruupataa), or (10) the fact that the view agrees with one's own ditthinijjhaanakkhanti).

In this manner, the Buddhism developed a very sophisticated philosophical system in which social ethics were integrated with rational investigation of human nature, social organization and the physical world. Buddhist ideas and concepts left a powerful impression on other Indian philosophical and religious belief systems, and over time, many commonalities developed amongst the competing ideologies.

However, there were also certain problems with the Buddhist world view which prevented its complete acceptance by intellectuals committed to the scientific method. For instance, although the Buddhists rejected the theory of past action determinism, they did posit the existence of a soul which survived a person's death and carried with it the merits and demerits of a person's past lives. Presumably this concept was essential to the Buddhist goal of encouraging right conduct but it was rejected by those who considered the soul as inseparable from the body and did not believe that the soul survived death.

Those who rejected the concept of transmigration of the soul naturally couldn't accept the idea that human destiny had anything to do with merits and demerits accumulated in previous incarnations of the "soul". In their view, morality and ethics were entirely social constructs and had to be dealt with accordingly. The realists (such as the Nyayavadis) who shared the Buddhist concern for morals and ethics in society argued that while morals and ethics ought to be encouraged, they could only be enforced through societal laws and judicial codes.

Another problem facing the Buddhists was that in many ways, their views were too advanced for their times. Society had not yet developed to the point where education was universal, and knowledge of the real world sufficient to prevent superstitions and irrational beliefs from being completely abandoned by the masses. In an era where society had only limited control over nature, it was inevitable that sections of society would continue with beliefs in deities and supernatural phenomenon in the hope that they may be spared from natural disasters or that their crops might withstand attacks from pests and disease. Thus although the Buddhists had a very important and salutatory effect on Indian society, the most advanced Buddhist concepts could be understood and practised by only a minority in society.

Over time, the spirit of inquiry and rational investigation that had spurred the early Buddhist scholars towards dialectical thinking and critical social analysis became more and more replaced by narrow and literalist interpretations of the earlier texts. For instance, advice against accepting something that appeared "logical" without personal verification was taken to mean that logic could be rejected.

Advice against wasting ones time on unsolvable metaphysical questions was also taken too literally and many Buddhist scholars remained aloof from the metaphysical debates pursued by other philosophical schools such as those of the Jains and the Nyaya Vaisheshikas. What they didn't anticipate was that some of these debates might lead to useful advances in mathematics or deeper understanding of human thought processes and new insights on human memory and psychology. These led to valuable advances in the interpretation of moods and emotions-thus benefiting Indian art, literature and music. In addition, later Buddhist monks lapsed into some of the very things that had been attacked by the early

Buddhists such as indulgence in unnecessary and elaborate rituals, belief in supra-natural phenomenon, and alienation of the priests from the masses. Activities such as meditation which were encouraged as a means to gaining wisdom became ends in themselves, and were turned into idealistic fetishes.

Although Buddhist monks dutifully delivered sermons on right conduct and right action, they often failed to engage in relevant and timely social criticism-and did not always connect the textual suggestions to concrete practice. Intra-Buddhist disputes developed around less significant details, even as some of the most important ideas that had initially shaped the philosophy were pushed into the background. As a result Buddhism as it was practised came to be associated with idealism and inaction. Whereas the early Buddhists saw no merit in worshipping god or its images, later Buddhism developed a pantheon of deities not very different from other Indian religions.

Thus even as Buddhism had spread almost throughout Asia by the 5th-6th C AD, it gradually began to lose its distinct edge and liberating influence on much of Indian society. Within the Indian subcontinent, strains of Buddhism survived in Sri Lanka, Bengal, Bhutan, Sikkim, parts of Bihar and Nepal, and parts of Sindh, Punjab, Kashmir and Afghanistan. In parts of Orissa and adjoining regions (such as Chhattisgarh and Telengana), Tantric (and other) influences reshaped the practice of Buddhism. Yet, Buddhism continued to have an impact outside India and developed pockets of influence as far West as Syria, as well as in much of Central Asia (including what is now Uzbekistan, Tajikistan, Kyrgyzia, Kazakhstan) and Tibet. In the East, its influence was felt on virtually every nation including Burma, Thailand, Malaya and Indonesia, Laos, Cambodia, Vietnam, China, Korea and Japan.

As noted earlier, the vast literature of Buddhism (like much of Hindu or Jain literature) was not a literature of revelation and authority. Its essays on social ethics and moral responsibilities, its treatises on philosophy and science, its art and poetry were but pointers to a path to wisdom. This gave Buddhism both flexibility and adaptability. Owing to its non-hegemonic character and humanist appeal, Buddhism was adopted without coercion or force. It was also successfully fused with Hinduism in many parts of South East Asia just as elements of it had been integrated into Hindu practices in India. In China, it was integrated with Taoism and Confucian principles; in Japan with Shinto beliefs.

For several centuries, within India and outside, several people followed multiple faiths and identified as both Buddhists and Hindus, or. as both Buddhists and Tantrics, (or Buddhists and Taoists) and so on. During the Gupta period (and in other reigns), philosophers from various schools of thought received royal patronage and temple grants were conferred for the construction of Buddhist and Hindu monuments alike.

It is also important to recognize that the form of Buddhism that was embraced in each nation was often quite different. For instance, in Western and Central Asia, it was not the philosophical or intellectual aspects of Buddhism that were popularized, but rather, its personal moral codes. Buddhist prosletysers imbued their stories of the Buddha with examples of miraculous healing and super-natural compassion so as to win more followers.

While such tendencies were also to be seen as Buddhism travelled within India or outwards, in Burma, Sri Lanka and Thailand, Buddhism developed organizational structures that appear to have been much more resilient. It was perhaps realized that the development of Buddhist virtue would require leadership and constant interaction with the community. In these nations, Buddhism did not degenerate into the extremes of mysticism or retreatism that became commonplace in certain parts of India (such as in the foothills of the Western Himalayas). Burmese and Thai monks maintained a practical and benevolent connection with the community, and thus retained a measure of respect within the community.

This also appears to be the case in Japan. In Korea, the emphasis on gaining wisdom was taken very seriously, and Buddhist monks took the lead in promoting mass literacy. This propelled the growth of technologies associated with the production of paper, writing instruments, inks, and furniture. And unlike in India, (where due to Upanishadic influences, "inner" wisdom came to be favoured over outer wisdom), Buddhist concern for disseminating the writings of the Buddha had significant positive secular impact. In Korean (and other Eastern) Buddhism, there was the correct realization that a Buddhist mindset, or that a Buddhist society could not be constructed overnight.

There was thus the emphasis on the (helical) upgradation of individuals and society towards greater "Buddhahood". This philosophical element was perhaps significant in that it prevented the sort of philosophical stagnation that occurred in India, where followers too often sought immediate succour, and thus not only became divorced from reality, but also lost sight of the strategic potential of the philosophy.

In addition, it ought to be noted that Buddhism in India also had to contend with strongly anarchic and ultra-democratic tendencies. Precisely because its philosophical structure emphasized the relative and changing nature of truth, different tendencies under the Buddhist mantle competed for leadership through argument and debate. Initially, this led to important advances in democratic practices within the Sanghas. But over time, it also led to clashes of egoes, hair-splitting and deadlock. While some Buddhist sects compromised and fused with other tendencies (even alien tendencies), others remained fiercely autonomous. To survive, Buddhism had to confront both the tendency to be co-opted, as well as the tendency to atomize.

However, the catastrophic demise of Buddhism in India was triggered by the onslaught of Islam which first obliterated the remnants of Buddhism in Central Asia, and then later in Afghanistan and India. By and large, Buddhism survived only in those countries that escaped invasions by Islamic conquerors. As a gentle faith that encouraged its followers to abjure violence, it was perhaps unable to protect itself from iconoclasts and proselytizers who intended to enforce a new religio-political order.

Accustomed to centuries of peaceful coexistence, India's Buddhists had not anticipated the need to develop viable strategies for self-defence that could have combated the violence of India's Islamic conquerors who virtually obliterated Buddhism from the land of its birth.

Yet, it also appears that (in large part) later Buddhism had deviated considerably from the rational principles outlined in the early texts. Monasteries often became isolated from mainstream society, and monks who focused exclusively on meditative practices and idealistic or esoteric philosophical speculation contributed little to social progress. Some have even argued that the monastic orders had degenerated into sheer parasitism and were becoming a heavy social drain. Consequently, value judgements on the demise of Buddhism and the rise of Islam in India need to be made with a measure of caution.

Nevertheless, it must be acknowledged that the ascent of Islam was concomitant with the eclipse of Buddhism, and since the influence of Buddhism was greatly dependant on the existence of the monastic orders, the destruction of monasteries and their conversion to mosques and institutions of Quranic learning simply lead to mass conversions to Islam.

In the long term, this could have had the effect of stunting India's future intellectual development, since the destruction of important institutions of Buddhist learning also led to a notable decline in the opportunity (and social sanction) to study secular subjects such as logic and epistemology (which were also taught at Buddhist universities-such as Bhagalpur).

It might also be observed that the destruction of Buddhist centres of learning coincided with the destruction of extremely valuable textual materials-which could have been potentially rediscovered, and revived or reinterpreted by future generations of Indians so as to achieve a society that was more thoughtful and learned. Islamic texts did not offer anything comparable in terms of causality or epistemology. Nor did they offer the psychological, sociological, or moral insights that had been developed under the ambit of Buddhism. Nor was there any comparable stress on seeking knowledge or constantly updating ones understanding of nature and human society.

One can, therefore, only speculate as to the full consequences of this profound sociological and cultural loss (and discontinuity). But East of India, Buddhism did survive, and in countries such Korea, Thailand and Burma, it continued to enjoy a loyal popular following. Philosophical innovations also took place, and as noted earlier, Buddhist scholars in China, Korea and Japan offered their own commentaries and somewhat individual interpretations of Buddhist concepts and formulations outlined in later (5-7th C.) Indian texts. And although the sacking of monasteries and centres of learning (such as Nalanda and Vikramshila in Bihar) led to records of the original Buddhist texts being permanently destroyed, it has been possible to reconstruct some of them from translations that survived outside India such as in Thailand and Tibet.

Notwithstanding the virtual erasure of Buddhism in India, it is possible to infer from these reconstructed texts and other archaeological records (and surviving monuments and artifacts) that Buddhism had a very powerful impact in shaping the destiny of India, and in triggering a social and cultural renaissance that would take Indian and other Asian civilizations to a higher level of social, cultural and material development.

6

The Philosophy of Buddhism

INTRODUCTION

From its inception, Buddhism has had a strong philosophical component. Buddhism is founded on the rejection of certain orthodox philosophical concepts, in which the Buddha had been instructed by various teachers. Buddhism rejects atheism, theism, monism, and dualism alike. The Buddha criticized all concepts of metaphysical being and non-being, and this critique is inextricable from the founding of Buddhism. Particular points of Buddhist philosophizing have often been the subject of disputes between different schools of Buddhism. Metaphysical questions such as "Is there a god?" and "Does the soul (Atman) really exist?" have divided the Buddha's followers even during his own lifetime, and epistemological debates over the proper modes of evidence have always been lively in Buddhism. Readers should note that theory for its own sake is not valued in Buddhism, but theory pursued in the interest of enlightenment for oneself or others is fully consistent with Buddhist values and ethics.

Buddhism as Philosophy?

Some have asserted that Buddhism as a whole is a practical philosophy rather than a religion. It is "practical" in that it has a specific method of application known as the Noble Eightfold Path (from which notions of divinity are entirely absent) of a particular set of philosophical principles (the Four Noble Truths). Proponents of such a view may argue that (a) Buddhism is non-theistic (i.e., it has no special use for the existence or non-existence of a god or gods) or atheistic and (b) religions necessarily involve some form of theism. Others might contest either part of such an argument. Other arguments for Buddhism "as" philosophy may claim that Buddhism does not have doctrines in the same sense as other religions; the Buddha himself taught that a person should accept a teaching only if one's own experience verifies it and it is praised by the wise.

HISTORICAL DEVELOPMENT OF BUDDHIST PHILOSOPHY

Early Development

The philosophical outlook of Earliest Buddhism was primarily negative, in the sense that it focused on what doctrines to *reject* more than on what doctrines to *accept*. This dimension has been preserved by the Madhyamaka school. It includes critical rejections of all views, which is a form of philosophy, but it is reluctant to posit its own. Only knowledge that is useful in achieving enlightenment is valued. The cycle of philosophical upheavals that in part drove the diversification of Buddhism into its many schools and sects only began once Buddhists began attempting to make explicit the implicit philosophy of the Buddha and the early Suttas.

After the death of the Buddha, attempts were made to gather his teachings and transmit them in a commonly agreed form, first orally, then also in writing (The Tripitaka). In addition to collecting the Buddha's speeches and rules for monastic life (Vinaya), monks soon undertook to condense what they considered the essential elements of Buddhist doctrine into lists of categories, provided with extensive commentary. This process took shape from about the 2nd century BCE to probably the 2nd century CE.

Later Developments

Very soon after, additional teachings began to be added to the list of important Buddhist texts. Many of these altered and refined Buddhist philosophy.

Comparison with other Philosophies

- Baruch Spinoza, though he argued for the existence of a permanent reality, asserts that all phenomenal existence is transitory. In his opinion sorrow is conquered "by finding an object of knowledge which is not transient, not ephemeral, but is immutable, permanent, everlasting." Buddhism teaches that such a quest is bound to fail.
- David Hume, after a relentless analysis of the mind, concluded that consciousness consists of fleeting mental states. Hume's Bundle theory is a very similar concept to anatta.
- Arthur Schopenhauer's philosophy was very similar to Buddhism.
- Ludwig Wittgenstein's "word games" map closely to the warning of intellectual speculation as a red herring to understanding, such as the *Parable of the Poison Arrow.*
- Friedrich Nietzsche, although himself dismissive of Buddhism as yet another nihilism, developed his philosophy of accepting life-as-it-exists and self-cultivation as extremely similar to Buddhism as better understood in the West today.

DHAMMA PHILOSOPHY

The non-aggressive, moral and philosophical system expounded by the Buddha, which demands no blind faith from its adherents, expounds no dogmatic creeds, encourages no superstitious rites and ceremonies, but advocates a golden mean that guides a disciple through pure living and pure thinking to the gain of supreme wisdom and deliverance from all evil, is called the Dhamma and is popularly known as Buddhism.

The all-merciful Buddha has passed away, but the sublime Dhamma which He unreservedly bequeathed to humanity, still exists in its pristine purity.

Although the Master has left no written records of His Teachings, His distinguished disciples preserved them by committing to memory and transmitting them orally from generation to generation.

Immediately after His demise 500 chief Arahats versed in the Dhamma and Vinaya, held a convocation to rehearse the Doctrine as was originally taught by the Buddha. Venerable Ananda Thera, who enjoyed the special privilege of hearing all the discourses, recited the Dhamma, while the Venerable Upali recited the Vinaya.

The *Tipitaka* was compiled and arranged in its present form by those Arahats of old.

During the reign of the pious Sinhala King Vattagamani Abhaya, about 83 BC, the Tipitaka was, for the first time in the history of Buddhism, committed to writing on palm leaves (ola) in Ceylon.

This voluminous *Tipitaka,* which contains the essence of the Buddha's Teaching, is estimated to be about eleven times the size of the Bible. A striking contrast between the Tipitaka and the Bible is that the former is not a gradual development like the latter.

As the word itself implies, the *Tipitaka* consists of three baskets. They are the Basket of Discipline *(Vinaya Pitaka),* the Basket of Discourses *(Sutta Pitaka),* and the Basket of Ultimate Doctrine *(Abhidhamma Pitaka).*

The *Vinaya Pitaka* which is regarded as the sheet anchor to the oldest historic celibate order — the Sangha — mainly deals with rules and regulations which the Buddha promulgated, as occasion arose, for the future discipline of the Order of monks *(Bhikkhus)* and nuns *(Bhikkunis).*

It described in detail the gradual development of the *Sasana* (Dispensation). An account of the life and ministry of the

Buddha is also given. Indirectly it reveals some important and interesting information about ancient history, Indian customs, arts, science, etc.

The Vinaya Pitaka consists of the five following books:

Vibhanga:

1. *Parajika* Pali — Major Offenses
2. *Pacittiya* Pali — Minor Offenses

Khandaka:

3. *Mahavagga* Pali – Greater Section
4. *Cullavagga* Pali – Shorter Section
5. *Parivara* Pali – Epitome of the Vinaya

The *Sutta Pitaka* consists chiefly of discourses, delivered by the Buddha himself on various occasions. There are also a few discourses delivered by some of His distinguished disciples such as the Venerable Sariputta, Ananda, Moggallana, etc., included in it. It is like a book of prescriptions, as the sermons embodied therein were expounded to suit the different occasions and the temperaments of various persons. There may be seemingly contradictory statements, but they should not be misconstrued as they were opportunely uttered by the Buddha to suit a particular purpose: for instance, to the self-same question He would maintain silence (when the inquirer is merely foolishly inquisitive), or give a detailed reply when He knew the inquirer to be an earnest seeker. Most of the sermons were intended mainly for the benefit of Bhikkhus and they deal with the Holy life and with the expositions of the doctrine. There are also several other discourses which deal with both the material and moral progress of His lay followers.

This Pitaka is divided into five Nikayas or collections, viz:

1. *Digha Nikaya* (Collection of Long Discourses).
2. *Majjhima Nikaya* (Collection of Middle-Length Discourses).
3. *Samyutta Nikaya* (Collection of Kindred Sayings).
4. *Anguttara Nikaya* (Collection of Discourses arranged in accordance with numbers).
5. *Khuddaka Nikaya* (Smaller Collection).

The fifth is subdivided into fifteen books:

1. *Khuddaka Patha* (Shorter texts)
2. *Dhammapada* (Way of Truth)
3. *Udana* (Paeans of Joy)
4. *Iti Vuttaka* ("Thus said" Discourses)
5. *Sutta Nipata* (Collected Discourses)
6. *Vimana Vatthu* (Stories of Celestial Mansions)

7. *Peta Vatthu (Stories of Petas)*
8. *Theragatha* (Psalms of the Brethren)
9. *Therigatha* (Psalms of the Sisters)
10. *Jataka* (Birth Stories)
11. *Niddesa* (Expositions)
12. *Patisambhida Magga* (Analytical Knowledge)
13. *Apadana* (Lives of Arahats)
14. *Buddhavamsa* (The History of the Buddha)
15. *Cariya Pitaka* (Modes of Conduct)

The *Abhidhamma Pitaka* is the most important and the most interesting of the three, containing as it does the profound philosophy of the Buddha's Teaching in contrast to the illuminating and simpler discourses in the Sutta Pitaka.

In the *Sutta Pitaka* is found the conventional teaching *(vohara desana)* while in the *Abhidhamma Pitaka* is found the ultimate teaching *(paramattha-desana)*. To the wise, Abhidhamma is an indispensable guide; to the spiritually evolved, an intellectual treat; and to research scholars, food for thought. Consciousness is defined. Thoughts are analyzed and classified chiefly from an ethical standpoint. Mental states are enumerated. The composition of each type of consciousness is set forth in detail. How thoughts arise, is minutely described. Irrelevant problems that interest mankind but having no relation to one's purification, are deliberately set aside. Matter is summarily discussed; fundamental units of matter, properties of matter, sources of matter, relationship between mind and matter, are explained.

The Abhidhamma investigates mind and matter, the two composite factors of the so-called being, to help the understanding of things as they truly are, and a philosophy has been developed on those lines. Based on that philosophy, an ethical system has been evolved, to realize the ultimate goal, Nibbana.

The *Abhidhamma Pitaka* consists of seven books:

1. *Dhammasangani* (Classification of Dhammas)
2. *Vibhanga* (The book of Divisions)
3. *Katha-Vatthu* (Points of Controversy)

4. *Puggala-Pannatti* (Descriptions of Individuals)
5. *Dhatu-Katha* (Discussion with reference to elements)
6. *Yamaka* (The Book of Pairs),
7. *Patthana* (The Book of Relations)

In the Tipitaka one finds milk for the babe and meat for the strong, for the Buddha taught His doctrine both to the masses and to the intelligentsia. The sublime Dhamma enshrined in these sacred texts, deals with truths and facts, and is not concerned with theories and philosophies which may be accepted as profound truths today only to be thrown overboard tomorrow.

The Buddha has presented us with no new astounding philosophical theories, nor did He venture to create any new material science. He explained to us what is within and without so far as it concerns our emancipation, as ultimately expounded a path of deliverance, which is unique. Incidentally, He has, however, forestalled many a modern scientist and philosopher.

Schopenhauer in his "World as Will and Idea" has presented the truth of suffering and its cause in a Western garb. Spinoza, though he denies not the existence of a permanent reality, asserts that all phenomenal existence is transitory. In his opinion sorrow is conquered "by finding an object of knowledge which is not transient, not ephemeral, but is immutable, permanent, everlasting."

Berkeley proved that the so-called indivisible atom is a metaphysical fiction. Hume, after a relentless analysis of the mind, concluded that consciousness consists of fleeting mental states. Bergson advocates the doctrine of change. Prof. James refers to a stream of consciousness.

The Buddha expounded these doctrines of Transiency, *(Anicca)*, Sorrow *(Dukkha)*, and No-Soul *(Anatta)* some 2500 years ago while He was sojourning in the valley of the Ganges.

It should be understood that the Buddha did not preach all that He knew. On one occasion while the Buddha was passing through a forest He took a handful of leaves and said:

"O Bhikkhus, what I have taught is comparable to the leaves in my hand. What I have not taught is comparable to the amount of leaves in the forest." He taught what He deemed was absolutely essential for one's purification making no distinction between an esoteric and exoteric doctrine.

He was characteristically silent on questions irrelevant to His noble mission. Buddhism no doubt accords with science, but both should be treated as parallel teachings, since one deals mainly with material truths while the other confines itself to moral and spiritual truths. The subject matter of each is different.

The Dhamma He taught is not merely to be preserved in books, nor is it a subject to be studied from a historical or literary standpoint. On the contrary it is to be learned and put into practice in the course of one's daily life, for without practice one cannot appreciate the truth. The Dhamma is to be studied, and more to be practiced, and above all to be realized; immediate realization is its ultimate goal. As such the Dhamma is compared to a raft which is meant for the sole purpose of escaping from the ocean of birth and death *(Samsara).*

Buddhism, therefore, cannot strictly be called a mere philosophy because it is not merely the "love of, inducing the search after, wisdom." Buddhism may approximate a philosophy, but it is very much more comprehensive.

Philosophy deals mainly with knowledge and is not concerned with practice; whereas Buddhism lays special emphasis on practice and realization.

BASIC BUDDHIST PHILOSOPHICAL DOCTRINES

There are some philosophical doctrines that are so early and so fundamental to Buddhism that denials of them tend to be regarded as profoundly non-Buddhist heterodoxies. All forms of Buddhism endeavour to maintain these principles.

Momentariness: Nothing exists for any length of time. There is no *substance* or duration to things. Each moment is an entirely new existence, which is succeeded by an entirely new existence. The only connection between one thing and the next is that one causes the next. This doctrine sounds much like the Greek philosopher Heraclitus. The "things" tend to be called the *dharmas* in Buddhist thought.

Relative Existence **or** ***No Self Nature***: Nothing has a *essence,* nature, or character by itself. Things in isolation are *shunya,* "empty." The nature of things only exists in relation to everything else that exists. Existence s wae know it is thus completely relative and conditioned by everything else.

Only *Nirvana* would be unconditioned, although we cannot know what it is like. The distinction between the conditioned reality that we know and the unconditioned reality that we do not know is similar to the distinction between *phenomena* and *things-in-themselves* made by the German philosopher Immanuel Kant.

The notion that the *dharmas* derive their nature from everything else has led to comparison with the "monads" of another German philosopher, Leibniz. The monads also represent the whole universe. However, since the *dharmas* are momentary, this is actually more like the actual entities postulated by Alfred North Whitehead (1861-1947) in his "Process" philosophy.

Shunyata, "Emptiness," is easily misunderstood. It is not nothingness. Emptiness is neither existence, nor non-existence, nor both existence and non-existence, nor neither existence nor non-existence. At the very least, this means that we don't know what is left when we take away all conditioned relations. Beyond that, it can mean that we *cannot* know what that is. No Self Nature means that there are no *essences,* just as Momentariness means that there are no *substances.*

No-Atman: There is no Self (*atman*) in Buddhism, either as an essence or as a substance. What we call our self is a collection of things, the "aggregates" (*skandhas*): 1) the body, or "form," 2) feelings, 3) ideas, 4) impressions, & 5) momentary consciousness. There is no enduring thing present in the aggregates. This critique of the self as just a collection is very similar to the view of the Scottish philosopher David Hume — though without Hume's critique of causality. An implication of No-Atman is that reincarnation cannot be *transmigration,* since there is nothing to migrate.

No-God: There is no Brahman or any other such ultimate enduring substance or nature to reality. *Nirvana* thus cannot be characterized as realizing either Self, Brahman, or God.

Dependent Origination: Everything has a cause. A momentary existence occurs as it does because of a previous momentary existence, but the cause itself is also momentary. Dependent Origination combines the doctrines of momentariness and relative existence and is why in the Second Noble Truth desire and ignorance cause each other. That relationship can be expanded:

1. ignorance (*avidya*), causes
2. impressions (*samakaras*), which cause
3. consciousness (*vijnana*), which causes
4. mind-body (*namarupa*), which causes
5. the sense organs (*sadayatana*), which cause
6. contact with objects (*sparsha*), which cause
7. experience (*vedana*), which causes
8. desire (*trsna*), which causes
9. clinging (*upadana*), which causes
10. the will to be born (*bhava*), which causes
11. rebirth (*jati*), which causes
12. suffering (*jaramarana*), which in turn causes
13. ignorance (*avidya*).

Nirvana is thus not the removal of an ultimate cause but the simultaneous removal of *all* causes, all of conditioned existence. The interpretation of Buddhist doctrine discussed above, that "suffering" is really more like unhappiness or dislocation, puts forward the notion that our understanding of Dependent Origination (now often called "Interdependent Arising") enables us to *adjust* to the world and thus live a happy and normal life. This may be a reasonable Mahayana or Japanese interpretation, but the point of the original teaching (the Third Noble Truth) is that *Nirvana* is to be attained by the removal of the causes of suffering, which means the entire *system of causation* in Dependent Origination — to be free of the world, not adjusted to it. The normal in this world is what the Buddha wanted to avoid.

Karma: Because there is no substance or duration in Buddhism, the Buddhist view of karma is different from that in Hinduism or Jainism. Karma is only causation, without the mediation of any substance (*apurva*, causal body, etc.). Reincarnation thus consists in our being *caused* by something in the past, and our karma is simply the effect now of past actions.

In the history of Buddhist philosophy, these doctrines created some difficulties. If there is no self, then what is it that attains enlightenment or Nirvana? It is not *me*, for I am already gone in an instant; and if it is *not* me, then why bother? Also, if there is no enduring self, then the rewards and punishments of karma are visited on *different* beings than those who merited them. Why do *I*, instead of someone else, deserve the karma of some past existence? The Buddha himself probably would have been irritated with the doctrines that created these difficulties, since he rejected theorizing (it did not "tend to edification"), and he would have expected no less than that such theories would lead to tangled and merely theoretical disputes.

The important philosophical lesson of these difficulties, however, is whether the concept of causality (which is accepted with none of the skepticism visited upon substance and essence) can be used as a substitute for the concept of substance. In all honesty, no. Something rather like the Buddhist position, however, can be formulated by Kant, for whom the concept of substance applies to phenomena but has only uncertain meaning when applied to things-in-themselves. Phenomena are only "provisional existence" to Buddhism, and the Buddhist doctrine of no enduring Self could easily be adapted to the Kantian transcendent.

When we use the term Buddhists, we do not mean to imply by it either the exoteric Buddhism instituted by the followers of Gautama Buddha, or the modern Buddhistic religion, but the secret philosophy of Sakyamuni, which in its essence is certainly identical with the ancient Wisdom-Religion of the sanctuary, the pre-Vedic Brahmanism. Neither Buddha, Pythagoras, Orpheus, Socrates, nor even Jesus, left behind them any writings. The esoteric teachings of Buddha were the *Gupta Vidya* (secret knowledge) of the ancient Brahmins, the key to which their modern successors have, with few exceptions, completely lost. And this *Vidya* has passed into what is now known as the *inner* teachings of the *Mahayana* school of Northern Buddhism.

In fact, Buddhism in the present age, cannot be justly judged by one or the other of its *exoteric* popular forms. Real Buddhism can be appreciated only by blending the philosophy of the Southern Church and the metaphysics of the Northern Schools. If one seems too iconoclastic and stern, and the other too metaphysical and transcendental, even to being overgrown with the weeds of Indian exotericism — many of the gods of its Pantheon having been transplanted under new names to Tibetan soil — it is entirely due to the popular expression of Buddhism in both Churches. The Hindu Reformer limited his public teachings to the purely moral and physiological aspect of the Wisdom-Religion, to Ethics and MAN alone. Things "unseen and incorporeal," the mystery of Being outside our terrestrial sphere, the great Teacher left entirely untouched in his public lectures, reserving the hidden Truths for a select circle of his Arhats.

Time and imagination made short work of the purity and philosophy of these teachings, once that they were transplanted from the secret and sacred circle of the Arhats, during the course of their work of proselytism, into a soil less prepared for metaphysical conceptions than India; *i.e.,* once they were transferred into China, Japan, Siam, and Burma. How the pristine purity of these grand revelations was dealt with may be seen in studying some of the so-called "esoteric" Buddhist schools of antiquity in their modern garb, not only in China and other Buddhist countries in general, but even in not a few schools in Tibet, left to the care of uninitiated Lamas and Mongolian innovators.

One great distinction between Theosophy and exoteric Buddhism is that the latter, represented by the Southern Church [Theravada], entirely denies *(a)* the existence of any Deity, and *(b)* any conscious *post-mortem* life, or even any self-conscious surviving individuality in man. Such at least is the teaching of the Siamese sect, not considered the *purest* form of exoteric Buddhism. And it is so, if we refer only to Buddha's public teachings. The schools of the Northern Buddhist Church, established in those countries to which his initiated Arhats retired after the Master's death, teach all that is now called Theosophical doctrines, because they form part of the knowledge of the initiates — thus proving how the truth has been sacrificed to the dead-letter by the too-zealous orthodoxy of Southern Buddhism. But how much grander and more noble, more philosophical and scientific, even in its dead-letter, is this teaching than that of any other Church or religion.

"The one Universal Light, which to Man is *Darkness,* is ever existent," says the Chaldean "Book of Numbers." From it proceeds periodically the ENERGY, which is reflected in the "Deep" or Chaos, the storehouse of future worlds, and, once awakened, stirs up and fructifies the latent Forces, which are the ever present eternal potentialities in it. Then awake anew the Brahmas and Buddhas — the co-eternal Forces — and a new Universe springs into being.... The doctrine of God being the Universal Mind diffused through all things, underlies all ancient philosophies. The Buddhist tenets which can never be better comprehended than when studying Pythagorean philosophy — its faithful reflection — are derived from this source as well as the Brahmanical religion and early Christianity. Archaic Occultism would remain incomprehensible to all, if it were rendered otherwise than through the more familiar channels of Buddhism and Hinduism. For the former is the emanation of the latter; and both are the children of one mother — ancient *Lemuro-Atlantean Wisdom.*

It is by the spirit of the teachings of both Buddha and Pythagoras that we can so easily recognize the identity of their doctrines. The all-pervading universal soul, the *Anima Mundi,* is Nirvana; and Buddha, as a generic name, is the anthropomorphized *monad* of Pythagoras. When resting in Nirvana, the final bliss, Buddha is the silent MONAD, dwelling in *darkness and silence.* He is also the formless Brahm, the sublime but *unknowable* Deity, which pervades invisibly the whole Universe. Whenever It is manifested, desiring to impress itself upon humanity in a shape intelligent to our intellect, whether we call it an *avatar,* or a King Messiah, or a *permutation* of Divine Spirit, *Logos,* Christos, it is all one and the same thing. In each case it is the "Father," who is in the *Son,* and the Son in "the Father." The immortal spirit overshadows the mortal man. It enters into him, and pervading his whole being, makes of him a god, who descends into his earthly tabernacle. Every man may become a Buddha, says the doctrine.

In the esoteric, and even exoteric Buddhism of the North, Adi Buddha, the One unknown, without beginning or end, identical with Parabrahm and Ain-Soph, emits a bright ray from its darkness. This is the *Logos* (the first), or Vajradhara, the Supreme Buddha. As the Lord of all Mysteries he cannot manifest, but sends into the world of manifestation his heart — the "diamond heart," Vajrasattva. This is the second *logos* of creation, from whom emanate the seven Dhyani Buddhas, called the Anupadaka, "the parentless." These Buddhas are the primeval monads from the world of *incorporeal being*, the *Arupa* world, wherein the Intelligences (on that plane only) have neither shape nor name, in the exoteric system, but have their distinct seven names in esoteric philosophy. These Dhyani Buddhas emanate, or create from themselves, by virtue of Dhyana, celestial Selves — the *superhuman* Bodhisattvas. These incarnating at the beginning of every human cycle on earth as mortal men, become occasionally, owing to their personal merit, Bodhisattvas among the Sons of Humanity, after which they may re-appear as *Manushi* (human) Buddhas. The Anupadaka (or Dhyani Buddhas) are thus identical with the Brahmanical *Manasaputra*, "mind-born sons" — whether of Brahma or either of the other two Trimurtian Hypostases, hence identical also with the Rishis and Prajapatis.

As the reader is supposed not to be acquainted with the Dhyani-Buddhas, it is as well to say at once that, *according to the Orientalists,* there are five Dhyanis who are the "celestial" Buddhas, of whom the human Buddhas are the manifestations in the world of form and matter. Esoterically, however, the Dhyani-Buddhas are seven, of whom five only have hitherto manifested, and two are to come in the sixth and seventh Root-races. They are, so to speak, the eternal prototypes of the Buddhas who appear on this earth, each of whom has his particular divine prototype. So, for instance, Amitabha is the Dhyani-Buddha of Gautama Sakyamuni, manifesting through him whenever this great Soul incarnates on earth as He did in Tzon-kha-pa [who was] the first and greatest Reformer who founded the "Yellow-Caps," Gyalugpas. He was born in the year 1355 A.D. in Amdo, and was the *Avatar* of Amitabha, the celestial name of Gautama Buddha.

The term Anupadaka, "parentless," or without progenitors, is a mystical designation having several meanings in the philosophy. By this name celestial beings, the Dhyan-Chohans or Dhyani-Buddhas, are generally meant. But as these correspond mystically to the human Buddhas and Bodhisattvas, known as the "Manushi (or human) Buddhas," the latter are also designated "Anupadaka," once that their whole personality is merged in their compound sixth and seventh principles— or Atma-Buddhi, and that they have become "diamond-souled" (Vajrasattvas), the full Mahatmas. The mystery in the hierarchy of the Anupadaka is great, its apex being the universal Spirit-Soul, and the lower rung the Manushi-Buddha; and even every Soul-endowed man is an Anupadaka in a latent state.

As the synthesis of the seven Dhyani-Buddhas, Avalokiteswara was the first Buddha (the Logos), so Amitabha is the inner "God" of Gautama, who, in China, is called Amita (-Buddha). They are, as Mr. Rhys Davids correctly states, "the glorious counterparts in the mystic world, free from the debasing conditions of this material life" of every earthly mortal Buddha — the liberated Manushi-Buddhas appointed to govern the Earth in this Round. They are the "Buddhas of Contemplation," and are all Anupadaka (parentless), *i.e.,* self-born of divine essence. The exoteric teaching which says that every Dhyani-Buddha has the faculty of creating from himself, an equally celestial son — a Dhyani-Bodhisattva — who, after the decease of the Manushi (human) Buddha, has to carry out the work of the latter, rests on the fact that owing to the highest initiation performed by one overshadowed by the "Spirit of Buddha" a candidate becomes virtually a Bodhisattva, created such by the High Initiator.

As to Gautama's being one of the true and undeniable SAVIOURS of the World, suffice it to say that the most rabid orthodox missionary, unless he is hopelessly insane, or has not the least regard for historical truth, cannot find one smallest accusation against the life and personal character of the "Buddha." Without any claim to divinity, allowing his followers to fall into atheism rather than into the degrading superstition of deva or idol-worship, his walk in life is from beginning to the end, holy and divine. During the forty-five years of his mission, it is as blameless and pure as that of a god — or as the latter should be. He is a perfect example of a divine, godly man. He reached Buddhaship — *i.e.,* complete enlightenment— entirely by his own merit and owing to his own individual exertions, no god being supposed to have any *personal* merit in the exercise of goodness and holiness. His is the only absolutely *bloodless* religion among all the existing religions: tolerant and liberal, teaching universal compassion and charity, love and self-sacrifice, poverty and contentment with one's lot, whatever it may be. No persecutions, and enforcement of faith by fire and sword, have ever disgraced it. No thunder-and-lightning-vomiting god has interfered with its chaste commandments; and if the simple, human philosophical code of daily life left to us by the greatest Man-Reformer ever known, should ever come to be adopted by mankind at large, then indeed an era of bliss and peace would dawn on humanity.

To become a Buddha one has to reach a complete detachment from all that is evanescent and finite, and live while yet on Earth in the immortal and everlasting alone, in a supreme state of holiness. To become a Buddha one has to break through the bondage of sense and personality; to acquire a complete perception of the REAL SELF and learn not to separate it from all other selves; to learn by experience the utter unreality of all phenomena of the visible Kosmos foremost of all. When the spiritual *entity* breaks loose for ever from every particle of matter, then only it enters upon the eternal and unchanging Nirvana. He exists in spirit, in *nothing;* as a form, a shape, a semblance, he is completely *annihilated,* and thus will die no more, for spirit alone is no *Maya,* but the only REALITY in an illusionary universe of ever-passing forms. Esoteric teachings claim that Buddha renounced Nirvana and gave up the Dharmakaya vesture to remain a "Buddha of Compassion" within the reach of the miseries of this world. And the religious philosophy he left to it has produced for over 2,000 years generations of good and unselfish men.

Every Orientalist and Pundit knows by heart the story of Gautama, the Buddha, the most perfect of mortal men that the world has ever seen, but none of them seem to suspect the esoteric meaning underlying his *prenatal* biography, *i.e.*, the significance of the popular story. The *Lalitavistara* tells the tale, but abstains from hinting at the truth. The 5,000 *Jatakas,* or the events of former births (re-incarnations) are taken literally instead of esoterically. Gautama, the Buddha, would not have been a mortal man, had he not passed through hundreds and thousands of births previous to his last. Yet the detailed account of these, and the statement that during them he worked his way up through every stage of transmigration from the lowest animate and inanimate atom and insect, up to the highest — or *man,* — contains simply the well-known occult aphorism, "a stone becomes a plant, a plant an animal, and an animal a man." Every human being who has ever existed has passed through the same evolution. But the hidden symbolism in the sequence of these rebirths *(jatakas)* contains a perfect history of the evolution on this earth, *pre* and *post* human, and is a scientific exposition of natural facts. One truth not veiled but bare and open is found in their nomenclature, *viz.,* that as soon as Gautama had reached the human form he began exhibiting in every personality the utmost unselfishness, self-sacrifice and charity. The name "Gautama" means — "on earth (gau) the most victorious (tama)."

The ethics of Theosophy are identical with those taught by Buddha, being the soul of the Wisdom-Religion, and once the common property of the initiates of all nations. But Buddha was the first to embody these lofty ethics in his public teachings, and to make them the foundation and the very essence of his public system. It is herein that lies the immense difference between the exoteric Buddhism and every other religion. For while in other religions ritualism and dogma hold the first and most important place, in Buddhism it is the ethics which have always been the most insisted upon. Christianity becomes every day more a religion of pure emotionalism; the root philosophy of both Adwaita and Buddhist scholars is *identical,* and both have the same respect for animal life, for both believe that every creature on earth, however small and humble, "is an immortal portion of the immortal matter" — for matter with them has quite another significance than it has with either Christian or materialist — and that every creature is subject to Karma.

20TH CENTURY PHILOSOPHY

The current era has seen radical changes in conceptions of human nature. Modern science has effectively rewritten the relationship of humankind to the natural world, advances in medicine and technology have freed us from the limitations and ailments of previous eras, and philosophy—particularly following the linguistic turn—altered how the relationships people have with themselves and each other is conceived. Questions about the meaning of life have seen equally radical changes, from attempts to reevaluate human existence in biological and scientific terms (as in pragmatism and logical positivism), to efforts to meta-theorize about meaning-making as an activity (existentialism, secular humanism).

Pragmatism

Pragmatism, originated in the late-19th-century U.S., to concern itself (mostly) with truth, positing that "only in struggling with the environment" do data, and derived theories, have meaning, and that *consequences*, like utility and practicality, are also components of truth. Moreover, pragmatism posits that *anything* useful and practical is not always true, arguing that what most contributes to the most human good in the long course is true. In practice, theoretical claims must be *practically verifiable*, i.e. one should be able to predict and test claims, and, that, ultimately, the needs of mankind should guide human intellectual inquiry. Pragmatic philosophers suggest that the practical, useful understanding of life is more important than searching for an impractical abstract truth about life. William James argued that truth could be made, but not sought. To a pragmatist, the meaning of life is discoverable only via experience.

Existentialism

Each man and each woman creates the essence (meaning) of his and her life; life is not determined by a supernatural god or an earthly authority, one is free. As such, one's ethical prime directives are *action, freedom,* and *decision,* thus, existentialism opposes rationalism and positivism.

In seeking meaning to life, the existentialist looks to where people find meaning in life, in course of which using only reason as a source of meaning is insufficient; the insufficiency gives rise to the emotions of anxiety and dread, felt in facing one's radical freedom, and the concomitant awareness of death. To the existentialist, existence precedes essence; the (essence) of one's life arises *only* after one comes to existence.

In existentialism, meaning is understood as the worth of life. Meaning in existentialism is unlike typical conceptions of "the meaning of life", because it is *descriptive.*

Due to the method of existentialism, prescriptive or declarative statements about meaning are unjustified. Meaning is only something that is for an individual, it only has a home in one person. Thus it is 'subjective' or should be understood to have an anti-system or anti-answer sensibility.

Soren Kierkegaard coined the term "leap of faith", arguing that life is full of absurdity, and one must make his and her own values in an indifferent world. One can live meaningfully (free of despair and anxiety) in an unconditional commitment to something finite, and devotes that meaningful life to the commitment, despite the vulnerability inherent to doing so.

Arthur Schopenhauer answered: "What is the meaning of life?" by determining that one's life reflects one's will, and that the will (life) is an aimless, irrational, and painful drive. Salvation, deliverance, and escape from suffering are in aesthetic contemplation, sympathy for others, and asceticism.

For Friedrich Nietzsche, life is worth living only if there are goals inspiring one to live. Accordingly, he saw nihilism ("all that happens is meaningless") as without goals. He discredited asceticism, because it denies one's living in the world; denied that values are objective facts, that are rationally necessary, universally-binding commitments: Our evaluations are interpretations, and not reflections of the world, as it is, in itself, and, therefore, all ideations take place from a particular perspective.

Absurdism

"... in spite of or in defiance of the whole of existence he wills to be himself with it, to take it along, almost defying his torment. For to hope in the possibility of help, not to speak of help by virtue of the absurd, that for God all things are possible – no, that he will not do. And as for seeking help from any other – no, that he will not do for all the world; rather than seek help he would prefer to be himself – with all the tortures of hell, if so it must be."

Soren Kierkegaard, the Sickness Unto Death

In absurdist philosophy, the Absurd arises out of the fundamental disharmony between the individual's search for meaning and the apparent meaninglessness of the universe. As beings looking for meaning in a meaningless world, humans have three ways of resolving the dilemma. Kierkegaard and Camus describe the solutions in their works, *The Sickness Unto Death* (1849) and *The Myth of Sisyphus* (1942):

- Suicide (or, "escaping existence"): a solution in which a person simply ends one's own life. Both Kierkegaard and Camus dismiss the viability of this option.
- Religious belief in a transcendent realm or being: a solution in which one believes in the existence of a reality that is beyond the Absurd, and, as such, has meaning. Kierkegaard stated that a belief in anything beyond the Absurd requires a non-rational but perhaps necessary religious acceptance in such an intangible and empirically unprovable thing (now commonly referred to as a "leap of faith"). However, Camus regarded this solution as "philosophical suicide".
- Acceptance of the Absurd: a solution in which one accepts and even embraces the Absurd and continues to live in spite of it. Camus endorsed this solution, while Kierkegaard regarded this solution as "demoniac madness": *"He rages most of all at the thought that eternity might get it into its head to take his misery from him!"*.

Secular Humanism

Per secular humanism, the human race came to be by

reproducing in a progression of unguided evolution as an integral part of nature, which is self-existing. Knowledge does not come from supernatural sources, but from human observation, experimentation, and rational analysis (the scientific method): the nature of the universe is what people discern it to be. Likewise, "values and realities" are determined "by means of intelligent inquiry" and "are derived from human need and interest as tested by experience", that is, by critical intelligence. "As far as we know, the total personality is [a function] of the biological organism transacting in a social and cultural context."

People determine human purpose, without supernatural influence; it is the human personality (general sense) that is the purpose of a human being's life; humanism seeks to develop and fulfil: "Humanism affirms our ability, and responsibility, to lead ethical lives of personal fulfilment that aspire to the greater good of humanity". Humanism aims to promote enlightened self-interest and the common good for all people. It is based on the premises that the happiness of the individual person is inextricably linked to the well-being of humanity, as a whole, in part, because humans are social animals, who find meaning in personal relations, and because cultural progress benefits everybody living in the culture.

The philosophical sub-genres posthumanism and transhumanism (sometimes used synonymously) are extensions of humanistic values. One should seek the advancement of humanity and of all life to the greatest degree feasible, to reconcile Renaissance humanism with the 21st century's technoscientific culture, thus, every living creature has the right to determine its personal and social "meaning of life".

From a humanistic-psychotherapeutic point of view, the question of the meaning of life could also be reinterpreted as "What is the meaning of *my* life?" Instead of becoming focused on cosmic or religious questions about overarching purpose, this approach suggests that the question is intensely personal. There are many therapeutic responses to this question, for example Viktor Frankl argues for "Dereflection", which largely translates as ceasing to endlessly reflect on the self, instead of engaging in life. On the whole, the therapeutic response is that the question of meaning of life evaporates if one is fully engaged in life. The question then morphs into more specific worries such as "What delusions am I under?", "What is blocking my ability to enjoy things?", "Why do I neglect loved-ones?".

Logical Positivism

Logical positivists ask: "What is the meaning of life?", "What is the meaning in asking?" and "If there are no objective values, then, is life meaningless?" Ludwig Wittgenstein and the logical positivists said: "Expressed in language, the question is meaningless"; because, *in* life the statement the "meaning of x", usually denotes the *consequences* of x, or the *significance* of x, or *what is notable* about x, etc., thus, when the meaning of life concept equals "x", in the statement the "meaning of x", the statement becomes recursive, and, therefore, nonsensical, or it might refer to the fact that biological life is essential to having a meaning in life.

The things (people, events) in the life of a person can have meaning (importance) as parts of a whole, but a discrete meaning of (the) life, itself, aside from those things, cannot be discerned. A person's life has meaning (for himself, others) as the life events resulting from his achievements, legacy, family, etc., but, to say that life, itself, has meaning, is a misuse of language, since any note of significance, or of consequence, is relevant only *in* life (to the living), so rendering the statement erroneous. Bertrand Russell wrote that although he found that his distaste for torture was not like his distaste for broccoli, he found no satisfactory, empirical method of proving this:

When we try to be definite, as to what we mean when we say that this or that is "the Good," we find ourselves involved in very great difficulties. Bentham's creed, that pleasure is the Good, roused furious opposition, and was said to be a pig's philosophy. Neither he nor his opponents could advance any argument. In a scientific question, evidence can be adduced on both sides, and, in the end, one side is seen to have the better case — or, if this does not happen, the question is left undecided. But in a question, as to whether this, or that, is the ultimate Good, there is no evidence, either way; each disputant can only appeal to his own emotions, and employ such rhetorical devices as shall rouse similar emotions in others... Questions as to "values" — that is to say, as to what is good or bad on its own account, independently of its effects — lie outside the domain of science, as the defenders of religion emphatically assert. I think that, in this, they are right, but, I draw the further conclusion, which they do not draw, that questions as to "values" lie wholly outside the domain of knowledge. That is to say, when we assert that this, or that, has "value", we are giving expression to our own emotions, not to a fact, which would still be true if our personal feelings were different.

Postmodernism

Postmodernist thought—broadly speaking—sees human nature as constructed by language, or by structures and institutions of human society. Unlike other forms of philosophy, postmodernism rarely seeks out *a priori* or innate meanings in human existence, but instead focuses on analysing or critiquing *given* meanings in order to rationalize or reconstruct them. Anything resembling a "meaning of life", in postmodernist terms, can only be understood within a social and linguistic framework, and must be pursued as an escape from the power structures that are already embedded in all forms of speech and interaction. As a rule, postmodernists see awareness of the constraints of language as necessary to escaping those constraints, but different theorists take different views on the nature of this process: from radical reconstruction of meaning by individuals (as in deconstructionism) to theories in which individuals are primarily extensions of language and society, without real autonomy (as in poststructuralism). In general, postmodernism seeks meaning by looking at the underlying structures that create or impose meaning, rather than the epiphenomenal appearances of the world.

NIRVNA IN THE MAHPARINIRVNA SUTRA

The nature of Nirvna assumes a differently aspected Mahayana focus in what alleges to be the final of all Mahayana sutras, allegedly delivered by the Buddha on his last day of life on earth-the *MahapariNirvna Sutra* or *Nirvna Sutra*. Here, as well as in a number of linked "tathagatagarbha" sutras, in which the Tathagatagarbha is equated with the Buddha's eternal Self or eternal nature, Nirvna is spoken of by the Mahayana Buddha in very "cataphatic", positive terms. Nirvna, or "Great Nirvna", is indicated to be the sphere or domain (vishaya) of the True Self. It is seen as the state which constitutes the attainment of what is "Eternal, the Self, Bliss, and the Pure". *Mah-Nirvna* ("Great Nirvna") thus becomes equivalent to the ineffable, unshakeable, blissful, all-pervading and deathless Selfhood of the Buddha himself-a mystery which no words can adequately reach and which, according to the *Nirvna Sutra*, can only be fully known by an Awakened Being-a perfect Buddha-directly.

Strikingly, the Buddha of the *Mahaparinirvna Sutra* gives the following definition of the attributes of Nirvna, which includes the ultimate reality of the Self (not to be confused with the "worldly ego" of the five skandhas):

> "The attributes of Nirvna are eightfold. What are these eight? Cessation (*nirodha*), loveliness/wholesomeness (*subha*), Truth (*satya*), Reality (*tattva*), eternity (*nitya*), bliss (*sukha*), the Self (*atman*), and complete purity (*parisuddhi*): that is Nirvna."

He further states: "Non-Self is Samsara (the cycle of rebirth); the Self (atman) is Great Nirvna."

An important facet of Nirvna in general is that it is not something that comes about from a concatenation of causes, that springs into existence as a result of an act of creation or an agglomeration of causative factors: it was never created; it always was, is and will be. But due to the moral and mental darkness of ordinary, samsarically benighted sentient beings, it remains hidden from unawakened perception. The Buddha of the Mahparinirvna sutra insists on its eternal nature and affirms its identity with the enduring, blissful Self, saying:

> *It is not the case that the inherent nature of Nirvna did not primordially exist but now exists. If the inherent nature of Nirvna did not primordially exist but does now exist, then it would not be free from taints (asravas) nor would it be eternally (nitya) present in nature. Regardless of whether there are Buddhas*

> *or not, its intrinsic nature and attributes are eternally present... Because of the obscuring darkness of the mental afflictions (kileshas), beings do not see it. The Tathagata, endowed with omniscient awareness (sarvajna-jnana), lights the lamp of insight with his skill-in-means (upaya-kauualya) and causes Bodhisattvas to perceive the Eternal, Bliss, the Self, and the Pure of Nirvna.*

Vitally, according to these Mahayana teachings, any being who has reached Nirvna is not blotted out or extinguished: there is the extinction of the impermanent and suffering-prone "worldly self" or ego, comprised of the five changeful skandhas, but not of the immortal "supramundane" Self of the indwelling Buddha Principle [*Buddha-dhatu*]. Spiritual death for such a Nirvna-ed being becomes an utter impossibility. The Buddha states in the "Mahyna Mahparinirvna Sutra" (Tibetan version): "Nirvna is deathless... Those who have passed into Nirvna are deathless. I say that anybody who is endowed with careful assiduity is not compounded and, even though they involve themselves in compounded things, they do not age, they do not die, they do not perish."

Paths to Nirvna in the Pali Canon

In the Visuddhimagga, Ch. I, v. 6 (Buddhaghosa & NGamoli, 1999, pp. 6-7), Buddhaghosa identifies various options within the Pali canon for pursuing a path to Nirvna, including:

1. by insight (*vipassana*) alone.
2. by jhana and understanding.
3. by deeds, vision and righteousness.
4. by virtue, consciousness and understanding.
5. by virtue, understanding, concentration and effort.
6. by the four foundations of mindfulness.

Depending on one's analysis, each of these options could be seen as a reframing of the Buddha's Threefold Training of virtue, mental development and wisdom.

Quotations

- Gautama Buddha:

- "Nirvna is the highest happiness."
- "Where there is nothing; where naught is grasped, there is the Isle of No-Beyond. Nirvna do I call it—the utter extinction of aging and dying."
- "There is, monks, an unborn—unbecome—unmade—unfabricated. If there were not that unborn—unbecome—unmade—unfabricated, there would not be the case that emancipation from the born—become—made—fabricated would be discerned. But precisely because there is an unborn—unbecome—unmade—unfabricated, emancipation from the born—become—made fabricated is discerned."
- This said: 'the liberated mind/will (citta) which does not cling' means Nibbana."
- "'The subjugation of becoming means Nirvna'; this means the subjugation of the five aggregates means Nirvna."
- "Parinibbuto thitatto"-"PariNirvna is to be fixed in the Soul."

• Said immediately after the physical death of Gautama Buddha wherein his mind (citta) is =pariNirvna=the essence of liberation:

- "No longer with (subsists by) in-breath nor out-breath, so is him (Gautama) who is steadfast in mind (citta), inherently quelled from all desires the mighty sage has passed beyond. With mind (citta) limitless (Brahman) he no longer bears sensations; illumined and unbound (nibbana), his mind (citta) is definitely (ahu) liberated."
- "The mind (citta) being so liberated and arisen from defilements, one is fixed in the Soul as liberation, one is quelled in fixation upon the Soul. Quelled in the Soul one is unshakable. So being unshakable, the very Soul is thoroughly unbound (parinirvna)."

• Sutta Nipata, tr. Rune Johansson:

- acc+ yath vtavegena khitto

atthaA paleti na upeti sankhaa
evaA muni namakaya kimutto
atthaA paleti na upeti sankhaa

- o atthan gatassa na pamGam atthi
ynea naA vajju taA tassan atthi
sabbesu dhammesu samkhatesu
samkhat vdapathpi sabbe
- o Like a flame that has been blown out by a strong wind goes to rest and cannot be defined, just so the sage who is freed from name and body goes to rest and cannot be defined.

  For him who has gone to rest there is no measure by means of which one could describe him; that is not for him. When all (dharmas) have gone, all signs of recognition have also gone.

- Venerable Sariputta:
  - o The destruction of greed, hatred and delusion is Nirvna.

MIDDLE WAY

In general, the Middle Way or Middle Path (Skt.: madhyama-pratipad; Pali: majjhima patipada) is the Buddhist practice of non-extremism. More specifically, in Theravada Buddhism, the Middle Way crystallizes the Buddha's Nirvana-bound path of moderation away from the extremes of sensual indulgence and self-mortification and toward the practice of wisdom, morality and mental cultivation. In Mahayana and Vajrayana Buddhism, the Middle Way refers to transcendental ways of approaching seemingly antithetical claims about reality.

Theravada Contexts

In Theravada Buddhism's Pali canon, the Middle Way was articulated by the Buddha in his first discourse, the Dhammacakkappavattana Sutta:

"Monks, these two extremes ought not to be practiced by one who has gone forth from the household life. (What are the two?) There is addiction to indulgence of sense-pleasures, which is low, coarse, the way of ordinary people, unworthy, and

> *unprofitable; and there is addiction to self-mortification, which is painful, unworthy, and unprofitable.*
>
> *"Avoiding both these extremes, the Tathagata (the Perfect One) has realized the Middle Path; it gives vision, gives knowledge, and leads to calm, to insight, to enlightenment and to Nibbana. And what is that Middle Path realized by the Tathagata...? It is the Noble Eightfold path, and nothing else, namely: right understanding, right thought, right speech, right action, right livelihood, right effort, right mindfulness and right concentration."*

Thus, for the attainment of Nibbana, the Middle Way involves:

- Abstaining from addictive sense-pleasures and self-mortification
- Nurturing the set of "right" actions that are known as the Noble Eightfold Path.

In this discourse (Pali: *sutta*), the Buddha identifies the Middle Way as a path for "one who has gone forth from the household life" (Pali: *pabbajitena*) although lay Buddhists may centre their lives on this path as well. In regards to the Buddha's admonition against the "indulgence of sense-pleasures" (Pali: *kamesu kama-sukha-allika*), Ven. Dr. Rewata Dhamma has written:

> *"...This kind of practice is the concern of so-called 'urban civilization,' which condones sensuous pleasues as the highest attributes of bliss; the greater the pleasures, the greater the happiness....*
>
> "The Buddha taught that indulgence in sensuous pleasures is not the practice of enlightened, noble ones (*ariyas*). Noble ones who live the worldly life do not have attachment to sense objects. For example, in the first stage of an enlightened noble life, the sotapanna, or stream winner, has not yet overcome lust and passions. Incipient perceptions of the agreeableness of carnal pleasures (*sukhasanna*) still linger. Nevertheless, the stream-winner will not feel the need to indulge in worldly pleasures."

When the Buddha delivered the Dhammacakkappavattana Sutta, he was addressing five ascetics with whom he had previously practiced severe austerities. Thus, it is this personal context as well as the broader context of Indian shramanic practices that gives particular relevancy to the caveat against the extreme (Pali: *anta*) of self-mortification (Pali: *atta-kilamatha*).

Mahayana Contexts

In Mahayana Buddhism, the Madhyamaka ("Middle Way") school posits a "middle way" position between metaphysical claims that things ultimately either exist or do not exist.

In the Tendai school, the "middle way" refers to the synthesis of the thesis that all things are "empty" and the antithesis that all things have phenomenal existence.

NOBLE EIGHT FOLD PATH

The Noble Eightfold Path (Pali: *Ariyo ammhaegiko maggo*; Sanskrit: *Arya 'cmaega marga*; Chinese: *Bazhengdao*; Japanese: Hasshodo; Thai: *Ariya Mugg Paad*; Mongolian *qutuctan-u naiman gesigun-u mor*) is, in the teachings of the Buddha, declared to be the way that leads to the end of *dukkha*, or suffering.

Essentially a practical guide of bringing about ethical and meditative discipline, the Noble Eightfold Path forms the fourth part of the Four Noble Truths, which have informed and driven much of the Buddhist tradition.

As the name indicates, there are eight elements in the Noble Eightfold Path, and these are divided into three basic categories as follows:

- Wisdom (Sanskrit: *prajna*, Pali: *panna*)
  1. Right view
  2. Right intention
- Ethical conduct (Sanskrit: *uila*, Pali: *sila*)
  3. Right speech
  4. Right action
  5. Right livelihood
- Mental discipline (Sanskrit and Pali: *samadhi*)
  6. Right effort
  7. Right mindfulness
  8. Right concentration

In all of the elements of the Noble Eightfold Path, the word "right" is a translation of the word *samyanc* (Sanskrit) or *samma* (Pali), which denotes completion, togetherness, and coherence, and which can also carry the sense of "perfect" or "ideal".

Though the path is numbered one through eight, it is generally not considered to be a series of linear steps through which one must progress; rather, as the Buddhist monk and scholar Walpola Rahula points out, the eight elements of the Noble Eightfold Path "are to be developed more or less simultaneously, as far as possible according to the capacity of each individual. They are all linked together and each helps the cultivation of the others".

In Buddhist symbolism, the Noble Eightfold Path is often represented by means of the Dharma wheel (Sanskrit: *dharmacakra*, Pali: *dhammacakka*), whose eight spokes represent the eight elements of the path.

Wisdom (Prajna-Panna)

The "wisdom" subdivision of the Noble Eightfold Path is constituted by those elements that refer primarily to the mental or cognitive aspect of a Buddhist practitioner's practice.

Right View

Right view (*samyag-dicmi-samm-dimmhi*) can also be translated as "right perspective" or "right understanding". This element of the Noble Eightfold Path refers explicitly to the Four Noble Truths of Buddhism, stating that these must be fully understood by the Buddhist practitioner. In the *Mahasatipahana Sutta*, one of the Buddha Uakyamuni's discourses, right understanding is explained directly in terms of the Four Noble Truths:

> *And what, O bhikkhus, is right understanding? To understand suffering, to understand the origination of suffering, to understand extinction of suffering, to understand the path leading to the extinction of suffering; this is called right understanding.*

Additionally, right understanding is sometimes considered to encompass an understanding of the Buddhist idea of the non-permanence, or even non-existence, of the self, an idea known as *anatman* in Sanskrit and *anatta* in Pali. There are two stages for every stage of the eightfold path, a preliminary stage and the higher stages gradually obtained through the journey towards enlightenment. The preliminary stage of Right Views or right understanding is the knowledge of the Four Noble Truths. The higher stage requires more than the comprehension of the Four Noble Truths, it also includes the knowledge and understanding of the not-self doctrine, impermanence, dependent origination, the five aggregates, "karma", rebirth, and so on.

Right Intention

Right intention (*samyak-sackalpa-samm-saekappa*) can also be translated as "right thought", "right resolve", or "right aspiration" or the exertion of our own will to change. This element of the Noble Eightfold Path deals, fundamentally, with the Buddhist practitioner's reasons for practicing Buddhism, and with his or her outlook towards the world. It enjoins renunciation of worldly things and an accordant greater commitment to spiritual matters; good will; and a commitment to non-violence, or *ahias*, towards other living beings. In the *Magga-vibhanga Sutta,* it is simply explained as follows:

> *And what is right thought? Being resolved on renunciation, on freedom from ill will, on harmlessness: This is called right thought.*

Ethical Conduct (Uila-Sila)

The "ethical conduct" (Uila) subdivision of the Noble Eightfold Path is considered the cornerstone or foundation upon which unwholesome thoughts and practices end and higher meditative states begin.

In AN 11.2 Cetana Sutta (An Act of Will) Buddha states it is virtue (without clinging to virtue) which gives freedom from remorse, which leads to joy, serenity and subsequent rapturous states of meditation. It is in the nature of things that freedom from remorse arises in a person endowed with virtue, consummate in virtue.

In Buddhism, this is also one of the Ten Recollections along with the Triple Gem.

"There is the case where the disciple of the noble ones recollects his own virtues, thus: '[They are] untorn, unbroken, unspotted, unsplattered, liberating, praised by the wise, untarnished, conducive to concentration.'

This aspect of the Noble Eightfold Path is the most outward-oriented aspect of the Noble Eightfold Path insofar as it deals directly with a Buddhist practitioner's relationship with other members of his or her society.

Right Speech

Right speech (*samyag-vac-sạmma-vaca*), as the name implies, deals with the way in which a Buddhist practitioner would best make use of his or her words. In the Pali Canon, this aspect of the Noble Eightfold Path is explained as follows:

And what is right speech? Abstaining from lying, abstaining from divisive speech, abstaining from abusive speech, abstaining from idle chatter: This, monks, is called right speech.

Other discourses in the Canon elaborate:

"Abandoning false speech, he abstains from false speech. He speaks the truth, holds to the truth, is firm, reliable, no deceiver of the world...."

"Abandoning divisive speech he abstains from divisive speech. What he has heard here he does not tell there to break those people apart from these people here. What he has heard there he does not tell here to break these people apart from those people there. Thus reconciling those who have broken apart or cementing those who are united, he loves concord, delights in concord, enjoys concord, speaks things that create concord...."

"Abandoning abusive speech, he abstains from abusive speech. He speaks words that are soothing to the ear, that are affectionate, that go to the heart, that are polite, appealing and pleasing to people at large....

"Abandoning idle chatter, he abstains from idle chatter. He speaks in season, speaks what is factual, what is in accordance with the goal, the Dhamma, and the Vinaya. He speaks words worth treasuring, seasonable, reasonable, circumscribed, connected with the goal...."

Regarding telling the truth about mundane knowledge, the *Cunda Kammaraputta Sutta* ascribes to the Buddha the following elaboration:

> *"There is the case where a certain person, abandoning false speech, abstains from false speech. When he has been called to a town meeting, a group meeting, a gathering of his relatives, his guild, or of the royalty, if he is asked as a witness, 'Come & tell, good man, what you know': If he doesn't know, he says, 'I don't know.' If he does know, he says, 'I know.' If he hasn't seen, he says, 'I haven't seen.' If he has seen, he says, 'I have seen.' Thus he doesn't consciously tell a lie for his own sake, for the sake of another, or for the sake of any reward. Abandoning false speech, he abstains from false speech."*

Regarding telling the truth about spiritual knowledge, the *Canki Sutta* ascribes to the Buddha the following cautionary statements:

> *"If a person has conviction, his statement, 'This is my conviction,' safeguards the truth. But he doesn't yet come to the definite conclusion that 'Only this is true; anything else is worthless.'..."*
>
> *"If a person likes something... holds an unbroken tradition... has something reasoned through analogy... has something he agrees to, having pondered views, his statement, 'This is what I agree to, having pondered views,' safeguards the truth. But he doesn't yet come to the definite conclusion that 'Only this is true; anything else is worthless.'..."*

Walpola Rahula glosses this path factor by stating that not engaging in such "forms of wrong and harmful speech" ultimately means that "one naturally has to speak the truth, has to use words that are friendly and benevolent, pleasant and gentle, meaningful and useful".

Right Action

Right action (*samyak-karmanta-samma-kammanta*)

can also be translated as "right conduct" and, as the name implies, deals with the proper way in which a Buddhist practitioner would act in his or her daily life. In the *Magga-vibhanga Sutta*, this aspect of the Noble Eightfold Path is explained as follows:

And what is right action? Abstaining from taking life, from stealing, & from illicit sex. This is called right action.

The Cunda Kammaraputta Sutta *expands:*

"And how is one made pure in three ways by bodily action?

"There is the case where a certain person, abandoning the taking of life, abstains from the taking of life. He dwells with his rod laid down, his knife laid down, scrupulous, merciful, compassionate for the welfare of all living beings."

"Abandoning the taking of what is not given, he abstains from taking what is not given. He does not take, in the manner of a thief, things in a village or a wilderness that belong to others and have not been given by them."

"Abandoning sensual misconduct, he abstains from sensual misconduct. He does not get sexually involved with those who are protected by their mothers, their fathers, their brothers, their sisters, their relatives, or their Dhamma; those with husbands, those who entail punishments, or even those crowned with flowers by another man."

Together with the idea of *ahias* and right speech, right action constitutes the Five Precepts (Sanskrit: *pancauila*, Pali: *pancasila*), which form the fundamental ethical code undertaken by lay followers of Buddhism, and which are as follows:

1. To refrain from destroying living beings.
2. To refrain from stealing.
3. To refrain from sexual misconduct (adultery, rape, etc.).
4. To refrain from false speech (lying).
5. To refrain from intoxicants, which lead to heedlessness.

Right Livelihood

Right livelihood (*samyag-ajiva-samma-ajiva*) is based around the concept of *ahias*, or harmlessness, and essentially states that Buddhist practitioners ought not to engage in trades or occupations which, either directly or indirectly, result in harm to other living beings or systems. Such occupations include "trading in arms and lethal weapons, intoxicating drinks, poisons, killing animals, [and] cheating", among others. "Business in human beings"—such as slave trading and prostitution—is also forbidden, as are several other dishonest means of gaining wealth, such as "scheming, persuading, hinting, belittling, [and] pursuing gain with gain".

Mental Discipline (Samadhi)

The "mental discipline" subdivision of the Noble Eightfold Path is constituted by those elements that deal with how a Buddhist practitioner can best go about shaping his or her outlook towards the world.

Right Effort

Right effort (*samyag-vyayama-samma-vayama*) can also be translated as "right endeavour", and involves the Buddhist practitioner's continuous effort to, essentially, keep his or her mind free of thoughts that might impair his or her ability to realize or put into practice the other elements of the Noble Eightfold Path; for example, wishing ill towards another living being would contradict the injunction—contained in the "Right thought" element—to have good will towards others, and the "Right effort" element refers to the process of attempting to root out such an ill wish and replace it with a good wish.

And what, monks, is right effort?

(i) There is the case where a monk generates desire, endeavours, activates persistence, upholds & exerts his intent for the sake of the non-arising of evil, unskilful qualities that have not yet arisen.

(ii) He generates desire, endeavours, activates persistence, upholds & exerts his intent for the sake of the abandonment of evil, unskilful qualities that have arisen.

(iii) He generates desire, endeavours, activates persistence, upholds & exerts his intent for the sake of the arising of skillful qualities that have not yet arisen.

(iv) He generates desire, endeavours, activates persistence, upholds & exerts his intent for the maintenance, non-confusion, increase, plenitude, development, & culmination of skillful qualities that have arisen: This, monks, is called right effort."

By making right effort, a Buddhist practitioner is considered to be engaging in an effort that is wholesome in terms of *karma;* that is, in terms of that effort's ultimate consequences to the practitioner. The four phases of Right Effort: (in simple English)

(1) make effort to prevent the evil that has not yet come.

(2) make effort to destroy the evil that has come.

(3) make effort to produce the good that has not yet come.

(4) make effort to cultivate the good that has come.

Right Mindfulness

Right mindfulness (*samyak-sm[ti-samma-sati*), also translated as "right memory", together with right concentration, is concerned broadly with the practice of Buddhist meditation.

Roughly speaking, "mindfulness" refers to the practice of keeping the mind alert to phenomena as they are affecting the body and mind.

In the *Magga-vibhanga Sutta,* this aspect of the Noble Eightfold Path is explained as follows:

And what, monks, is right mindfulness?

(i) There is the case where a monk remains focused on (his/her) *body* in and of itself... ardent, aware, and mindful... having already put aside worldly desire and aversion.

(ii) (He/she) remains focused on *feelings* in and of themselves... ardent, aware, and mindful... having already put aside worldly desire and aversion.

(iii) (He/she) remains focused on *the mind* in and of itself... ardent, aware, and mindful... having already put aside worldly desire and aversion.

(iv) (He/she) remains focused on *mental qualities* in and of themselves... ardent, aware, and mindful... having already put aside worldly desire and aversion.

This, monks, is called right mindfulness.

This is also an important aspect of what constitutes the concept of "self" or Buddhist concept of Atman:

"And how, Ananda, is a bhikkhu an island unto himself, a refuge unto himself, seeking no external refuge; with the

Dhamma as his island, the Dhamma as his refuge, seeking no other refuge?

"When he dwells contemplating the body in the body, earnestly, clearly comprehending, and mindfully, after having overcome desire and sorrow in regard to the world; when he dwells contemplating feelings in feelings, the mind in the mind, and mental objects in mental objects, earnestly, clearly comprehending, and mindfully, after having overcome desire and sorrow in regard to the world, then, truly, he is an island unto himself, a refuge unto himself, seeking no external refuge; having the Dhamma as his island, the Dhamma as his refuge, seeking no other refuge. (DN 16 Maha-parinibbana Sutta)

Bhikkhu Bodhi, a monk of the Theravadin tradition, further glosses the concept of mindfulness as follows:

The mind is deliberately kept at the level of bare attention, *a detached observation of what is happening within us and around us in the present moment. In the practice of right mindfulness the mind is trained to remain in the present, open, quiet, and alert, contemplating the present event. All judgments and interpretations have to be suspended, or if they occur, just registered and dropped.*

Right Concentration

Right concentration (*samyak-samadhi-samma-samadhi*), together with right mindfulness, is concerned broadly with the practice of Buddhist meditation.

And what, monks, is right concentration?

(i) Quite withdrawn from sensuality, withdrawn from unwholesome states, a monk enters in the first jhana: rapture and pleasure born from detachment, accompanied by movement of the mind onto the object and retention of the mind on the object.

(ii) With the stilling of directed thought and evaluation, (he/she) enters and remains in the second jhana: rapture and pleasure born of concentration; fixed single-pointed awareness free from movement of the mind onto the object and retention of the mind on the object; assurance.

(iii) With the fading of rapture, (he/she) remains in equanimity, mindful and fully aware, and physically sensitive of pleasure. (He/She) enters and remains in the third jhana which the Noble Ones declare to be "Equanimous and mindful, (he/she) has a pleasurable abiding."

(iv) With the abandoning of pleasure and pain...as with the earlier disappearance of elation and distress...(he/she) enters and remains in the fourth jhana: purity of equanimity and mindfulness, neither in pleasure nor in pain.

This, monks, is called right concentration.

The Ninth and Tenth Elements

In the *Great Forty Sutra* (Mahacattarisaka Sutta), which appears in the Pali Canon, the Buddha explains that cultivation of the Eightfold Path leads to the development of two further stages once enlightenment has been reached. These also fall under the category of panna and are *Right Knowledge* (sammnga) and *Right Liberation* (or *Right Release*; sammavimutti). Some consider *Right Association* as an implicit ninth aspect of the Path. To further the foregoing, Bucknell & Martin (1986: p.6) state:

> *The Eightfold Path as described gives an impression of orderliness and completeness. However, closer study of the texts indicates that it is not after all a complete account of Gautama's course of practice. A number of suttas describe a Tenfold Path. This differs from the Eightfold Path in having two further stages following right concentration, namely right insight or knowledge or wisdom (sammnga) and right liberation (samma vimutti). These two extra stages are nowhere described, nor is any explanation given for their frequent omission. The tenth state, right liberation, is presumably to be equated with the final goal, nirvgna. However, the ninth stage, right insight, which appears from its position in the list to be of crucial importance, remains unaccounted for.*

7

Buddhism in Bangladesh

About 0.5% of Bangladesh population adheres to the Theravada school of Buddhism. Most of the practitioners are from the south-eastern district of Chittagong and Chittagong Hill Tracts.

DEMOGRAPHIC OVERVIEW

Most of the followers of Buddhism in Bangladesh live in the south-eastern region, especially in the Chittagong district. Also, there are people of Arakanese descent living in the sub-tropical Chittagong Hill Tracts.

Most of these people belong to the Chakma, Chak, Marma, Tenchungya and the Khyang, who since time immemorial have practiced Buddhism. Other tribals, notably those who practice Animism, have come under some Buddhist influence, and this is true in the case of the Khumi and the Mru, and to a lesser extent on the other tribals.

History

Bangladesh (historical Bengal) has a unique place in the history of Buddhism, mainly for two reasons. Firstly, Bengal was the last stronghold of Indian Buddhism where it could survive as a socio-cultural force until the 12th century, despite its disappearance from other parts of the Indian subcontinent. Secondly, it is generally claimed that Bengal was the home of a form of Buddhism, namely, the Tantric Buddhism. Tantric Buddhism is a later development in Bengal and therefore it remains to be seen what specific factors are responsible for turning the pure form of Buddhism into tantricism and whether the mystic and esoteric practices in the Buddhism of Bangladesh are of distinctively Bengali origin.

Early Origins

In the early days of Buddhism, many kings and rulers like Bimbisara, Ashoka, Kanishka patronized the spread of Buddha's teaching. This continued until the Palas and Chandras of Bengal in the 12th century. Of course, Buddhism faced hostility from some of the rulers, but throughout the first millennium and beyond, Buddhism thrived in Bengal.

It is possible that Buddhism entered Bengal before Asoka's time. After attaining enlightenment, the Buddha is said to have delivered his first sermon at Saranath and then moved to Magadha, Kosala, Vaishali and other places within what was known as Majjhimadesha or Madhyadesha. In the Divyavadana, the eastern boundary of the Majjhimadesha is said to have extended as far as pundravardhana (North Bengal). Furthermore, the Buddha is said to have received considerable support from King Bimbisara of Magadha who not only dedicated Venuvana as a residence for monks, but also remained his close friend and a great patron of his Dhamma throughout his life. Since Bengal was adjacent to Magadha, it is possible that the Buddha had visited parts of Bangladesh as suggested by Hiuen Tsang, who notes that Asoka had erected stupas at various places in Bengal and Orissa to commemorate these visits.

Asoka's Reign and the Post-Maurya Period Epigraphic and other sources reveal that Buddhism had established a powerful footing in Bengal during Asoka's reign. The discovery of a Mauryan inscription in Brahmi characters at Mahasthangarh in the district of Bogra bearing the name Pudanagala (Pundranagara) and the recovery of many Mauryan coins and other artifacts dating from the fourth and third centuries BC suggest that the Gangetic delta was under the control of the Mauryan empire. The Chinese traveller, I-tsing, is said to have noticed Asoka's stupas near tamralipti (Tamluk) and Karnasuvarna (modern Burdwan and Murshidabad districts) in current West Bengal, in Pundravardhana (North Bengal) and in Samatata (Bangladesh). The port of Tamralipti to the west of the Bhagirathi-Hooghli river, in particular, played an important role during Asoka's rule. It was from here, according to Mahavangsa, that the Buddhist mission from Asoka's capital city, Pataliputra, sailed for Sri Lanka to spread the message of the Buddha.

POST-MAURYAN PERIOD

With the decline of the Maurya Empire, Buddhism lost the royal patronage which it once enjoyed. Pusyamitra, after killing his master, Brhadratha, declared himself the emperor and ascended the throne of Magadha. He founded the Sunga dynasty in the 2nd century BC. With the resurgence of the Sungas, Buddhism met with its first major setback. Buddhism, once a thriving religion, declined in the absence of the royal patronage, as also because of the unfavourable attitude of the Sunga kings towards Buddhism and the Sangha.

Contrary to this position, some Indian scholars are of the view that the orthodox Sunga kings were not intolerant towards Buddhism, and that Buddhism continued to prosper even during the time of the Sunga kings. During the Sunga period, Buddhism was in existence in Bengal, and this can also be inferred from a terracotta tablet that was found at a place called Tamralipti. This terracotta tablet is currently on exhibit at the Aṣutosh Museum, University of Calcutta.

The Kushana period (around 1st century) gave further impetus to Buddhism when Kanishka raised Buddhism to the status of the state religion, erected stupas and chaityas, built monasteries and, like Asoka, sent missions abroad. The discovery of Buddha images, copper and gold coins and inscriptions, belonging to this period, indicate the flourishing status of Buddhism during the reign of Kaniska.

Gupta Dynasty

Kings of the Gupta dynasty were devout adherents of a Brahminical faith, sometimes called as *Parama Bhagavatas*, and they patronized and revived Brahminism, but they also possessed a tolerant outlook which allowed Buddhism to flourish. In the meantime, rise of the two powerful Hindu cults of Saivism and Vaisnavism, brought Buddhism closer to Hinduism. In its spiritual nihilism, Buddhism was approximated to the Bhakti movements so much so that, by the middle of the 6th century, the Buddha was accepted as an avatar of Vishnu.

According to Chinese sources, Maharaja Gupta, also known as Shri Gupta, the first ruler of the Gupta dynasty, built a Buddhist temple and offered it to Buddhist monks from China along with a gift of twenty four villages. This temple is believed to have remained a sacred place till the 7th century.

Samudra Gupta, although a devout worshipper of Vishnu, also proved to be a great patron of Buddhism. It was during his reign that cultural relations between India and Ceylon were established. His teacher and guide, the celebrated Buddhist scholar Vasubandhu, was appointed minister, and, with the permission of the Ceylonese King Meghavanna, a monastery was built at Bodh Gaya for the monks and pilgrims of Ceylon. Chandra Gupta II who, like his father Samudra Gupta, was a devout Vaisnava by faith, gave full freedom to the practice of other faiths in his empire.

Fa-hien's Account

During his visit to Bengal, Fa-hien is said to have travelled eastward along the course of the Ganges river, and during his journey, he came across Buddhist stupas and monks at several places. In a place named Tamralipti, Fa-hien is said to have spent two years, and visited twenty-two monasteries, inhabited by monks who lived in accordance with the Buddhist Vinaya.

Archaeological evidences also support Fa-hien's account about the thriving state of Buddhism in the Gupta period. An inscription found at Gunaigarh near Comilla, bearing the year 188 of the Gupta era (corresponding to 506 or 507 of the Christian era), records a gift of land by Maharaja Vainya Gupta in favour of the Buddhist Avaivarttika Sangha of the Mahayana sect.

The Sangha, founded by the Acharya Shantideva and housed in a monastery called *Ashrama Vihara*, was dedicated to Avalokiteshvara. The inscription also refers to other Buddhist monasteries, one of which was known as *Raja Vihara*, which literally translates into *Royal Vihara*. Two Buddhist sculptures, a standing image of the Buddha found at Biharail in Rajshahi district and a gold-plated bronze image of Manjushri discovered at Balai Dhap mound at Mahasthana in Bogra, also bear testimony to the flourishing state of Buddhism during the rule of the Gupta kings.

Both the Hinayana and Mahayana sects of Buddhism flourished during the Gupta period. A number of Buddhist inscriptions, seals, images and manuscripts in Gupta characters, discovered at various archaeological excavations sites, testify to the thriving state of the early Hinayana schools, namely, the Sarvastivadins, the Sammatiyas (or the Vatsiputriyas) and Sthavirvadins. Gradually, Hinayana lost its hold, and Mahayana took ascendancy over Hinayana. Mahayana, with its ultra-altruistic principles, its scope for devotion and worship, and its opening of the state of Bodhisattvahood began to capture the imagination of common people, and acquired the status of an important religious movement. As Mahayana grew popular, Bodhisattvas such as Manjusri, Avalokitesvara and the goddess Prajnaparamita rose to occupy important positions.

The *Adi Buddha* and Amitabha Buddha also received special attention. Worship of Bodhisattva images along with the image of the Buddha turned into a common practice. The Mahayanists are said to have revered the Prajna texts just as the Hinayanists revered their Vinaya and Abhidharma books. The Mahayanists are also said to have practised spells (dharanis) for religious purposes.

Hiuen Tsang visited India in the 7th century and visited almost all the major places associated with Buddhism in Bangladesh. According to him, there were six or seven Buddhist monasteries at Kajangala near Rajmahal, housing over three hundred monks.

In the northern part of the country, he also claimed to have seen a belvedere built of stone and brick, with a broad and high base, artistic ornamentation and distinct carved images of the Buddha and the devas. At Pundravardhana he is said to have found twenty Buddhist monasteries with more than 3,000 monks who practised both Hinayana and Mahayana. The magnificent Po-shi-po, with spacious halls and storeyed chambers, occupied by over 700 monks, was located in the vicinity of the capital of

Pundravardhana. There is also mention of a temple with an image of Avalokitesvara not far from this establishment, which attracted visitors from far and near.

Fa-hien visited India in the 5th century, and found that some of the old Buddhist centres like Kapilavastu and Saraswati were in a neglected and ruinous state, while Pataliputra, Mathura, Bodh Gaya, Sarnath and Nalanda were flourishing as active centres of Buddhism.

The great monastery of Nalanda, which was founded by Kumara Gupta Mahendraditya, rose to prominence in the Gupta period and in course of time turned into a university and became the greatest centre of Buddhist learning in Asia. From an early date, the Buddhists of Bengal were closely linked with this great institution, although it was situated in Magadha.

Prior to Hiuen Tsang's visit to Nalanda, Acharya Dharmapala had been the high priest of its monastery. He was succeeded by his disciple Acharya shilabhadra, a scion of a Brahmana king of Samatata. It was under Silabhadra's guidance that Hiuen Tsang studied Buddhist philosophy, including the vedas and Sangkhya Shastras, for five years. Not only scholars from Bengal but also its kings, the Guptas, the Palas etc., contributed to the development of the great institutions at Nalanda.

POST-GUPTA PERIOD

During the post-Gupta period, Harsavardhana gave Buddhism a new impetus. But, in the 6th century, Shashanka came to the throne, who was hostile to Buddhism. According to Hiuen Tsang's account, Shashanka ordered the extermination of the Buddhist monks in and around Kushinagar; he cut down the holy Bodhi tree of Bodh Gaya and threw into the Ganges a sacred stone bearing the footprints of the Buddha. He is also said to have removed a Buddha image from a temple close to the Bodhi tree and replaced it with an image of Hindu god Lord Shiva.

Contrary to this, the reign of Emperor Harsavardhana (606-647) was one of resurgence and renewed progress and development. Despite being a worshipper of Shiva and Surya, Harsavardhana had great leanings towards Buddhism, and his elder brother, Rajyavardhana, and sister Rajyashri both were being devout Buddhists. Harsa was at first a follower of the Hinayana sect, but, in later life, became an ardent follower of Mahayana.

Some of his notable contributions to the cause of Buddhism include erecting stupas on the banks of the Ganges, building monasteries at places sacred to Buddhism, and forbidding the slaying of animals. Another of his important contributions to Buddhism was his convening regularly the quinquennial convocation in which he gave away in religious alms everything he possessed. Harsa used to summon Buddhist monks once a year for religious discussions. Harsa was specially attached to Nalanda and extended help liberally.

After Harsavardhana, the Khadga dynasty is said to be the first Buddhist dynasty to rule an independent Bengal between the 7th and 8th centuries AD. The discovery of two copperplates, one at Ashrafpur, 30 miles north-east of Dhaka and another at Deulbari, 14 miles south of Comilla, gives valuable information about this royal dynasty.

These copperplates mention the names of three kings, Khadgodyama, Jatakhadga and Devakhadga, and include the names of the queen and the son of Devakhadga, Prabhavati and Rajaraja or Rajarajabhata. I-tsing's account notes that as many as fifty-six Buddhist priests from China visited India and its neighbouring areas in the latter half of the 7th century AD. One of these monks, Sheng-chi, who visited Samatata, mentions Rajabhata as its king and describes him as an ardent worshipper of the three gems (*Triratna*), that is, the Buddha, Dhamma and Sangha. There were 30 monasteries with more that 4,000 monks in Samatata alone during the pilgrim's visit.

Pala Dynasty

The Pala Dynasty ruled Bengal from 8th to 12th century, and this period is regarded as the golden age of Buddhism in Bengal. The Pala rulers were devout Buddhists (*Parama-saugata*), and were also equally sympathetic to other religious faiths. Palas invoked the Buddha at the beginning of their official records and proceedings. Under the royal patronage of the Pala kings,

Buddhism and all institutions associated with Buddhism continuously flourished and thrived in Bengal for four centuries under the patronage of the Pala kings. During the same period, Buddhism was almost wiped out in other parts of the Indian subcontinent, and at the same time, it also became a dominant force in neighbouring regions, extending its influence to Tibet in the north and the Malaya peninsula in the south.

Archaeological and epigraphic discoveries indicate the generous support of the Pala rulers towards Buddhism, and instances of the Palas' patronage of Buddhism are numerous. According to Tibetan Buddhist tradition, King Gopala (750-770) built a monastery at Nalanda and established many schools for dissemination of Buddhist principles. According to Taranatha, many distinguished Buddhist teachers flourished during the reign of King Gopala, prominent among them were Danashila, Vishesamitra, Sura and Prajavarman. The Odantapuri Vihara was an example of rare architectural beauty. The famous Sam-ye monastery of Tibet is believed to have been built on the model of this great Vihara.

King Dharmapala (770-781) continued the religious policy of his father, and he also extended liberal support to Buddhist establishments. He founded the famous Vikramshila Vihara on a hill top on the bank of the Ganges river in Magadha. This Vihara soon rose to prominence as an international centre of learning and emerged as a university, second only to Nalanda. Vikramshila University maintained contact with Tibet and several Tibetan scholars participated in the affairs of the university throughout the rule of the Pala dynasty. Several of Vikramashila scholars, who once numbered 3000 in the 12th century, composed numerous books in Sanskrit, and also translated them into Tibetan. The curricula of the university included logic, metaphysics, grammar, tantras, and rituals. Importantly, the reigning monarch of the land awarded degrees to the students.

A monastery, built by King Dharmapala at Somapura Rajshahi district, and now better known as the Somapura Mahavihara (Naogaon) and which became a model for many such monasteries in South-east Asia, stands as a magnificent testament to the Pala patronage of Buddhism. King Dharmapala is also said to have established at least fifty religious schools designed to teach Buddhist philosophy, and to study Prajnaparamita in particular. He was a great patron of the Buddhist writer, Haribhadra, and, during his reign, as in his father's, many distinguished Buddhist teachers, such as Purnavardhana, Prabhakara, Kalyanagupta, Sagaramegha, Bhuddhajapada, flourished.

Under King Devapala (810-850), the Pala empire reached the zenith of its glory, and Bengal became a paramount power. King Devapala is said to have granted an endowment of five villages for the upkeep of a monastery founded by King Balaputradeva of Java, Sumatra and Malaya. Not only did he complete the Somapura establishment, he also showed keen interest in the well-being of the Vikramshila Vihara.

Mahipala I, the ninth king of the Pala dynasty and rightly called the founder of the second Pala empire, is responsible for the revival of the past glory of the Buddhist establishments. He repaired the Buddhist monuments at Nalanda and constructed two new temples at Bodh Gaya. Many famous monasteries were built during the Pala period of which mention may be made of Jagaddala, Traikutaka, Pandita, Devikota, Pattikeraka, Sannagara, Phullahari and Vikramapuri.

Chandra Dynasty

Buddhism flourished during the reign of the Chandra dynasty in Harikela (eastern and southern parts of Bengal). The discovery of a large Buddha stupa, Salbana Vihara and other inscriptions at the Mainamati hills, four miles to the west of Comilla, still bears testimony to the condition of Buddhism during the Chandra kings. According to Tibetan sources, Buddhist tantricism flourished under the Chandra rule. The famous Buddhist scholar of Vikramapura, Atish Dipankar Srigyan, is believed to be related to the Chandra dynasty.

The Pala Kingdom was not only the last stronghold of dying Buddhism in India, it was also responsible for the rise of Tantric Buddhism. This new phase of Mahayana Buddhism has been variously designated by Charles Eliot and others as 'late', 'degenerate', and 'corrupt'. Such allegations are based on the assumption that when Buddhism entered Bengal, it gradually came under the powerful influence of tantric beliefs and practices, including what are known as sexo-yogic practices, which made it fall away from the purity of its early form and eventually develop into what came to be known as esoteric or magical Buddhism.

Professor Trevor Ling opines that in Bengal from the time of Asoka to the Pala period, both the Hinayana and Mahayana, not the tantric, forms of Buddhism were practised.

He describes the classical pattern of Buddhism as a three-cornered relationship between Sanga, king and people and emphasizes that the Buddhism of the Pala period was a true representative example of this classical pattern. Trevor Ling and many others believe that the Pala rule in Bengal heralded an era of progress in culture, religion, education, literature, art and sculpture.

Amongst other achievements of the Palas, Ling has particularly mentioned their active patronage of Bangla language and literature. It was in a popular new language, a proto-Bangla form, that the Buddhist poets composed what are known to be the first poems of Bangla literature, the famous charyapada, a Tantric work of twenty-three Buddhist Tantrikists known as Siddhas.

Decline and Revival

The Sena Dynasty gained prominence after the decline of the Palas. The Senas were orthodox followers of Saivaism or Vaisnavism. Under them, the royal support for Buddhism ended. As a consequence, Buddhism soon began to decline and disintegrate. Another contributing factor was the coming of Islam through the subsequent defeat of the Sena dynasty at the hands of Muhammad bin Bakhtyar Khalji. After that, many of the surviving Buddhist monks fled to Nepal, Tibet or Bhutan. The Buddhist laity were either converted to Islam or were integrated into the fold of Brahmanism. Buddhism, as a separate entity, was almost extinct, surviving in many debased forms of popular practices such as dharma thakur puja or the puja of jagannath.

The decline of Buddhism, however, did not result in its total disappearance from the land of its birth, and it continued to survive in various forms of popular worship, rites and rituals until its resurgence in modern India. With its rediscovery in its parent country, the traditions of Buddhism were significantly recognized so that the Asokan pillar, the sacred Wheel of Law (Dharmachakra) and the Singhanada sculpture from Saranatha are now a part of Indian national life and heritage.

The renewal of Buddhism in India today is attributed to Dr. BR Ambedkar, the architect of the Indian Constitution, who led the mass conversion of millions of untouchables or 'Scheduled Castes' to Buddhism in 1956. In Bengal, however, the revival of Buddhism seems to have taken place centuries before Dr. BR Ambedkar's introduction of the neo-Buddhist movement in Maharastra and other places. In the districts of Chittagong and the Chittagong Hill Tracts, the south-eastern parts of Bangladesh, a Buddhist minority had been practising Theravada long before the Moghuls and the British arrived in Bengal. In course of time, these Buddhists reformed their Sangha and in 1887 founded the Chittagong Buddhist Association, believed to be the first Buddhist society to be formed in the South Asian sub-continent.

8

Tibetan Buddhism

Tibetan Buddhism is the body of Buddhist religious doctrine and institutions characteristic of Tibet and certain regions of the Himalayas, including northern Nepal, Bhutan, and India (particularly in Arunachal Pradesh, Laddakh, Dharamsala, Lahaul and Spiti in Himachal Pradesh, and Sikkim). It is the state religion of Bhutan.

It is also practiced in Mongolia and parts of Russia (Kalmykia, Buryatia, and Tuva) and Northeast China. Texts recognized as scripture and commentary are contained in the Tibetan Buddhist canon, such that Tibetan is a spiritual language of these areas. A Tibetan diaspora has spread Tibetan Buddhism to many Western countries, where the tradition has gained popularity. Among its prominent exponents is the 14th Dalai Lama of Tibet. The number of its adherents is estimated to be between ten and twenty million.

THE PRACTICE OF TIBETAN BUDDHIST NUNS

In the long course of human history, each area and nation has its own different religious Life-style and their different manifestation in different times. After Buddhism entered Tibet, it had chosen its existence in the process of Tibetanization. As the religious females and women practitioners who acted as one of vehicle spreading and implementing Buddhism, they had set up their optimal value of life and religion behavioral pattern,with distinctive individuality. The book will illustrate the practice of the Tibetan Buddhist nuns from 3 aspects.

Practice in Early Times

The practice of Tibetan Buddhist nuns can be traced back to the 8th century AD and the most representative figures are Yeshe Tsogyal and Zhuosa khri gyal mo tsun who were once the consorts of Trisong Deutsen.

They actively promoted Tibetan Buddhism and made special contributions to the development of it. From their stories, we can learn about the early practice of Tibetan Buddhist nuns, whose practice life reflected very distinct features and characteristics.

The Practice Centred on Sects

In the 1st half of the 10th century AD, the Tibetan Buddhist nuns began its revival and development with the renaissance of Tibetan Buddhism.

Especially with the rise of Tibetan Buddhist sects, the Tibetan nuns also shaped into various sects such as Nyingma AUU the Bka'-gdams AUU Sakya AUU Zhibyed AUU Gcod-Yulh AUU Kaggu AUU Jonang, Gelug and Gogra AUU Zhalu or Bulu AUU Bodong sects. Therefore, the practice of nuns was connected with their own sect and the sect-centred nunneries, organizational institutions as well as religious ceremonies were set up, which made their practice more organized, institutionalized and standardized.

The Variety of Practice

Tibetan Buddhist nuns observe the principles of their respective sects, and in the meantime construct distinct practice mode. The writer have made field investigation on Tibetan nuns and nunneries over years and divided the Tibetan nuns into several types as follows according to their different practice forms: female Rinpoche, the Buddhist practicing in monasteries, Buddhist ascetic, wandering Buddhist and nunnery community Buddhist, Buddhist practicing at home etc., so as to study their practice in all aspects.

It is believed that the practice of Tibetan Buddhist nuns and their distinct practice pattern have been influenced by Tibetan Buddhism and constrained by individual choice and Buddhist qualities.

However, socio-economy and geographical environment are the fundamental factors which diversified the practice of Tibetan Buddhist nuns and directly affected the practice pattern.

Although the nuns different from each other in the content as well as the pattern of their practice, with the same purpose they wish to satisfy the religious life of individual and community through the performance of these religious consciousnesses. This is their common psychological basis and the reflection of Tibetan Buddhist nuns' personal value orientation and life attitude.

THE MYTHOLOGY OF TIBETAN MOUNTAIN GODS

There are countless high mountains in Tibet, and ancient Tibetans believed that gods resided on every one of them. The worship of mountain gods was one of the most important forms of nature worship among ancient Tibetans; it was fundamental to their entire belief system. Each mountain god possessed his own territory and was in charge of particular affairs. Around each god sprang up myths, legends, sacrificial rites and procedures. Analysis of Tibetan mountain god worship should lead to a fuller understanding of Tibetan mythology, and to a vision of the larger structures of that mythology.

As ancient Tibetan society grew ever more complex, individual, autonomous Tibetan mountain gods became associated in a complex hierarchy. Classification and stratification heralded the emergence of a single, supreme deity. Different geographical circumstances, and complex social developments and contradictions in the religion, however, brought about similarities, differences, and contradictions in characteristics and functions among the deities in the upper echelons of the system. According to traditional, pre-Buddhist Tibetan belief, there are four great mountain gods in the Tibetan region; each one is identified with a specific sacred mountain1: yar-lha-sham-po in central Tibet; gnyan-chenthang-lha, in Byang-thang in the north; sku-lha-ri-rgya in the south; vod-degung-rgyal in the south. These four gods, together with five other famous mountain gods—rma-chen-spon-ra (or Anyesrmachen), shyogs-chen-ldongra, sgan-po-lha-rje, zhogs-lha-rgyug-po, and shevu-kha-rag—form the core of the Tibetan mountain-god system; together they were called "the nine creator-gods" (srid-pa-chags-po-lha-dgu). In addition, geographical differences between each Tibetan region gave rise to individual local gods, such as the great mountain god gnyan-po-g'ywu-rtse-rdza-re, worshipped by the Tibetan go-log tribe, and the sacred mountain of gangs-dkar-ti-se in western Tibet.

The study of Tibetan mountain gods presents two principal problems. First, previous research on Tibetan mythology has had little to say about them, and what data does exist is quite heterogeneous. In addition, the features of the myths have certainly been diluted over time. Buddhist myths and rituals muffled the original character of the Tibetan myths; for example, almost all mountain gods are now Buddhist guardians. These twin obstacles require that our investigation must start with the place of mountain gods in relevant folk beliefs, myth, ritual, and customs. Some Tibetan literature and ritual scriptures also help to reveal the outline of the involved mythology. In what follows, all these sources are employed in providing an introduction to and analysis of some well-known mountain god myths and rituals.

The Myth of yar-lha-sham-po Located in the vphyongs-rgyal county, yar-lha-sham-po "the great god sham-po," ranks second among the nine creator-gods mentioned above, behind only the mountain god vod-de-gung-rgyal. Yar-lha-sham-po is an old mountain god, often mentioned in the classic Tibetan scriptures of Dunhuang from the sixth to the ninth centuries CE. The scriptures state that "yar-lha-sham-po is the highest god" (Yar-lha-sham-po-ni-gtsug-lha-vo),2 but, in fact, yar-lha-sham-po is not the highest mountain peak in Tibet; it is, rather, largely due to its location in central Tibet that it became one of the greatest Tibetan gods.

The Tibetan mountain gods belong to two principal classes. One arose from the deification of mountains believed to act as the benefactors of mankind. Such mountains are most often located in proximity to temperate valleys and fertile pastureland that benefit from the reservoirs of water held in the snowy mountaintops. The natural advantages conferred by the fertile land and mountain waters led the local inhabitants to deify the snowy mountains, creating mountain gods. These gods, obviously, were seen as benefactors of mankind. The other major class occupies mountains located in dense forests or in wild and desolate lands uninhabited by mankind.

MYTHOLOGY OF TIBETAN MOUNTAIN GODS

These gods are usually considered to be evil. Yar-lha-sham-po is located in the Yar-lung River Valley, an agricultural region said to be the cradle of the Tibetan people. The material bounty that nature afforded the ancient inhabitants of this river valley induced them to deify the surrounding mountains, and yar-lha-sham-po was venerated as the greatest god. With the later interaction and amalgamation between the Yar-lung tribe and other tribes, the Yar-lung developed and prevailed, eventually becoming the rulers of the entire Tibetan people. Their principal mountain god, consequently, became the principal god for all Tibetan tribes.

In Tibetan historiography, the mountain god yar-lha-sham-po is often called the royal god, and represents the power of the royal family. At the beginning of the spread of Buddhism into Tibet, many members of the royal house, adherents of the native Tibetan religion, Bon-po, remained averse to Buddhism. This situation gave rise to the story of how the Buddhist deity pad-ma-vdyung-gnas encountered resistance from yar-lha-sham-po, who caused a flood to destroy a Buddhist palace. The emergence and triumph of yar-lha-sham-po as the supreme mountain god is also the history of the development and strength of the yar-lung tribe. Absent a unified Tibetan power and a wise king skilled in military strategy, the Tibetan mountain god yar-lha-sham-po would not have become such a preeminent fixture.

A distinctive feature of Tibetan mythology is that the images of mountain gods are based on religious elements other than the physical mountains themselves. They are often embodied as animals or totems. In this respect the mythology is not one-dimensional but exemplifies complex forms. A good example is the image of yar-lha-sham-po. According to a popular regional myth, yar-lha-sham-po is portrayed as a white yak, from whose mouth and nose snowstorms continuously blow. He is endowed with extraordinary magical powers: he can destroy rocks, cause floods, and even transform himself into a white man in order to have sexual intercourse with women and father babies. As the paramount god, yar-lha-sham-po ruled all local gods (yul-lha) and village gods (sa-bdag) in the Yar-lung region. Here is a description of yar-lha-sham-po in the throes of resisting pad-mavbyung-gnas as the new god tries to enter Tibet:

After that, master pad-ma-vbyung-gna
Knew beforehand that it was time to defeat the monster,
Came to the dangerous road of lam-vphrang.
Yar-lha-sham-po sent out ambushing thunders.
He turned into a white yak as large as a mountain,
Became wild and smashed rocks,
Blocked the road and left no passage;
Air pumped from his mouth and nostrils as dense as fog-fall;
It was heavy with rain and snow that let you see nothing of the road.

The portrayal of yar-lha-sham-po—as a white yak who can change shape at will—reveals something of early Tibetan beliefs about mountain gods.

As the myths about the mountain developed, images of yar-lha-shampo also changed; a white yak was replaced by a man-god clothed in white with a body as white as a conch, holding a short spear with colourful silk flags and a crystal sword in his hands. This human image of yar-lha-shampo is typically accompanied by a wife and children. His wife is gnam-smanthog-gi-bu-yug, the primary goddess. She is clothed in light red attire, holds lightning in her right hand and hailstones in her left, and flies on bolts of lightning.

The Myth of gnyan-chen-thang-lha If yar-lha-sham-po is the supreme god, indeed the royal god, then the most famous mountain god is gnyan-chen-thang-lha; he is also known as thang-lha-val-shur or thang-lha-yab-shur. Gnyan-chen-thang-lha was first worshipped as a god of hail, one of eighteen deities in charge of hail. When people passed by the mountain thang-lha, they would burn incense and offer all kinds of sacrifices to him. In Tibetan mythology gnyan-chen-thang-lha is a guardian of treasure. A prayer text describes the image and lineage of this mountain god:

To your father vod-de-gung-rgyal pray.
Plead to your mother, The single-winged jade bird.
To yourself, God yar zhur gnyan gyu, pray.
With respect I mention your residence, vdam shod snar mo lags.
An eagle as green as turquoise is soaring in between.
It is full of light there, Though in winter it is as green as spring.
O mountain god, the land you inhabit is delightful!
I call upon your name, and your name is known to the gods,
The heavenly musician king mtshan gsol ba.
I call upon your secret name, rdo rje vbar ba rtsal.
O mountain god, what clothes do you wear?
You wear white, a silk dress and a white cotton coat.
If you want to ride, what are you going to ride, mountain god?
You ride on a magic horse with four white hooves, Galloping across the three worlds.
Your white dress sends out brightness.
You hold a cane in the right hand
And hold a crystal rosary in the left.

The Myth of the Five Sisters of Longevity

The myth of the Five Sisters of Longevity (tshe-ring-mched-lnga) is popular in the Mount Everest region. The five sisters are identifed with particular mountains in the area. The greatest of them is bkra-shis-tshe-ringma, who oversees the welfare and longevity of mankind. Iconographically, she is young and beautiful, and rides a white lion.

In her left hand she holds a sacred arrow used for taking auspices; dice made of white conch and a mirror are tied to the tail of the arrow. She wears white silk garments, a cloak made of peacock feathers, and a white scarf wrapped around her head. Bkra-shis-tshe-ring-ma belongs to a group of guardian goddesses who offer cleverness and wisdom to mankind. Among the sisters of longevity are mting-gi-zhal-bzang-ma, typically represented as a green goddess holding a magical mirror and riding a wild horse;

the yellow goddess mi-g'yu-blo-bzang-ma, a giver of grain who rides a golden tiger; the red goddess cod-pan-mgrin-bzang-ma, a goddess of wealth who holds a plate full of treasures and rides a red doe; and another green goddess, gtaddkar-vgro-bzang-ma, who holds a sacred arrow in her hand, rides a dragon, and possesses dominion over the animals. The Five Sisters of Longevity live on the peak of Mount Everest. Myth tells that at its foot lie five icy lakes, each a different colour corresponding to the colours of the five goddesses.

The Eminence of the Mountain Gods

In Tibetan mythology, the mountain gods have immense power and rule all other deities; this power stems from their control of weather phenomena—the wind, the clouds, thunder, hail, and so on. Accordingly, they have become the principal gods of Tibetan mythology, and their veneration is the most important form of nature worship in Tibet.

In this regard Tibetan mythology is no different from myths of peoples all over the world, since the principal gods in most cultures are usually nature gods. Because of their massive "bodies" and because of the illusions created by the weather around the peaks, mountain gods have changeable images in ritual. In time an amalgamation of mountain god worship with animal worship occurred: animals such as sheep, yaks, and wild horses all but replaced the old images. This animal imagery in turn gave way to anthropomorphism, as the animal forms became accompanying gods or the beasts that the mountain god rides. Changes in ritual imagery notwithstanding, the preeminence of the mountain gods in Tibetan mythology is unquestioned. Sacrifices to them are a collective rather than an individual matter, for a mountain god is not usually considered to be an individual guardian; instead, he or she is the guardian of a particular tribe or even an entire people.

The Mountain Gods and the Heavenly Rope

The Origin, Development, and Etymology of the Heavenly Rope Owing to the lofty heights of the mountains and the sometimes illusory influences of weather conditions, ancient Tibetans connected the mountain gods to the more abstract conceptual class of heavenly gods, believing the peaks to be sites for passage from this world to the heavens above, sites where a rope (or step) was connected directly to heaven. Myths about this heavenly rope (dmu-thag in Tibetan) were, not surprisingly, especially prevalent among the various ethnic groups that lived near the mountains themselves.

Early Tibetan mythology differentiated mountain gods from heavenly gods: heavenly gods were chiefly symbolic and less directly connected to the material life of early Tibet. Over time, however, the apparent physical proximity, together with similarities in ritual worship, led to increased identification between the mountain gods and the heavenly gods, the result being that the latter now possess a large measure of the features of the preeminent mountain gods; it is even held that mountain gods and heavenly gods can transform from one into the other. The mountain gods sometimes rise to the status of heavenly gods, and the heavenly gods sometimes descend to become mountain gods. Vod-de-gung-rgyal, for example, is a patriarchal god ranked among the so-called "nine creator-gods." However, judging from the word vod-de-gung-rgyal, this mountain god is also a heavenly god, for in Tibetan, gung means "heaven," and gung-rgyal signifies "heavenly king."

Here it may be appreciated that the way the Tibetans understand the heavenly gods is somewhat different from that of peoples who live in other geographical conditions. The Tibetans' understanding of the heavenly gods developed on the basis of their mountain god worship. After developing the conception of the heavenly gods through this kind of worship, ancient Tibetans postulated a tie between the two sets of gods. Hence the myth of the heavenly rope.

The phrase for "heavenly rope" in Tibetan is dmu-thag-smu-thag. The word dmu appears relatively late in Tibetan literature. Dmu is written as mu in Dunhuang literature, and etymological comparisons between various Tibeto-Burmese languages strongly suggests that mu-in Tibetan refers to "the heavenly god." As for the word dmu-thag, I believe it to be closely connected to the Tibetan word for "rainbow" (vjav). A rainbow could well be understood by early societies as a rope connecting heaven to earth, a rope sent down by the heavenly gods. Literally, dmu-thag means "the heavenly gods' rope." According to Tibetan literature, when the Tibetan king btsanpo died he looked like a rope under the "rainbow," and he went up to the heavens along the dmu-thag.

It seems, then, that there is an intimate relationship between dmu-thag and vjav. In Pelliot's Tibetan text no. 126.2 ("The Formation of Dmu-thag"), we read that "from the lights in the sky and fog over the sea came the white curdle of the Bon religion. It is stretched by the wind, woven into threads, and wound round a tree. It is known as Dmuthag or g.yang thag ("fortune rope")." This text clearly identifies dmuthag with the rainbow.

The Myth of the Heavenly Rope and the Royal Genealogy of Ancient Tibet Like the Hans, the Tibetans also have their own tradition of historiography. Beginning in the seventh to ninth centuries CE and continuing for more than 1000 years, Tibetan culture produced a wide variety of historical texts. The Tibetan historiographical tradition is closely linked to the cultural exchanges between the Tibetan and Han peoples; as early as the sixth and seventh centuries, Tibetan scholars were translating Chinese historical texts into the Tibetan language. Chronological texts similar to those in Chinese also began to appear.

In much the same way that Han historians historicized their ancient mythology, Tibetan historians, when recording their own ancestral deeds and the genealogy of the royal family, historicized Tibetan mythology, but the historiographical methods, approaches, and processes they adopted differed somewhat. It will be useful to turn now to an analysis of the historicizing of Tibetan mythology and its relation to the mythology of the heavenly rope.

At an early stage of the heavenly rope myth, gods that travelled between the heaven and the earth appeared largely in a natural shape, taking the form of such animals as yaks and wild horses; etiologically, then, these animals were considered to be descended from the heavens. According to the myth known as The Horse and the Wild Horse, for example, the horse lived in the heavens and the wild horse lived in the middle air, and they descended to the divine land of gong-thang. With the emergence of more complex societies, anthropomorphic gods with magical powers replaced animal-shaped gods.

In Tibet, the currents of military and economic development fostered the emergence of a "high" culture, and people began to keep track of their ancestral history. In a system rooted in tribal confederacies, the concept of consanguinity meant that Tibetan historiography gave special attention to the recording of genealogies. New cultural contacts also played a part. Tibetan historians employed new chronological methods, recording folk tales and myths as history with extreme rigor and accuracy. They ranked mythological figures among their ancient kings and thus brought them into the historical record. As a result, many Tibetan history books hold that the first generation of Tibetan kings (btsan-po) descended from the heavens to the sacred mountains. For example, in Tibetan Historical Texts in a Duhuang Version we find that nyag-khri-btsan-po descended to the mountain of lha-ri-byang-mtheo ("the sacred mountain towering high in the north"). In sum, the inheritance of royal Tibetan genealogy in ancient times was founded on the basis of the mythology surrounding the mountain gods; indeed, the mountain gods were crucial to the development of the heavenly gods and the mythology of the heavenly rope.

TIBETAN CULTURE

Tibetan culture developed under the influence of a number of factors. Tibet's specific geographic and climactic conditions-its altitude, short growing season, and cold weather-have encouraged reliance on pastorialism, as well as the development of a different cuisine from surrounding regions. Contact with neighboring countries and cultures-including India, China, and Mongolia-have influenced the development of Tibetan culture, but the Himalayan region's remoteness and inaccessibility have preserved distinctive local influences. Buddhism has exerted a particularly strong influence on Tibetan culture since its introduction in the 7th Century. Art, literature, and music all contain elements of Buddhist religion, and Buddhism itself has adopted a unique form in Tibet, influenced by the Bon tradition and other local beliefs.

TIBETAN ART

Tibetan art refers to the art of Tibet and other present and former Himalayan kingdoms (Bhutan, Laddakh, Nepal, and Sikkim). Tibetan art is first and foremost a form of sacred art, reflecting the over-riding influence of Tibetan Buddhism on these cultures.

The art of Tibet may be studied in terms of influences which have contributed to it over the centuries.

MAHAYANA BUDDHIST INFLUENCE

As Mahayana Buddhism emerged as a separate school in the 4th century BC it emphasized the role of bodhisattvas, compassionate beings who forego their personal escape to Nirvana in order to assist others. From an early time various bodhisattvas were also subjects of statuary art. Tibetan Buddhism, as an offspring of Mahayana Buddhism, inherited this tradition. But the additional dominating presence of the Vajrayana (or Buddhist tantra) may have had an overriding importance in the artistic culture. A common bodhisattva depicted in Tibetan art is the deity Chenrezig (Avalokitesvara), often portrayed as a thousand-armed saint with an eye in the middle of each hand, representing the all-seeing compassionate one who hears our requests. This deity can also be understood as a Yidam, or 'meditation Buddha' for Vajrayana practice.

Tantric Influence

More specifically, Tibetan Buddhism contains Tantric Buddhism, also known as Vajrayana Buddhism for its common symbolism of the *vajra,* the diamond thunderbolt (known in Tibetan as the dorje). Most of the typical Tibetan Buddhist art can be seen as part of the practice of tantra. Vajrayana techniques incorporate many visualizations/imaginations during meditation, and most of the elaborate tantric art can be seen as aids to these visualizations; from representations of meditational deities (yidams) to mandalas and all kinds of ritual implements.

A surprising aspect of Tantric Buddhism is the common representation of wrathful deities, often depicted with angry faces, circles of flame, or with the skulls of the dead. These images represent the *Protectors* (Skt. dharmapala) and their fearsome bearing belies their true compassionate nature. Actually their wrath represents their dedication to the protection of the dharma teaching as well as to the protection of the specific tantric practices to prevent corruption or disruption of the practice. They are most importantly used as wrathful psychological aspects that can be used to conquer the negative attitudes of the practitioner.

Bon Influence

The indigenous shamanistic religion of the Himalayas is known as Bon. Bon contributes a pantheon of local tutelary deities to Tibetan art. In Tibetan temples (known as lhakhang), statues of the Buddha or Padmasambhava are often paired with statues of the tutelary deity of the district who often appears angry or dark. These gods once inflicted harm and sickness on the local citizens but after the arrival of Padmasambhava these negative forces have been subdued and now must serve Buddha.

Thangka paintings, a syncrestism of Chinese scroll-painting with Nepalese and Kashmiri painting, appeared around the 11th century. Rectangular and painted on cotton or linen, they are usually traditional motifs depicting religious, astrological, and theological subjects, and sometimes the Mandala. To ensure that the image will not fade, organic and mineral pigments are added, and the painting is framed in colourful silk broadcades.

The art of Tibet may be studied in terms of influences which have contributed to it over the centuries.

CUISINE

Tibetan cuisine, is quite distinct from neighbouring styles, since few crops grow at the high altitudes that characterize Tibet, although some areas in Tibet are low enough to grow such crops as rice, oranges, bananas, and lemon. The most important crop is barley. Flour milled from roasted barley, called *tsampa,* is the staple food of Tibet. *Balep* is Tibetan bread eaten for breakfast or even for lunch. *Thukpa* is mainly consumed for dinner. It consists of noodles of various shapes, vegetables and meat in broth. Tibetan *thukpas* can be of different shape like pasta. Meat dishes are likely to be yak, goat, or mutton, often dried, or cooked in a spicy stew with potatoes. Mustard seed is cultivated in Tibet, and therefore features heavily in its cuisine. Yak yoghurt, butter and cheese are frequently eaten, and well-prepared yoghurt is considered something of a prestige item. As well as consumed in Tibet, varieties of Tibetan dishes are consumed in Laddakh, Sikkim and Arunachal Pradesh in India.

Other Tibetan foods include:

- Sha Balep-a bread stuffed with seasoned beef.
- Balep korkun-a central Tibetan flatbread cooked on a skillet rather than in an oven.
- Momos-a type of steamed dumpling, a heavier version of the Chinese jiaozi.
- Thenthuk-a type of cold-weather soup made with noodles and various vegetables.
- Shab Tra-Stir-fried meat tossed with celery, carrots and fresh green chili.

In larger Tibetan towns and cities many restaurants now serve Sichuan-style Chinese food. Western imports and fusion dishes, such as fried yak and chips, are also popular. Nevertheless, many small restaurants serving traditional Tibetan dishes persist in both cities and the countryside.

Beverages

Most Tibetans drink many cups of yak butter tea each day. Jasmine tea is also sometimes available.

"Brick tea is made by methods only distantly related to those employed in China or Ceylon. When the water boils, a great handful of the stuff is crumbled into it and allowed to stew for between five and ten minutes, until the whole infusion is so opaque that it looks almost black. At this stage a pinch of salt is added; the Tibetans always put salt, never sugar, in their tea. I have been told that they sometimes add a little soda, in order to give the beverage a pinkish tinge, but I never saw this done in Sikang. They very seldom, on the other hand, drink tea without butter in it. If you are at home, you empty the saucepan into a big wooden churn, straining the tea through a colander made of reed or horsehair. Then you drop a large lump of butter into it, and, after being vigorously stirred, this brew is transferred to a huge copper teapot and put on a brazier to keep it hot. When you are travelling, you do not normally take a churn with you, so everyone fills his wooden bowl with tea, scoops a piece of butter out of a basket, puts it in the bowl, stirs the mixture gently with his finger, and, finally, drinks the tea."

Alcoholic beverages include:

- Chang, a beer usually made from barley
- Pinjopo, a rice wine.

CALENDAR

The Tibetan calendar is a lunisolar calendar, that is, the Tibetan year is composed of either 12 or 13 lunar months, each beginning and ending with a new moon. A thirteenth month is added every two or three years, so that an average Tibetan year is equal to the solar year.

The Tibetan New Year celebration is Losar (*lo-gsar*). The Tibetan civil year starts with the first day of the first Hor month. During the Yar-lung Dynasty the Tibetan year started in summer. According to almanacs the year starts with the third Hor month. There were many different traditions in Tibet to fix the beginning of the year.

Years

There were different traditions of naming years in Tibet. During the time of the Yar-lung Dynasty years were named by the 12 animals of the Chinese zodiac. From the 12th century onwards, we observe the usage of two sixty-year cycles. The 60-year cycle is known as the Brhaspati cycle and was first introduced into Tibet by an Indian Buddhist by the name of Chandra Nath and Chilu Pandit of Tibet in 1025 CE. The first cycle is the *rab-byung* cycle. The first year of the first *rab-byung* cycle started in 1027. This cycle was adopted from India. The second cycle was derived from China and was called *drug-cu skor*. The first year of the first *drug-cu skor* cycle started in 1024. The cycles were counted by ordinal numbers, but the years within the cycles were never counted but referred to by special names.

Years with Cardinal Numbers

Three relatively modern notations of cardinal numbers are used for Tibetan years.

On Tibetan banknotes from the first half of the 20th century cardinal numbers can be seen, with year 1 at 225 AD, which is a reference to the 28th king of Tibet, Thothori Nyantsen. A year 1659 means 1659 years have elapsed after the foundation of Tibetan monarchy and gives the year of 1659 + 255 " 1 = 1913. The introduction of this year notation is without doubt related to the proclamation of Tibetan independence by the 13th Dalai Lama in 1912.

Since the second half of the 20th century another year notation has been used, where the year of, for example, 2009 coincides with the Tibetan year of 2136. This relatively modern year notation is referred to as *Bot Gyalo* (*bod rgyal lo*). In this era the first year is 127 BC, referring to in this case the first king of Tibet Nyatri Tsenpo.

In Tibetan calendars of the second half of the 20th century and on Tibetan coins cardinal year numbers are found with the indication of *rab lo,* where the first year coincides with the first year of the *rab byung*-cycle, that is 1027. *Rab lo* 928, for example, is the year of 1954 on the western Gregorian calendar.

9

Chinese Buddhism

Chinese Buddhism, as a branch of Buddhism, is an important religion in China and one of the three major schools of thought along with Confucianism and Taoism. It has affected and been affected by Chinese culture, politics, literature and philosophy for almost two millennia.

PRESENT-DAY BUDDHISM

Periods of Buddhist History

The history of Buddhism in China may be divided into four periods. Buddhism entered China, as we have seen, in the second century B.C. The first period, that of the translation and propagation of the faith, ended in 420 A.D. The second period, that of interpenetration, lasted to the beginning of the T'ang dynasty, 618 A.D. The third, the period of establishment, ended with the close of the five dynasties, in 960 A.D. The fourth period, that of decay, has extended to the present day.

The Progress of the Last Twenty-five Years

There are signs of a revival of Buddhism in China. Whether this is a tide, or a wave, only the future can reveal. In 1893 Dharmapala, an Indian monk, stopped in Shanghai on his way back from the Congress of Religions in Chicago. It was his purpose to make a tour of China, to arouse the Chinese Buddhists to send missionaries to India to restore Buddhism there, and then to start a propaganda throughout the whole world. He addressed the monks of Shanghai. Dr. Edkins, the veteran missionary, acted as his interpreter. Dharmapala was surrounded by a horde of curious monks who were more interested in his strange appearance and in the cost of his garments than they were in his great ideals. They were also feeling the iron heel of the Confucian government and at once inquired about the attitude of the government toward such an innovation. Dharmapala did not go beyond Shanghai.

Japanese Buddhists, especially the members of the Hongwanji sect, have taken a deep interest in Chinese Buddhists. Count Otani once visited the chief monasteries of China. Numerous Japanese Buddhists have made such visits. In 1902, the Empress Dowager, fired by a reforming zeal, decided to confiscate Buddhist property and to use the proceeds for the spread of modern education. The Buddhist monasteries put themselves under the protection of Japanese monks in order to hold their property. When by 1906 the Empress Dowager saw the consequences of her edict, she at once issued a new edict, reversing the former one, and the Japanese monks took their departure.

The Japanese Buddhists have been fired by missionary zeal for China. In many of the large cities of China are the temples of the Hongwanji sect. Established primarily for the Japanese, these temples are intended to serve as points of departure for a nation-wide missionary work. The twenty-one demands made upon China included two significant items in the last group which the Chinese refused to sign: "Art. 2: Japanese hospitals, churches and schools in the interior of China shall be granted the right of owning land." "Art. 7: China agrees that Japanese subjects shall have the right of missionary propaganda in China."

Under Japanese influence there was established in 1907 at Nanking, under the leadership of Yang, a lay Buddhist devotee, a school for the training of Buddhist missionaries. The students were to go to Japan for further training, and the more promising ones were to study in India. This project was discontinued after the death of Yang on account of the lack of funds.

When the republic was established Buddhism felt a wave of reform. The monasteries established schools for monks and children. A magazine was published which appeared irregularly for several numbers and then stopped. A national organization was formed with headquarters at Peking. A survey of monasteries was begun. The activities in lecturing and propaganda were increased, but Yuan Shih-kai issued twenty-seven regulations for the control of Buddhist monasteries, which markedly dampened the ardor of the reformers. The world war which accentuated the spirit of nationalism had the added effect of stirring up Buddhist enthusiasm. There are at present signs of new activity among them in China.

Present Activities

While Buddhism may be standing still or even dying in certain parts of China, it is showing signs of new life in the provinces of Kiangsu and Chekiang and in the large cities. Such revival in centers subject to the influence of the modern world shows that Buddhism in China as in Japan has sufficient vitality to adjust itself to modern conditions. Let us consider some of these activities.

(a) The Reconstruction of Monasteries._—During the T'ai Ping rebellion, which devastated China in 1850-1865, the monasteries suffered with the towns. Not only were the monasteries burned to the ground, but their means of support were taken away and the monks were scattered. There are still many of these ruined monasteries in the Yangtze valley and in southern and western China. Quite a number of them have been rebuilt. Perhaps the most notable example is that at Changchow which was destroyed during the rebellion. Today it is the largest monastery in China, having about two thousand monks. In Fukien several new monasteries have been built in the last few decades. In the provinces of Chekiang and Kiangsu, in the large cities and about Peking there are building activities, showing that the monasteries are feeling a new wave of prosperity.

T'ai Hsu, one of the leaders' of modern Buddhism, is holding up an ideal program for Buddhism in this time of reconstruction. He proposes that there should be 576 central monasteries, 4608 preaching places, 72 Buddhist hospitals and 72 orphanages.

(b) Accessions._—Regarding the number of monks it is almost impossible to obtain any reliable figures. A conservative estimate, based upon partial returns, makes the number of monks about 400,000 and that of nuns about 10,000. The impression among the Buddhists is that the number of monks is increasing. That is quite probable in view of the rebuilding and repairing which is now in progress.

More significant is the number of accessions from the learned class. Many officials, disheartened by the present confused political situation, have sought refuge in the monasteries. Some of them are now abbots of monasteries and are using their influence to build them up. All over China there are Confucian scholars who are giving themselves to the study of Buddhism and to meditation. Some of the Chinese students who have studied in Buddhist universities in Japan are propagating Buddhism by lecture and pen.

(c) Publications._—Quite as significant is the increase in the publication of Buddhist literature of all kinds. Many of the monasteries have printing departments where they publish the sutras needed for their own use. In addition, there are eight or more publishing centers where Buddhist literature is printed. The most famous are Yang's establishment at Nanking, the Buddhist Press in Yangchow and that in Peking. In these establishments about nine hundred different works are being published. The most noteworthy recent publication has been that of the Chinese Buddhist Tripitaka in Shanghai.

Among these publications are a few modern issues. The Chung Hua Book Company has published several works on Buddhism. Other books have been issued for the sake of harmonizing Buddhism with western science and philosophy. In this enterprise Japanese influence is visible. In 1921 a Shanghai press published a dictionary of Buddhist terms containing 3302 pages, based on the Japanese Dictionary of Buddhism. Other works also show the influence of Japanese scholarship.

Among the publications have appeared two magazines. One published at Ningpo, is called "New Buddhism." This is struggling and may have to succumb. The other is known as the "Sound of the Sea Tide," now published in Hankow. Moreover, in all the large cities there are Buddhist bookshops where only Buddhist works are sold. These all report a good business. This literary activity reveals an interest among the reading classes of China. Few such books are purchased by the monks. The Chinese scholars read them for their style and for their deep philosophy, but also for light and for help in the present distracting political situation of their country.

(d) Lectures._—Along with publication goes the spread of Buddhism by lectures in the monasteries and the cities of China. A few years ago Buddhist sermons, however serious, were only listened to by monks and by a few pious devotees. Today such addresses are advertised and are usually well attended by the intellectuals. Often many women are found listening. Monks like T'ai Hs?Yuan Ying have a national reputation. Not only monks, but laymen trained in Japan are delivering lectures on the Buddhist sutras. The favorites are the Awakening of Faith and the Suddharma Pundarika sutra.

(e) Buddhist Societies._—With the lectures goes the organization of Buddhist societies for all sorts of purposes. There is a central society in Peking which has branches in every province. The connection is rather loose. Buddhism has never been in favor of centralization. Nor for that matter would the government have allowed it. The chief ends aimed at by these societies are fellowship, devotion, study, propagation, and service. Such societies, often short lived, are springing up in many quarters. They meet for lectures on Buddhism or to conduct a study class in some of the sutras. Occasionally the more ambitious conduct an institute for several months. Some spend part of the time in meditation together. Several schools for children are supported by these societies. They also encourage work of a religious nature among prisoners, distributing tracts and holding services. Such activities are especially appreciated by those who are to suffer the death penalty. The societies are also doing publishing work. The two magazines are supported by the members of the larger societies.

(f) Signs of Social Ambition._—Social work is a prominent feature of some of these Buddhist societies. They have raised money for famine stricken regions, have opened orphanages, and assist in Red Cross work. One of the largest Chinese institutions for ministering to people who are sick and in trouble is located at Hankow. Around a central Buddhist temple is a modern-built hospital, an orphanage and several schools for poor children. It may not maintain western standards of efficiency, but it certainly represents the outreach of modern Buddhism.

Perhaps their most far-reaching advance has been made because of the realization that leaders are needed and that they must be trained. Several schools for this purpose have sprung into existence. Such schools are necessarily very primitive and are struggling with the difficulties of finding an adequate staff and equipment and of obtaining the best type of students.

Another sign of new life has been the making of programs for the future development of Buddhism. One of the most comprehensive appeared a short time ago. For the individual it proposes the cultivation of love, mercy, equality, freedom, progressiveness, an established faith, patience and endurance. For all men it proposes (1) an education according to capacity; (2) a trade suited to ability; (3) an opportunity to develop one's powers; (4) a chance for enlightenment for all. For society it urges the cultivation of cooperation, social service, sacrifice for the social weal, and the social consciousness in the individual. On behalf of the country it urges patriotism, participation in the government, and cooperation in international movements. For the world it advocates universal progress. As to the universe it specifies as a goal the bringing of men into harmony with spiritual realities, the enlightenment of all and the realization of the spiritual universe.

A Buddhist writer sums up the aims of new Buddhism as follows:

> *"Formerly Buddhism desired to escape the sinful world. Today Buddhism not only desires to escape this world of sin, but longs to transform this world of sin into a new world dominated by the ideals of Buddhism. Formerly Buddhism was occupied with erecting and perfecting its doctrines and polity as an organization. Today it not only hopes to perfect the doctrines and polity, but desires to spread the doctrines and ideals abroad so as to help mankind to become truly cultured."*

The Attitude of Tibetan Lamas

Not only the Chinese Buddhists, but the Lamas of Mongolia and Tibet are feeling the impulses of the new age. Quite recently an exhibition was held in the Lama temple at Peking which attracted thousands of visitors. Its object was to obtain money to repair the temple, and thus to give its work a fresh impulse. That these impulses are not necessarily hostile to Christianity is shown by a letter written by the Kurung Tsering Lama of Kokonor district to the Rev. T. S?sen of Szechuan:

> *"I, your humble servant, have seen several copies of the Scriptures and, having read them carefully, they certainly made me believe in Christ. I understand a little of the outstanding principles and the doctrinal teaching of the One Son, but as to the Holy Spirit's nature and essence, and as to the origin of this religion, I am not at all clear, and it is therefore important that the doctrinal principles of this religion should be fully explained, so as to enlighten the unintelligent and people of small mental ability.*
>
> *"The teaching of the science of medicine and astrology is also very important. It is therefore evident if we want this blessing openly manifested, we must believe in the religion of the only Son of God. Being in earnest, I therefore pray you from my heart not to consider this letter lightly. With a hundred salutations."*

Enclosed with this letter was a poem written in most elegant language.

> *"O thou Supreme God and most precious Father, The truth above all religions, The Ruler of all animate and inanimate worlds! Greater than wisdom, separated from birth and death, Is his son Christ the Lord shining in glory among endless*

beings. Incomprehensible wonder, miraculously made! In this teaching I myself also believe—As your spirit is with heaven united, My soul undivided is seeking the truth Jesus the Savior's desire fulfilling, For the coming of the Kingdom of Heaven I am praying. Happiness to all."

The Buddhist World Versus the Christian World

Looking back over the last twenty-five years we see rising quite distinctly a Buddhist world growing conscious of itself, of its past history and of its mission to the world. This Buddhist, world has much more of a program than it had twenty-five years ago. Its object is to unite the Mahay¡+ and the H?y¡+ branches of Buddhism and to spread Buddhist propaganda over the world. At present the leadership of this movement is in Japan. It is in part a political movement. There is no question that Christianity is not at all pleasing to the Japanese militarists. It is regarded by them as the advance post of western industrialism and political ambition. Quite naturally such leaders desire to make the Buddhist world a unit. It is also a social movement.

The spirit of the Japanese Buddhist has been brought to consciousness by the new position of Japan. Japan is seeking to take its place in the world as a first rate power. By this not only will Japan's industry and commerce profit, but its spiritual values must also be adapted to the world. The movement then has its spiritual side. Japanese travelers and people are going to all parts of the world. They carry with them the religious ideals which have been shaped by Buddhism. Buddhism in the past was one of the great religions of salvation with an inspiring missionary message. It is again awakening to this task of evangelization. Under the leadership of Japanese scholars and religious statesmen the Japanese are seeking to unite the Buddhist world so that it shall become a force in the new world. Japan is thus trying to give back what it has received in the past. At present in Buddhist countries there is a strong force working against this movement. Nationalism is a new force to be reckoned with. Still even with the spirit of nationalism permeating every group, the Buddhist world is getting together and will strive to make its contribution to the life of the whole world.

THE ENTRANCE OF BUDDHISM INTO CHINA

Buddhism was not an indigenous religion of China. Its, founder was Gautama of India in the sixth century B.C. Some centuries later it found its way into China by way of central Asia. There is a tradition that as early as 142 B.C. Chang Ch'ien, an ambassador of the Chinese emperor, Wu Ti, visited the countries of central Asia, where he first learned about the new religion which was making such headway and reported concerning it to his master. A few years later the generals of Wu Ti captured a gold image of the Buddha which the emperor set up in his palace and worshiped, but he took no further steps.

According to Chinese historians Buddhism was officially recognized in China about 67 A.D. A few years before that date, the emperor, Ming-Ti, saw in a dream a large golden image with a halo hovering above his palace. His advisers, some of whom were no doubt already favorable to the new religion, interpreted the image of the dream to be that of Buddha, the great sage of India, who was inviting his adhesion. Following their advice the emperor sent an embassy to study into Buddhism. It brought back two Indian monks and a quantity of Buddhist classics. These were carried on a white horse and so the monastery which the emperor built for the monks and those who came after them was called the White Horse Monastery. Its tablet is said to have survived to this day.

This dream story is worth repeating because it goes to show that Buddhism was not only known at an early date, but was favored at the court of China. In fact, the same history which relates the dream contains the biography of an official who became an adherent of Buddhism a few years before the dream took place. This is not at all surprising, because an acquaintance with Buddhism was the inevitable concomitant of the military campaigning, the many embassies and the wide-ranging trade of those centuries. But the introduction of Buddhism into China was especially promoted by reason of the current policy of the Chinese government of moving conquered populations in countries west of China into China proper, The vanquished peoples brought their own religion along with them. At one time what is now the province of Shansi was populated in this way by the Hsiung-nu, many of whom were Buddhists.

The introduction and spread of Buddhism were hastened by the decline of Confucianism and Taoism. The Han dynasty (206 B. C.-221 A. D.) established a government founded on Confucianism. It reproduced the classics destroyed in the previous dynasty and encouraged their study; it established the state worship of Confucius; it based its laws and regulations upon the ideals and principles advocated by Confucius. The great increase of wealth and power under this dynasty led to a gradual deterioration in the character of the rulers and officials. The sigid Confucian regulations became burdensome to the people who ceased to respect their leaders. Confucianism lost its hold as the complete solution of the problems of life. At the same time Taoism had become a veritable jumble of meaningless and superstitious rites which served to support a horde of ignorant, selfish priests. The high religious ideals of the earlier Taoist mystics were abandoned for a search after the elixir of life during fruitless journeys to the isles of the Immortals which were supposed to be in the Eastern Sea.

At this juncture there arose in North China a sect of men called the Purists who advocated a return from the vagaries of Taoism and the irritating rules of Confucianism to the simple life practised by the Taoist mystics. When these thoughtful and earnest minded men came into contact with Buddhism they were captivated by it. It had all they were claiming for Taoist mysticism and more. They devoted their literary ability and religious fervor to the spreading of the new religion and its success was in no small measure due to their efforts. As a result of this early association the tenets of the two religions seemed so much alike that various emperors called assemblies of Buddhists and Taoists with the intention of effecting a union of the two religions into one. If the emperor was under the influence of Buddhism he tried to force all Taoists to become Buddhists. If he was favorable to Taoism he tried to make all Buddhists become Taoists.

But such mandates were as unsuccessful as other similar schemes have been. In the third century A. D. after the Han dynasty had ended, China was broken up into several small kingdoms which contended for supremacy, so that for about four hundred years the whole country was in a state of disunion. One of the strong dynasties of this period, the Northern Wei (386-535 A. D.), was distinctly loyal to Buddhism. During its continuance Buddhism prospered greatly. Although Chinese were not permitted to become monks until 335 A. D., still Buddhism made rapid advances and in the fourth century, when that restriction was removed, about nine-tenths of the people of northwestern China had become Buddhists. Since then Buddhism has been an established factor in Chinese life.

HISTORY OF BUDDHISM IN CHINA

Arrival Along the Silk Road

The arrival of Buddhism in China was a consequence of the first contacts between China and Central Asia which occurred with the opening of the Silk Road in the 2nd century BCE, following the travels of Zhang Qian between 138 and 126 BCE. Chinese murals in the Tarim Basin city of Dunhuang describe the Emperor Han Wudi (156-87 BCE) worshipping Buddhist statues, "golden men brought in 120 BCE by a great Han general in his campaigns against the nomads". However, there is no such mention of Han Wudi worshipping the Buddha in Chinese historical literature. The Hou Hanshu then records the visit of Yuezhi envoys to the Chinese capital in 2 BCE, who gave oral teachings on Buddhist sutras to a student, suggesting that some Yuezhi had already started to disseminate the Buddhist faith in eastern Asia during the 1st century BCE (Baldev Kumar (1973), exact source needed).

The Hou Hanshu describes the enquiry about Buddhism made around 70 CE by the emperor Emperor Ming (58-75 CE):

> *"There is a current tradition that Emperor Ming dreamed that he saw a tall golden man the top of whose head was glowing. He questioned his group of advisors and one of them said: "In the West there is a god called Buddha. His body is sixteen chi high (3.7 metres or 12 feet), and is the colour of true gold." The Emperor, to discover the true doctrine, sent an envoy to Tianzhu (Northwestern India) to inquire about the Buddha's doctrine,*

after which paintings and statues [of the Buddha] appeared in the Middle Kingdom." (Hou Hanshu, trans. John Hill)

This encounter is further described in a 6th century CE account by Yang Xuanzhi:

"The establishment of the BaimI-Sì by Emperor Ming (58-75 CE) of the Han marked the introduction of Buddhism into China. The temple was located on the south side of the Imperial Drive, three leagues (li) outside the Xiyang Gate. The Emperor dreamt of the golden man sixteen Chinese feet tall, with the aureole of sun and moon radiating from his head and his neck. A "golden god", he was known as Buddha. The emperor dispatched envoys to the Western Regions in search of the god, and, as a result, acquired Buddhist scriptures and images. At the time, because the scriptures were carried into China on the backs of white horses, White Horse was adopted as the name of the temple." (Translation: Ulrich Theobald).

These Chinese emissaries are said to have visited the country of the Yuezhi, and to have brought back with them two missionnaries named Dharmaraksa and Kasyapa Matanga (also called Moton and Chufarlan), together with sutras written with 600,000 Sanskrit words. The two missionnaries wrote "The Sutra of forty-two sections spoken by the Buddha", to provide guidance on the ideas of Buddhism and the conduct of monks. It is the first Buddhist text in the Chinese language, although its authenticity is a matter of debate.

Their arrival in 67 CE marks Buddhism's official introduction in China. Historians generally agree that by the middle of the 1st century, the religion had penetrated to areas north of the Huai River. Emperor Ming's brother Liu Ying the Prince of Chu was the first high-profile believer of Buddhism, although there is some evidence that Emperor Ming himself might have been as well.

The first documented translation of Buddhist scriptures into Chinese occurs in 148 CE, with the arrival of the Parthian missionary An Shih Kao in China, probably on the heels of the Kushan expansion into the Tarim Basin. An Shi Kao established Buddhist temples in Loyang and organized the translation of Buddhist scriptures into Chinese, testifying to the beginning of a wave of

Central Asian Buddhist proselitism that was to last several centuries. Traces of Buddhist iconography can also be seen in works of art from this period.

By the end of the second century, a prosperous community had been settled at Pengcheng (modern Xuzhou, Jiangsu).

Relation to Confucianism and Taoism

Most of the Chinese gentry were indifferent to the Central Asian travellers and their religion. Not only was their religion unknown, but much of it seemed alien and amoral to Chinese sensibilities. Concepts such as monasticism and individual spiritual enlightenment directly contradicted the core Confucian principles of family and emperor. Confucianism promoted social stability, order, strong families, and practical living. Chinese officials questioned how a monk's personal attainment of nirvana benefited the empire. Buddhism was less antithetical to Daoism, the other major religion of China. Indeed, upon first encountering Buddhism, many Chinese scholars regarded it as merely a foreign equivalent of Daoism.

Local Interpretation of Indian Texts

To thrive in China, Buddhism had to transform itself into a system that could exist within the Chinese way of life. Thus highly regarded Indian sutras that advocated filial piety became core texts in China. Buddhism was made compatible with ancestor worship and participation in China's hierarchical system. Works were written arguing that the salvation of an individual was a benefit to that individual's society and family and monks thus contributed to the greater good. It is conjectured that the shocking collapse of the Han Dynasty in 220 and the resulting period of social upheaval and political unrest known as the Three Kingdoms period may have helped the spread of Buddhism. Buddhism was a minor force, however, compared with Daoism which was directly associated with efforts to defy the emperor (cf. Yellow Turban Rebellion). The Daoist Zhang family self-governed the Hanzhong Commandry for nearly 20 years until invasion by the renowned Chinese warlord Cao Cao.

A reason for the lack of interest mostly stemmed from the ruling entity and gentry. All the rulers were Han Chinese and had simply never heard of or knew too little of the religion. The Nine-grade controller system, by which prominent individuals in each local administrative area were given the authority to rank local families and individuals in nine grades according to their potential for government service, further consolidated the importance of Confucianism. Daoism too remained a strong force among the population and philosophers.

LAMAISM (TIBETAN BUDDHISM) IN CHINA

Lamaism, also known as Tibetan Buddhism, is a form of Mahayana Buddhism that is practiced mainly in Tibet, Mongolia, Gansu, Qinghai, and parts of Yunnan and Sichuan provinces. The practice is named after the 'lama', the Tibetan word for teacher. Buddhism was established as the official religion in Tibet in 641 A.D., under King Songtsen Gampo. Prior to that, Tibetans had traditionally practiced the shamanistic religion of Bon. While Buddhism grew, it did not completely supplant Bon, which is still practiced today by more than 130,000 people in Tibet, according to a 2007 report by the Chinese government.

Around 760, a Buddhist mystic known as Padmasambhava or Guru Rinpoche travelled to Tibet from India to establish a monastery near Lhasa known as the Nyingma School. Padamasambhava combined aspects of Buddhism, Tantric Buddhism and Bon to form the unique practice of Tibetan Buddhism. While Tibetan Buddhism grew, there were continued conflicts with Bon shamans and followers. Some lamas even attempted to eliminate any aspect of Bon practices from Tibetan Buddhism.

In the 1200s the Mongols who populated north-central Asia adopted Tibetan Buddhism. Under the Mongolian-led Yuan Dynasty (1271-1368) Lamaism became the official religion of China. It was during this Dynasty that the Manchus, who lived in Northeast China, also adopted Tibetan Buddhism. Under the later Manchu-led Qing Dynasty (1644-1911) Tibetan Buddhism was also practiced in the Chinese imperial court.

Political Changes

In 1949, following the defeat of the Nationalists by Chinese Communists in the Chinese Civil War, China became a Socialist and atheist nation. These changes quickly conflicted with traditional Tibetan society which consisted of estates with lords and laborers. In 1950 the Chinese defeated Tibetan fighters and initiated policies, such as land reform, to bring Tibet into further into the People's Republic of China. In 1951, the Chinese government and representatives of the 14th Dalai Lama, the religion's spiritual leader, underwent talks that resulted in the Seventeen Point Agreement that includes a statement of China's sovereignty over Tibet. The agreement was later ratified in Lhasa.

But many Tibetans continued to resist Chinese rule and staged a failed uprising in 1959, which led to a violent Chinese military crackdown on Tibet. It was during this period that the Dalai Lama fled to India with help from the U.S. Central Intelligence Agency. After leaving Tibet, the Dalai Lama discredited the Seventeen Point Agreement saying it was forced and never valid.

In Dharamsala, India, the Dalai Lama established the Tibetan Government in Exile, officially known as the Central Tibetan Administration. Meanwhile, in China, the 10th Panchen Lama, the second most powerful lama after the Dalai Lama, became the figurehead of Tibet.

Religious Practices

Tibetan Buddhism differs from traditional Buddhism in its shamanistic and mystical elements, much of which was taken from the traditional Bon religion and Tantric Hinduism. Ritualistic practices are common, including prayer, drumming and meditation. Followers also worship guardian deities and believe in living incarnations of the Buddha.

There are many Tibetan Buddhist holidays, including Year End celebrations and Losar or New Year celebrations in February and March that mark the start of spring. There are also a Horse Racing Festival in June, a Water Feast in August which marks the start of Autumn, and the Lhabab Duchen in the winter which commemorates the Buddha's descent from Heaven.

Within Tibetan Buddhism are several different schools including the dominant Gelugpa or Yellow Hat Sect, the Kagyupa school, the Nyingmapa school, and the Sakyapa school. The Kagyupa, Nyingmapa and Sakyapa are collective known as followers of the Red Hat Sect. The use of hat in its name refers to the colour of the hats that followers wear during ceremonies. The oldest teachings is the Nyingmapa school, which dates to the 8th century from the Buddhist mystic Padmasambhava. This belief is based on the first translations of Buddhist teachings from the original Sanskrit into the Tibetan language. Most of the followers of this order today are in Kham in eastern Tibet.

The Kagyupa school was created in the 11th Century during a second period of translation from the original Sanskrit into Tibetan. The Kagyu school uses oral lineage and guru devotion, and focuses on tantric teachings. The Sakyapa sect was also created in the 11th Century. It is located in southern Tibet where the Sakya Monastery was built. It was founded by Drogmi, a translator of texts who had also studied in India. Sakya monks were influential in collecting Buddhist and Tantric texts.

The Gelugpa or Yellow Hat sect is currently the most powerful in Tibetan Buddhism. It developed in the 15th Century because many followers viewed the other sects as corrupt. This sect was developed by the religious leader Tsongkhapa who created stricter rituals for religious practices. He also included rules of celibacy. It was under the Yellow Sect that the Dalai Lama and Panchen Lama lineages were established.

Structure

Traditional Tibetan Buddhism had a hierarchy that begins with the Dalai Lama, followed by the Panchen Lama. They are followed by a higher clergy and a lower clergy, and then by Tibetan Buddhist followers.

The Dalai Lama and the Panchen Lama are both viewed as reincarnations. The Dalai Lama is the reincarnation of all previous lamas starting with Avalokitesvara, the Buddha of Compassion.

The Panchen Lama is the reincarnation of all previous Panchen Lamas starting with Amitabha, the Buddha of Light.

When a Dalai Lama and Panchen Lama dies, leaders seek out their reincarnation among boys in the region. When they find potential candidates they give the child a series of tests to affirm they are reincarnations.

The issue of reincarnation has become political in light of the conflict between China and Tibetan leaders. In 1995, China rejected a boy that the Dalai Lama confirmed as the new Panchen Lama, which led to a selection of a different boy. China later created policy that only monasteries in China could apply for approval for future reincarnations.

In 2007, the Dalai Lama has hinted that his successor or reincarnate could be found before he dies and it could even be a girl.

Tibetan Buddhism Today

Tibetans and Chinese continue to have conflicts. Most recently, riots in Tibet in March 2008 led to the death of 18 Chinese and the subsequent crackdown by the Chinese military, which Tibetan leaders in exile say have killed more than 140 Tibetans.

Since the riots, Chinese leaders and the Dalai Lama have had three different talks to find a solution to the conflict. To address younger Tibetans in exile who believe that the Dalai Lama could be more forceful, the Dalai Lama called a meeting of exiles in November 2008 to discuss their future.

Following the meeting, most of the members seemed to continue to support the Dalai Lama's "Middle Path" approach which aims to peacefully resolve the issue by pushing co-existence between Tibetans and the Chinese government.

BUDDHISM GAINS POLITICAL TRACTION IN THE NORTH

Subsequent chaotic periods of Sixteen Kingdoms and Southern and Northern Dynasties changed the situation, resulting in state support of Buddhism. Most rulers and population of the Wu, Hu, and the Northern dynasties originated from more than ten distinct ethnic groups including either non-Han Chinese "barbarians", or Han Chinese after generations of "barbarian" influence. They did not propagate nor trust the combined philosophical concept of Confucianism and Daoism as zealously as their rivals in the south. Official support of Buddhism would eventually mould a new Chinese populace with a common ideology out of the diversely ethnic population, which would in turn consolidate these dynasties.

It is instructive that Buddhism propagated faster in northern China than in the south. Social upheaval in northern China worked to break down cultural barriers between the elite ruling families and the general populace, in contrast to the south where elite clans and royal families firmly monopolized politics. Daoist and Confucian political ideology had long consolidated the political status of elite clans in the south. Support of another religion would have unknown and possibly adverse effects, for which these clans would not risk their privileges. Furthermore pro-Buddhist policy would not be backed by the bureaucracy, which had been staffed by members of the clans. Southern rulers were in weaker positions to strive for their legitimacy-some were even installed by the clans. It was not until the reign of Emperor Wu of the Liang Dynasty that saw the official support of Buddhism. Rebellion of Hou Jing near the end of Emperor Wu's reign wreaked havoc on the political and social privileges of the elite clans, which indirectly assisted the spread of Buddhism. But Buddhism spread pretty well in the peasant populace, both in the north and the south.

Monks and Rulers Join Forces

Arrivals of several prestigious monks in the early 5th century also contributed to the propagation of the religion and were welcomed by rulers of the Sixteen Kingdoms and Northern Dynasties. Fo Tu Cheng was entrusted by the tyrant Shi Hu of Later Chao. Kumarajiva was invited by Lu Guang, the founder of Later Liang, and later by Yao Xing, second ruler of Later Qin. Biographies of these monks, among others, were the subject of the *Memoirs of Eminent Monks*.

The direct experiential impact of contact with practicing monks should not be underestimated. Confucianism had no equivalent to holy men — the archetypical best and brightest was a wise government minister, not a saint. Daoist priests were more immediate, but given to relativism. It is notable that when another "foreign " religion, Nestorianism, sought to extol the virtues of one of its main benefactors they claimed he was so moral that "...even among the most pure and self-denying of the Buddhists, such excellence was never heard of;" Through the actions and example of monks, Buddhists successfully laid claim to the high moral ground in society.

In this way Buddhism grew to become a major religion in China. By the start of the 6th century, Buddhism had grown in popularity to rival Daoism. We know they were successful because the monks were soon accused of falling into extravagance and their lands and properties confiscated by Emperor Wu of the Northern Zhou dynasty and Wuzong of the Tang Dynasty.

During the early Tang dynasty the monk Xuanzang journeyed to Nalanda in India and other important sites to bring back scriptures. He sought to expand influence of Mahayana over Theravada, though the Yogacara school he preferred differs significantly from the later Chinese Mahayana schools that developed such as Pure Land. The Tang capital of Chang'an (today's Xi'an) became an important centre for Buddhist thought. From there Buddhism spread to Korea, and Japanese embassies of Kentoshi helped gain footholds in Japan. Buddhist ideology began to merge with Confucianism and Daoism, due in part to the use of existing Chinese philosophical terms in the translation of Buddhist scriptures. Various Confucian scholars of the Song dynasty, including Zhu Xi (wg: Chu Hsi), sought to redefine Confucianism as Neo-Confucianism.

The popularization of Buddhism in this period is evident in the many scripture-filled caves and structures surviving today. The Mogao Caves near Dunhuang in Gansu province, the Longmen Grottoes near Luoyang in Henan and the Yungang Grottoes near Datong in Shanxi are the most renowned of the Northern, Sui and Tang Dynasties. The Leshan Giant Buddha, carved out of a hillside in the 8th century during Tang Dynasty and looking down on the confluence of three rivers, is still the largest stone Buddha statue in the world. As a side note, duplications of Buddhist texts were considered to bring meritorious karma. Printing from individually carved wooden blocks, from movable clay type and from movable metal type, proved much more efficient and eventually eclipsed hand copying. The *Diamond Sutra* of AD 868, a Buddhist scripture discovered in AD 1907 inside the Mogao Caves, was the first dated example of block printing.

THE ESTABLISHMENT OF BUDDHISM AS THE PREDOMINATING RELIGION OF CHINA

Even the historical influences noted above do not account entirely for the spread of Buddhism in China. In order to understand this and the place which Buddhism occupies, we need to review briefly the different forms which religion takes in China and to note how Buddhism has related itself to them.

The World of Invisible Spirits

The Chinese believe _in_ a surrounding-world of spirits, whose origin is exceedingly various. They touch life at every point. There are spirits which are guardians of the soil, tree spirits, mountain demons, fire gods, the spirits of animals, of mountains, of rivers, seas and stars, of the heavenly bodies and of many forms of active life. These spirits to the Chinese mind, of today are a projection, a sort of spiritual counterpart, of the many sided interests, practical or otherwise, of the groups and communities by whom they are worshipped. There are other spirits which mirror the ideals of the groups by which they are worshipped. Some of them may have been incarnated in the lives of great leaders. There are spirits which are mere animations, occasional spirits, associated with objects crossing the interests of men, but not constant enough to attain a definite, independent life as spiritual beings. Thus surrounding the average Chinese peasant there is a densely populated spirit world affecting in all kinds of ways his, daily existence.

This other world is the background which must be kept in mind by one who would understand or attempt to guide Chinese religious experience. It is the basis on which all organized forms of religious activity are built. The nearest of these to his heart is the proper regard for his ancestors.

The Universal Sense of Ancestor Control

The ancestral control of family life occupies so large and important a place in Chinese thought and practice that ancestor worship has been called the original religion of the Chinese. It is certain that the earliest Confucian records recognize ancestor worship; but doubtless it antedated them, growing up out of the general religious consciousness of the people.

The discussion of that origin in detail cannot be taken up here. It may be followed in the literature noted in the appendix or in the volume of this series entitled "Present-Day Confucianism." Ancestor worship is active today, however, because the Chinese as a people believe that these ancestors control in a very real way the good or evil fortunes of their descendants, because this recognition of ancestors furnishes a potent means of promoting family unity and social ethics, and, most of all, because a happy future life is supposed to be dependent upon descendants who will faithfully minister to the dead. Since each one desires such a future he is faithful in promoting the observance of the obligation.

Consequently, ancestor worship, like the previously mentioned belief in the invisible spiritual world, underlies all other religious developments. No family is so obscure or poor that it does not submit to the ritual or discipline which is supposed to ensure the favor of the spirits belonging to the community. Likewise, every such family is loyal to the supposed needs of its deceased ancestors. In a very intimate way these beliefs are interwoven with the private and social morality of every family or group in Chinese society, and must be taken into account by any one who seeks to bring a religious message to the Chinese people.

Degenerate Taoism

Taoism is that system of Chinese religious thought and practice, beginning about the fifth century B. C., which was originally based on the teachings of Lao Tzu and developed in the writings of Lieh Tzu and Chuang Tzu and found in the Tao T'hing. It is really in this original form a philosophy of some merit. According to its teaching the Tao is the great impersonal background of the world from which all things proceed as beams from the sun, and to which all beings return. In contrast to the present, transient, changing world the Tao is unchangeable and quiet. Originally the Taoists emphasized quiescence, a life in accordance with nature, as a means of assimilating themselves to the Tao, believing that in this way they would obtain length of days, eternal life and especially the power to become superior to natural conditions.

There is a movement today among Chinese scholars in favor of a return to this original highest form of Taoism. It appeals to them as a philosophy of life; an answer to its riddles. Among the masses of the people, however, Taoism manifests itself in a ritual of extreme superstition. It recommends magic tricks and curious superstitions as a means of prolonging life. It expresses itself very largely in these degrading practices which few Chinese will defend, but which are yet very commonly practiced.

The Organizing Value of Confucianism

Confucianism brought organization into these hazy conceptions of life and duty. It took for granted this spiritual-unspiritual background of animism, ancestor-worship and Taoism, but reshaped and adapted it as a whole so that it might fit into that proper organization of the state and nation which was one of its great objectives. Just as Confucianism related the family to the village, the village to the district, and the district to the state, so it organized the spiritual world into a hierarchy with Shang Ti as its head. This hierarchy was developed along the lines of the organization mentioned above. Under Shang Ti were the five cosmic emperors, one for each of the four quarters and one for heaven above, under whom were the gods of the soil, the mountains, rivers, seas, stars, the sun and moon, the ancestors and the gods of special groups. Each of the deities in the various ranks had duties to those above and rights with reference to those below. These duties and rights, as they affected the individual, were not only expressed in law but were embodied in ceremony and music, in daily religious life and practice in such a way that each individual had reason to feel that he was a functioning agent in this grand Confucian universe. If any one failed to do his part, the whole universe would suffer. So thoroughly has this idea been adopted by the Chinese people that every one joins in forcing an individual, however reluctant or careless, to perform his part of each ceremony as it has been ordered from high antiquity.

The emperor alone worshipped the supreme deity, Shang Ti; the great officers of state, according to the dignity of their office, were related to subordinate gods and required to show them adequate respect and reverence. Confucius and a long line of noted men following him were semi-deified [Footnote: Confucius was by imperial decree deified in 1908.] and highly reverenced by the literati, the class from which the officers of state were as a rule obtained, in connection with their duties, and as an expression of their ideals. To the common people were left the ordinary local deities, while all classes, of course, each in its own fashion reverenced, cherished and obeyed their ancestors. It should be remarked at this point that Confucianism of this official character has broken down, not only under the impact of modern ideas, but under the longing of the Chinese for a universal deity. The people turn to Heaven and to the Pearly Emperor, the popular counterpart of Shang Ti.

Viewed from another angle, Confucianism is an elaborate system of ethics. In writings which are virtually the scriptures of the Chinese people Confucius and his successors have set forth the principles which should govern the life of a people who recognize this spiritual universe and system. These ethics have grown out of a long and, in some respects, a sound experience. Much can be said in their favor. The essential weaknesses of the Confucian system of ethics lie in its sectional and personal loyalties and its monarchical basis. The spirit of democracy is a deadly foe to Confucianism. Another element of weakness is its excessive dependence upon the past. Confucius reached ultimate wisdom by the study of the best that had been attained before his day. He looked backward rather than forward. Consequently a modern, broadly educated Confucianist finds himself in an anomalous position. He does not need absolutely to reject the wisdom which Confucianism embodies, but he can no longer accept it as a sound, reliable and indisputable scheme of thought and action. Yet its simple ethical principles and its social relationships are basal in the lives of the vast masses of the Chinese.

Buddhism an. Inclusive Religion

Upon this, confused jumble of spiritism, superstition, loyalty to ancestors and submission to a divine hierarchy Buddhism was superimposed. It quickly dominated all because of its superior excellence. The form of Buddhism which became established in China was not, to be sure, like the Buddhism preached by Gautama and his disciples, or like that form of Buddhism which had taken root in Burma or Ceylon. Except in name, the Buddhism of Southern Asia and the Buddhism which developed in China were virtually two distinct types of religion. The Buddhism of Burma and Ceylon was of the conservative H?y¡+ ("Little Vehicle" of salvation) school, while that of China was of the progressive Mahb.na ("Great Vehicle" of salvation) school. Their differences are so marked as to be worthy of a careful statement.

The Hinayana, which is today the type of Buddhism in Ceylon, Burma and Siam, has always clung closely to tradition as expressed in the original Buddhist scriptures. Its basic ideas were that life is on the whole a time of suffering, that the cause of this sorrow is desire or ignorance, and that there is a possible deliverance from it. This deliverance or salvation is to be attained by following the eightfold path, namely, right knowledge, aspiration, speech, conduct, means of livelihood, endeavor, mindfulness and meditation. To the beatific state to be ultimately attained Gautama gave the name Nirvana, explained by his followers variously either as an utter extinction of personality or as a passionless peace, a general state of well-being free from all evil desire or clinging to life and released from the chain of transmigration. Hinayana Buddhism appeals to the individual as affording a way of escape from evil desire and its consequences by acquiring knowledge, by constant discipline, and by a devotedness of the life to religious ends through membership in the monastic order which Buddha established. It encourages, however, a personal salvation worked out by the individual alone. The Mahb.na school of Buddhists accept the general ideas of the Hinayana regarding life and salvation, but so change the spirit and objectives as to make Buddhism into what is virtually another religion. It does not confine salvation to the few who can retire from the world and give themselves wholly to good works, but opens Buddhahood to all. The "saint" of Hinayana Buddhism is the _arhat_ who is intent on saving himself. The saint of Mahb.na Buddhism is the candidate for Buddhahood (Bodhisattva) who defers his entrance into the bliss of deliverance in order to save others. Mahb.na Buddhism is progressive. It encourages missionary enterprise and was a secret of the remarkable spread of Buddhism over Asia. Moreover, while the H?y¡+ school recognizes no god or being to whom worship is given, the Maha.n#(ame to regard Gautama himself as a god and salvation as life in a heavenly world of pure souls. Thus the Mahb.na type of thinking constitutes a bridge between H?y¡+ Buddhism and Christianity. In fact, a recent writer has declared that H?y¡+ Buddhists are verging toward these more spiritual conceptions. [Footnote: See Saunders, _Buddhism and Buddhists in Southern Asia,_ pp. 10, 20.]

After the death of Sù*amuni [Footnote: Sù*amuni is the name by which Gautama, the Buddha, is familiarly known in China.] Buddhism broke up into a number of sects usually said to be eighteen in number. When Buddhism came to China some of these sects were introduced, but they assumed new forms in their Chinese environment. Besides the sects brought, from India the Chinese developed several strong sects of their own. Usually they speak of ten sects although the number is far larger, if the various subdivisions are included.

To indicate the manifold differences between these groups in Buddhism would take us far afield and would not be profitable. It will be of interest, however, to consider some of the chief sects. One of the sects introduced from India is the Pure Land or the Ching T'u which holds before the believer the "Western Paradise" gained through faith in Amit¨(a. Any one, no matter what his life may have been, may enter the Western Paradise by repeating the name of Amit¨(a. This sect is widespread in China. In Japan there are two branches of it known as the Nishi-Hongwanji and the Higashi-Hongwanji with their head monasteries in Kyoto. They are the most progressive sects in Japan and are carrying on missionary work in China, the Hawaiian Islands and in the United States.

Another strong sect is the Meditative sect or the Ch'an Men (Zen in Japan). This was introduced by Bodhidharma, or Tamo, who arrived in the capital of China in the year 520 A.D. On his arrival the emperor Wu Ti tried to impress the sage with his greatness saying: "We have built temples, multiplied the Scriptures, encouraged many to join the Order: is not there much merit in all this?" "None," was the blunt reply. "But what say the holy books? Do they not promise rewards for such deeds?" "There is nothing holy." "But you, yourself, are you not one of the holy ones?" "I don't know." "Who are you?" "I don't know." Thus introduced, the great man proceeded to open his missionary-labors by sitting down opposite a wall arid gazing at it for the next nine years. From this he has been called the "wall-gazer." He and his successors promulgated the doctrine that neither the scriptures, the ritual nor the organization, in fact nothing outward had any value in the attainment of enlightenment. They held that the heart of the universe is Buddha and that apart from the heart or the thought all is unreal. They thought themselves back into the universal Buddha and then found the Buddha heart in all nature. Thus they awakened the spirit which permeated nature, art and literature and made the whole world kin with the spirit of the Buddha.

"The golden light upon the sunkist peaks,
The water murmuring in the pebbly creeks,
Are Buddha. In the stillness, hark, he speaks!"

Such pantheism and quietism often lead to a confusion in moral relations, but these mystics were quite correct in their morals because they checked up their mysticism with the moral system of the Buddha.

Still another important sect originated in the sixth century A. D. on Chinese soil, namely, the T'ien T'ai (Japanese Tendai), so called because it started in a monastery situated on the beautiful T'ien T'ai mountains south of Ningpo. Chih K'ai, the founder, realized that Buddhism contained a great mass of contradictory teachings and practice, all attributed to the Buddha. He sought for a harmonizing principle and found it in the arbitrary theory that these teachings were given to different people on five different occasions and hence the discrepancies. The practical message of this sect has been that all beings have the Buddha heart and that the Buddha loves all beings, so that all beings may attain salvation, which consists in the full realization of the Buddha heart latent in them.

There was a time when these sects were very active and flourishing in China. At the present time the various tendencies for which they stood have been adopted by Buddhism as a whole and the various sectaries, though still keeping the name of the sect, live peacefully in the same monastery.

All the monasteries practice meditation, believe in the paradise of Amit¨(a, and are enjoying the ironic calm advocated by the T'ien T'ai. While the struggle among the sects of China has been followed by a calm which resembles stagnation, those in Japan are very active and the reader is referred to the volume of this series on Japanese Buddhism for further treatment of the subject.

When Buddhism entered China it brought with it a new world. It was new _practical_ and new spiritually. It brought a knowledge unknown before regarding the heavenly bodies, regarding nature and regarding medicine, and a practice vastly above the realm of magical arts.

In addition to these practical benefits, Buddhism proclaimed a new spiritual universe far more real and extensive than any of which the Chinese had dreamed, and peopled with spiritual beings having characteristics entirely novel. In comparison with this new universe or series of universes which Indian imagination had created, the Chinese universe was wooden and geometric. Since it was an organized system and a greater rather than a different one, the Chinese people readily accepted it and made it their own.

Buddhism not only enlarged the universe and gave the individual a range of opportunity hitherto unsuspected, but it introduced a scheme of religious practice, or rather several of them, enabling the individual devotee to attain a place in this spiritual universe through his own efforts. These "ways" of salvation were quite in harmony with Chinese ideas. They resembled what had already been a part of the national practice and so were readily adopted and adapted by the Chinese.

Buddhism rendered a great service to the Chinese through its new estimate of the individual. Ancient China scarcely recognized the individual. He was merged in the family and the clan. Taoists, to be sure, talked of "immortals" and Confucianism exhibited its typical personality, or "princely man," but these were thought of as supermen, as ideals. The classics of China had very little to say about the common people. The great common crowd was submerged. Buddhism, on the other hand, gave every individual a distinct place in the great wheel _dharma,_ the law, and made it possible for him to reach the very highest goal of salvation. This introduced a genuinely new element into the social and family life of the Chinese people.

Buddhism was so markedly superior to any one of the four other methods of expressing the religious life, that it quickly won practical recognition as the real religion of China. Confucianism may be called the doctrine of the learned classes. It formulates their principles of life, but it is in no strict sense a popular religion. It is rather a state ritual, or a scheme of personal and social ethics. Taoism recognizes the immediate influence of the spirit world, but it ministers only to local ideals and needs. In the usages of family and community life, ancestor worship has a definite place, but an occasional one. Buddhism was able to leave untouched each of these expressions of Chinese personal and social life, and yet it went far beyond them in ministering to religious development. Its ideas of being, of moral responsibility and of religious relationships furnished a new psychology which with all its imperfections far surpassed that of the Chinese. Buddhism's organization was so satisfying and adaptable that not only was it taken over readily by the Chinese, but it has also persisted in China without marked changes since its introduction. Most of all it stressed personal salvation and promised an escape from the impersonal world of distress and hunger which surrounds the average Chinese into a heaven ruled by Amit¨(a [Footnote: Amit¨(a, meaning "infinite light," is the Sanskrit name of one of the Buddhas moat highly revered in China. The usual Chinese equivalent is Omi-To-Fo.] the Merciful. The obligations of Buddhism are very definite and universally recognized. It enforces high standards of living, but has added significance because it draws each devotee into a sort of fellowship with the divine, and mates not this life alone, but this life plus a future life, the end of human activity. Buddhism, therefore, really expresses the deepest religious life of the people of China.

It will be worth while to note some illustrations of the conviction of the Chinese people that there are three religions to which they owe allegiance and yet that these are essentially one. They often say, "The three teachings are the whole teaching." An old scholar is reported to have remarked, "The three roads are different, but they lead to the same source."

A common story reports that Confucius was asked in the other world about drinking wine, which Buddhists forbid but Taoists permit. Confucius replied: "If I do not drink I become a Buddha. If I drink I become an Immortal. Well, if there is wine, I shall drink; if there is none, I shall abstain." This expresses characteristically the Chinese habit of adaptation. Such a decision sounds quite up to date.

The Ethical Culture Society of Peking, recently organized, has upon its walls pictures of Buddha, Lao Tzu, Confucius and Christ. Its members claim to worship Shang Ti as the god of all religions. An offshoot of this society, the T'ung Shan She, associates the three founders very closely with Christ. It claims to have a deeper revelation of Christ than the Christians themselves. A new organization, the Tao Yuan, plans to harmonize the three old religions with Mohammedanism and Christianity.

Buddhism has consistently and continually striven to bring about a unity of religion in China by interpenetrating Confucianism and Taoism. Quite early the Buddhists invented the story that the Bodhisattva Ju T'ung was really Confucius incarnate. There was at one time a Buddhist temple to Confucius in the province of Shantung. The Buddhists also gave out the story that Bodhisattva Kas'yapa was the incarnation of Lao Tzu, the founder of Taoism. An artist painted Lao Tzu transformed into a Buddha, seated in a lotus bud with a halo about his head. In front of the Buddha was Confucius doing reverence. A Chinese scholar, asked for his opinion about the picture, said: "Buddha should be seated; Lao Tzu should be standing at the side looking askance at Buddha; and Confucius should be grovelling on the floor."

A monument dating from 543 A. D., illustrates this tendency of Buddhism to represent its own superiority in Chinese religious life. At the top of the monument is Brahma, lower down is Sù*amuni with his disciples, Ananda and Kas'yapa on one face, and on the other Sù*amuni again, conversing with Buddha Prabhutaratna and worshipped by monks and Bodhisattvas. On the pedestal are Confucian and Taoist deities, ten in number. Thus Buddhism sought to rank itself clearly above the other two religions. From the early days Buddhism regarded itself as their superior and began the processes of interpenetration and absorption. In consequence the values originally inherent in Buddhism have come to be regarded as the natural possession of the Chinese. It does express their religious life, especially in South China, where outward manifestations of religion are perhaps more marked than in the north.

THE DAOIST RELIGION OF CHINA

In Chinese history there have been various religions such as Buddhism, Buddhism, Islam and Christianity, both Catholic and Protestant, but among them only Buddhism is the religion of the Chinese people.* To be more precise, Buddhism is a religion of the Han people and has certain concrete features that come from this association. It has had a large influence on Chinese culture, psychology, customs, science and technology, medicine and hygiene, philosophy and even on Chinese politics and economics. How did the Daoist religion arise and what are its particular characteristics relative to other religions?

Daoist religion was born at the time of the Han Emperor Shun-di at the end of the first century A.D. At this time China already had a written history of about 2,000 years. At the end of the Warring States period (that is, the third and second centuries B.C.) there had existed people called "immortals" who claimed that by certain practices they could `extend their lives and not die.' These `immortals' were only individuals practicing by themselves; they never formed any kind of religious organization. However, at the end of the Western Han period (at the beginning of the first century A.D.) Buddhism came to China from India. The entry of Buddhism had a transformative effect and sped up the foundation of a Chinese religion. Because Buddhism was a foreign culture entering China, however, it elicited a strong reaction among the Chinese people.

The interaction of Chinese culture with a foreign culture led to both borrowing and criticizing. We can see both of these in the earliest of the Daoist religious writings, the Taiping Jing. In this work Daoists borrowed such Buddhist terms as the `three realms', but also criticized Buddhists for their so-called `four practices.' (These were the unfilial abandonment of father and mother to become a monk, the abandoning of wife and therefore the cutting off of future generations, the practice of begging, and the practice of eating excrement).

The Daoists said that this was contravening the spiritual way of heaven. In particular, once established the Daoist religion set forth the doctrine of `Laozi (Lao Tzu) converting the barbarians' in order to criticize Buddhism. They said that Laozi (Lao Tzu), the original teacher of Buddhism in the Zhou period (the sixth century B.C.), had left China through the Hangu Pass and gone to India, where he had taught Shakyamuni, the historical Buddha. Therefore, the Buddha was the disciple of Laozi (Lao Tzu).

The founder of the Daoist religion is generally recognized to be Zhang Daoling.

There are two views in the Chinese scholarly community as to where the Daoist religion originated. The scholar Chen Yinge claims that the Daoist religion originated in Shandong, Jiangsu and other coastal areas. Another scholar, Meng Wentong, claims that it originated in Sichuan and was influenced by the customs and practices of minority peoples there. I think that the Daoist religion originated in the coastal areas because the immortals were active in this area. Further, Zhang Daoling himself was from Feng County in Jiangsu and only later went to Sichuan, where he formally established the organization of the Daoist religion. It is quite possible that certain elements of minority peoples' customs were absorbed into his teachings at that time.

The Daoist religion that later developed in Sichuan and the Han River area is called Five Pecks of Rice Buddhism because people on entering the sect made an offering of five pecks of rice. It is also called Heavenly Teacher Buddhism because the leader of this sect, Zhang Daoling, was called the Heavenly Teacher. Heavenly Teacher Buddhism was passed on from Zhang to his son, Zhang Heng, and again transmitted to Zhang Lu, the latter's son. Zhang Lu established a Daoist kingdom in the Han River area, which he ruled for thirty years. Eventually he was defeated by Cao, to whom he surrendered. Zhang Lu's son, Zhang Sheng, fled to Longhu Mountain in Jiangxi where he became the fourth generation Heavenly Teacher. At the present time this sect of Buddhism has already been transmitted to its sixty-fifth generation. The sixty-fourth generation Heavenly Teacher is in Taiwan. His nephew is on the Chinese mainland continuing the tradition as the sixty-fifth generation Heavenly Teacher. This young Heavenly Teacher, a man in his twenties, came to my home to study the Daoist religion.

After the Five Pecks of Rich school, in Yan (Hebei), Qi (Shandong), Jiang (Jiangsu), and Huai (Huaihe, Anhui), another sect of the Daoist religion was founded by Zhang Jiao called Taiping Buddhism. Zhang Jiao used the Daoist religion to organize an extremely large-scale peasant uprising. When this was put down, Taiping Buddhism largely disappeared.

In the Three Kingdoms and Western Jin periods (the third century A.D.) the Daoist religion was hemmed in by imperial rulers and developed very little. However, in the Eastern Jin period (fourth century A.D.) the Daoist religion began to develop speedily and many nobles adhered to it. For example, the most famous aristocratic families of the time for generations believed in Buddhism. The most famous calligrapher in Chinese history, Wang Xizhi, was also a follower of the Daoist religion. One story recounts that Wang Xizhi particularly loved geese and wanted to buy the dozen or so geese raised by a Daoist priest. The priest would not sell, and Wang asked a second and a third time. Finally the priest said that if Wang would copy out for the whole Dao De Jing (Tao Te Ching) he would give him the geese. So Wang copied the entire work.

An interesting development occurred in the Tang period (618-907), whose rulers had the surname Li. At this time the leaders of the Daoist religion were looking for a mythological figure they could venerate as the founder of the religion, and they came upon Laozi (Lao Tzu), who was also named Li. This was not a coincidence. First of all, even before the Daoist religion was formally established, Laozi (Lao Tzu) had been mythologized. Second, the Han dynasty had venerated Confucian thought as orthodoxy, which, of course, honored Confucius. The Daoists claimed that Laozi (Lao Tzu) was Confucius's teacher, thus hoping to overcome the Confucianists. Now, according to the Shiji, Laozi (Lao Tzu) was surnamed Li with a given name of Erh. Since the Tang emperors were also surnamed Li, in order to increase their own importance they said that they were descendants of Laozi (Lao Tzu). Because of this, the Tang emperors took the Daoist religion relatively seriously: emperor Xuanzong even wrote his own commentary on the Dao De Jing (Tao Te Ching).

After the Daoist religion was established, on the one hand, it struggled with Buddhism and, on the other, it absorbed Buddhist thought. But the Daoist religion also has its own definite characteristics. Many religions seek to understand or answer such questions as What happens to human beings after death? For example, Buddhists seek to answer the question: What can people do after death to keep from being reborn into this world? The Daoists, however, seek to answer this question: How can people keep from dying? The ideal in the Daoist religion is for people to `extend their lives and not die,' to `fly up in this very body'--that is, to become an immortal.

Regarding this question the Daoist religion has certain theories. Daoists claim that people have both a spirit or soul and a body, both of which are constructed from qi. The qi that makes up the spirit or soul is called soul-qi. The qi that makes up the body is called form-qi. Only when the soul-qi and the body-qi are joined together in a single person do we have life. People should seek two things--to live forever and to obtain good fortune. If you die, everything is finished, so in order to seek to extend life, first, you must get a body that does not decay so that the spirit or soul will have a place to abide. Then seek a method for the soul to stay with the body, otherwise you will be dead and not be able to achieve any kind of good fortune.

Because of this Daoists seek ways to keep body and soul together, and Buddhism has various methods to accomplish this purpose. The most basic of these are of two sorts: the outer pill and the inner pill. The outer pill consists of using various minerals, especially mercury, in order to concoct a potion. It is hoped that by ingesting various potions one can keep one's body from decaying, and then the soul can continue forever in its midst. They claim that if you put a bronze mud on your feet and soak your feet in water for a very long time, you will not decay. If you can find the so-called golden pill, once you eat it your whole body will be able to live forever without decaying.

The inner pill is a series of practices that cause the qi within the human body to circulate through certain channels. This is called "working on your qi' and is the same kind of thing that is known these days as qigong. If the qi continually circulates in the human body, the whole body will be suffused with the light of an extremely fine qi. The body itself will become as light as qi and the person will be able to ascend to heaven, which is called "to fly up in this very body."

When Buddhism became a religion it had to have its own deities to venerate. At first the deity most venerated was the mythologized Laozi (Lao Tzu), called `Laojun' or 'Taishang Laojun.' Afterwards, under the influence of Buddhism, very many other deities were added. Originally Buddhism had only Shakyamuni as the Buddha, but afterwards they said that before Shakyamuni there had been seven other Buddhas. Towards the end of the Northern and Southern Dynasties a Daoist priest named Tao Hongjing wrote a book called Zhenling Weiye Tu in which he divided Daoist deities into seven levels.

The highest level contained three deities. In the center was one called Yuanshi Tiandao. On his left was Gaoshang Daojun and on his right was Yuanhuang Daojun. Laozi (Lao Tzu), or Taishang Laojun, was placed below on the fourth level. Today in Daoist temples the formal hall is called the Hall of the Three Pure Ones, and most sects worship these three deities. However, not all Daoist sects are alike. Some still claim Taishang Laojun as the highest deity, saying that he existed before Heaven and Earth were dreaded and that in different times he has different causes. Originally he was Pan'gu Xiansheng. Heaven and Earth were separated by him, and he has various spiritual powers.

The Daoist religion has one female deity of particular power who is named Xiwang Mu (Queen Mother of the West). Xiwang Mu existed as a deity before the founding of the Daoist religion. In the Shanhaijing (from the fourth to the second century B.C.) Xiwang Mu is not yet a female deity, but either of undifferentiated sex. or male.

Only after the Mutianzi Zhuan does Xiwang Mu become a female deity. This book recounts the story of the Zhou King Mu (of about 1000 B.C.) who went to the Kunlun Mountains to seek Xiwang Mu. In the earliest Daoist scriptures, however, where it is said there that the character `Mu' indicates the proof of the longevity of the deity Xiwang Mu is merely a deity of long life. Thus `Mu' here does not necessarily mean a female deity. Only in the Jin and Northern and Southern Dynasties, when the Daoist religion set up Dongwang Gong as a counterpart to Xiwang Mu, did Xi-Wang Mu emerge as an important female deity.

The Daoist religion took the human body and its cultivation very seriously, as in such matters as exilers, the inner and outer pill, and qigong. Because of this it has had a great influence on ancient medicine, pharmacology, chemistry and the nourishment of the human body. Many great Daoist leaders such as Ge Hong, Tao Hongjing and Sun Simiao were important scientists of Old China. Because of this, people today who research the history and development of Chinese science and technology cannot but study the history of the Daoist religion. The English historian of science, Joseph Needham, in his Science and Civilization in China, has relied extensively on the writings of the Daoist religion.

Daoists have written many works. The earliest collection of Daoist works, called the Zhengtong Daozang, has five thousand volumes. It was compiled in 1445 in the tenth year of the Zhengtong Emperor of the Ming. Later, in the Wanli period, a supplement appeared. These are important resources for the study of the history of Chinese religion.

In China today Daoism (Taoism) is one of the important religions. About three thousand people who have formally become Daoist priests, and several important Daoist temples have been restored. In Beijing there is a Daoist temple, called the Temple of the White Clouds (Baiyun Guan), which was established in the Yuan dynasty (the thirteenth century) and belongs to the Guanzhen sect of Daoism (Taoism). Its Hall of the Three Pure Ones is very fine; it also has two areas for the display of historical objects of the Daoist religion. In Chengdu, Sichuan there is the Green Goat palace and in Wuahn the Temple of Eternal Spring, both of which have been very well restored and belong to the Guanzhen Daoist sect. In Xian a Daoist temple called Louguan Tai belongs to the Northern sect of Daoism (Taoism). It was first built in the Northern Zhou dynasty (fifth century A.D.), but what exists now was rebuilt in the Ming (fifteenth and sixteenth centuries). It is said that in the Louguan Tai, Laozi (Lao Tzu), before he left for the West, dictated the Dao De Jing (Tao Te Ching) to the gatekeeper, named Yixi.

Longhu Mountain in Jiangxi is the birthplace of the Zhengyi sect of Daoism (Taoism). Maoshan in Jiangsu is the birthplace of Tao Hongjing's Maoshan sect. Hangzhou has a Daoist temple in Geling where, it is said, Ge Hong refined the pill. At each of these Daoist temples are Daoist priests, young and old, male and female. At Beijing's Temple of the White Clouds a school of Daoist religion teaches priests how to read Daoist scriptures. Beijing also has a Daoist Association, a national organization publishing the Journal of the Chinese Daoist Association. At Sichuan University the Institute for the Study of Religion is dedicated solely to the Daoist religion and is editing a Daoist dictionary. Beijing University has established an Institute for the Study of the History of the Daoist Religion, where I teach. The Institute for the Study of World Religions at the Chinese Academy of Social Sciences in Beijing is doing a synopsis of the five thousand volumes of the Daoist canon. Two national conferences have been devoted to the study of the Daoist religion, one at Beijing University. Thus the study of Daoist currently is developing very quickly.

MODERN CHINESE BUDDHISM (BRANCHES AND SECTS)

Today the most popular form of Buddhism in both mainland China and Taiwan is a mix of the Pure Land and Chan school. Its central scripture, the Amitabha Sutra was first brought to China by An Shigao, circa 147, however the school did not become popular until later.

GRECO-BUDDHISM

Greco-Buddhism, sometimes spelled Graeco-Buddhism, is the cultural syncretism between Hellenistic culture and Buddhism, which developed over a period of close to 800 years in Central Asia in the area corresponding to modern-day Afghanistan and Pakistan, between the 4th century BCE and the 5th century CE. Greco-Buddhism influenced the artistic (and, possibly, conceptual) development of Buddhism, and in particular Mahayana Buddhism, before it was adopted by Central and Northeastern Asia from the 1st century CE, ultimately spreading to China, Korea and Japan.

Historical Outline

The interaction between Hellenistic Greece and Buddhism started when Alexander the Great conquered Asia Minor and Central Asia in 334 BCE, crossing the Indus and Jhelum rivers, and going as far as the Beas, thus establishing direct contact with India, the birthplace of Buddhism. Alexander founded several cities in his new territories in the areas of the Oxus and Bactria, and Greek settlements further extended to the Khyber Pass, Gandhara and the Punjab. These regions correspond to a unique geographical passageway between the Himalayas and the Hindu Kush mountains, through which most of the interaction between India and Central Asia took place, generating intense cultural exchange and trade.

Following Alexander's death on June 10, 323 BCE, the *Diadochoi* (successors) founded their own kingdoms in Asia Minor and Central Asia. General Seleucus set up the Seleucid Kingdom, which extended as far as India. Later, the Eastern part of the Seleucid Kingdom broke away to form the Greco-Bactrian Kingdom (3rd–

2nd century BCE), followed by the Indo-Greek Kingdom (2nd–1st century BCE), and later the Kushan Empire (1st–3rd century CE). The interaction of Greek and Buddhist cultures operated over several centuries until it ended in the 5th century CE with the invasions of the White Huns, and later the expansion of Islam.

Religious Interactions

The length of the Greek presence in Central Asia and northern India provided opportunities for interaction, not only on the artistic, but also on the religious plane.

Alexander the Great in Bactria and India (331-325)

When Alexander conquered the Bactrian and Gandharan regions, these areas may already have been under Buddhist influence. According to a legend preserved in Pali, the language of the Theravada canon, two merchant brothers from Bactria, named Tapassu and Bhallika, visited the Buddha and became his disciples. They then returned to Bactria and built temples to the Buddha (Foltz).

In 326 Alexander invaded India. King Ambhi, ruler of Taxila, surrendered his city, a notable centre of Buddhist faith, to Alexander. Alexander fought an epic battle against Porus, a ruler of a region in the Punjab in the Battle of Hydaspes in (326 BC). Alexander continued on to conquer all the headwaters of the Indus River.

Several philosophers, such as Pyrrho, Anaxarchus and Onesicritus, are said to have been selected by Alexander to accompany him in his eastern campaigns. During the 18 months they were in India, they were able to interact with Indian religious men, generally described as Gymnosophists ("naked philosophers"). Pyrrho (360-270 BCE), returned to Greece and became the first Skeptic and the founder of the school named Pyrrhonism. The Greek biographer Diogenes Laertius explained that Pyrrho's equanimity and detachment from the world were acquired in India. Few of his sayings are directly known, but they are clearly reminiscent of eastern, possibly Buddhist, thought:

> *"Nothing really exists, but human life is governed by convention"*

> *"Nothing is in itself more this than that" (Diogenes Laertius IX.61)*

Another of these philosophers, Onesicritus, a Cynic, is said by Strabo to have learnt in India the following precepts:

> *"That nothing that happens to a man is bad or good, opinions being merely dreams"*
>
> *"That the best philosophy [is] that which liberates the mind from [both] pleasure and grief" (Strabo, XV.I.65)*

These contacts initiated the first direct interactions between Greek culture and Indian religions, which were to continue and expand for several more centuries.

The Mauryan Empire (322–183 BCE)

The Indian emperor Chandragupta, founder of the Mauryan dynasty, re-conquered around 322 BCE the northwest Indian territory that had been lost to Alexander the Great. However, contacts were kept with his Greek neighbours in the Seleucid Empire, Chandragupta received the daughter of the Seleucid king Seleucus I after a peace treaty, and several Greeks, such as the historian Megasthenes, resided at the Mauryan court.

Chandragupta's grandson Ashoka converted to the Buddhist faith and became a great proselytizer in the line of the traditional Pali canon of Theravada Buddhism, insisting on non-violence to humans and animals (ahimsa), and general precepts regulating the life of lay people.

According to the Edicts of Ashoka, set in stone, some of them written in Greek, he sent Buddhist emissaries to the Greek lands in Asia and as far as the Mediterranean. The edicts name each of the rulers of the Hellenic world at the time:

> *"The conquest by Dharma has been won here, on the borders, and even six hundred yojanas (4,000 miles) away, where the Greek king Antiochos (Antiyoga) rules, and beyond there where the four kings named Ptolemy (Turamaya), Antigonos (Antikini), Magas (Maka) and Alexander (Alikasu[n]dara) rule, likewise in the south among the Cholas, the Pandyas, and as far as Tamraparni." (Rock Edict Nb.13).*

Ashoka also claims he converted to Buddhism Greek populations within his realm:

> *"Here in the king's domain among the Greeks, the Kambojas, the Nabhakas, the Nabhapamkits, the Bhojas, the Pitinikas, the Andhras and the Palidas, everywhere people are following Beloved-of-the-Gods' instructions in Dharma." Rock Edict Nb13 (S. Dhammika).*

Finally, some of the emissaries of Ashoka, such as the famous Dharmaraksita, are described in Pali sources as leading Greek ("Yona") Buddhist monks, active in Buddhist proselytism (the Mahavamsa, XII).

The Greek Presence in Bactria (325 to 125 BCE)

Alexander had established in Bactria several cities (Ai-Khanoum, Begram) and an administration that were to last more than two centuries under the Seleucids and the Greco-Bactrians, all the time in direct contact with Indian territory.

The Greeks sent ambassadors to the court of the Mauryan empire, such as the historian Megasthenes under Chandragupta Maurya, and later Deimakos under his son Bindusara, who reported extensively on the civilization of the Indians.

Megasthenes sent detailed reports on Indian religions, which were circulated and quoted throughout the Classical world for centuries:

> *"Megasthenes makes a different division of the philosophers, saying that they are of two kinds, one of which he calls the Brachmanes, and the other the Sarmanes..." Strabo XV. 1. 58-60*

The Greco-Bactrians maintained a strong Hellenistic culture at the door of India during the rule of the Mauryan empire in India, as exemplified by the archaeological site of Ai-Khanoum.

When the Mauryan empire was toppled by the Sungas around 180 BCE, the Greco-Bactrians expanded into India, where they established the Indo-Greek kingdom, under which Buddhism was able to flourish.

The Indo-Greek Kingdom and Buddhism (180 BCE –10 CE)

The Greco-Bactrians conquered parts of northern India from 180 BCE, whence they are known as the Indo-Greeks. They controlled various areas of the northern Indian territory until 10 CE. Buddhism prospered under the Indo-Greek kings, and it has been suggested that their invasion of India was intended to protect the Buddhist faith from the religious persecutions of the new Indian dynasty of the Sungas (185–73 BCE) which had overthrown the Mauryans.

Coinage

The coins of the Indo-Greek king Menander (reigned 160 to 135 BCE), found from Afghanistan to central India, bear the inscription "Saviour King Menander" in Greek on the front. Several Indo-Greek kings after Menander, such as Zoilos I, Strato I, Heliokles II, Theophilos, Peukolaos, Menander II and Archebios display on their coins the title of "Maharajasa Dharmika" (lit. "King of the Dharma") in the Prakrit language and in the Kharoshthi script.

Some of the coins of Menander I and Menander II incorporate the Buddhist symbol of the eight-spoked wheel, associated with the Greek symbols of victory, either the palm of victory, or the victory wreath handed over by the goddess Nike. According to the Milinda Panha, at the end of his reign Menander I became a Buddhist arhat, a fact also echoed by Plutarch, who explains that his relics were shared and enshrined.

The ubiquitous symbol of the elephant in Indo-Greek coinage may also have been associated with Buddhism, as suggested by the parallel between coins of Antialcidas and Menander II, where the elephant in the coins of Antialcidas holds the same relationship to Zeus and Nike as the Buddhist wheel on the coins of Menander II. When the zoroastrian Indo-Parthians invaded northern India in the 1st century CE, they adopted a large part of the symbolism of Indo-Greek coinage, but refrained from ever using the elephant, suggesting that its meaning was not merely geographical. Finally, after the reign of Menander I, several Indo-Greek rulers, such as

Amyntas, King Nicias, Peukolaos, Hermaeus, Hippostratos and Menander II, depicted themselves or their Greek deities forming with the right hand a benediction gesture identical to the Buddhist vitarka mudra (thumb and index joined together, with other fingers extended), which in Buddhism signifies the transmission of Buddha's teaching.

Cities

According to Ptolemy, Greek cities were founded by the Greco-Bactrians in northern Pakistan. Menander established his capital in Sagala, today's Sialkot in Punjab, one of the centres of the blossoming Buddhist culture (Milinda Panha). A large Greek city built by Demetrius and rebuilt by Menander has been excavated at the archaeological site of Sirkap near Taxila, where Buddhist stupas were standing side-by-side with Hindu and Greek temples, indicating religious tolerance and syncretism.

Scriptures

Evidence of direct religious interaction between Greek and Buddhist thought during the period include the Milinda Panha, a Buddhist discourse in the platonic style, held between king Menander and the Buddhist monk Nagasena. Also the Mahavamsa records that during Menander's reign, "a Greek ("Yona") Buddhist head monk" named Mahadharmaraksita (literally translated as 'Great Teacher/Preserver of the Dharma') led 30,000 Buddhist monks from "the Greek city of Alexandria" (possibly Alexandria-of-the-Caucasus, around 150km north of today's Kabul in Afghanistan), to Sri Lanka for the dedication of a stupa, indicating that Buddhism flourished in Menander's territory and that Greeks took a very active part in it.

Several Buddhist dedications by Greeks in India are recorded, such as that of the Greek meridarch (civil governor of a province) named Theodorus, describing in Kharoshthi how he enshrined relics of the Buddha. The inscriptions were found on a vase inside a stupa, dated to the reign of Menander or one his successors in the 1st century BCE:

"Theudorena meridarkhena pratithavida ime sarira sakamunisa bhagavato bahu-jana-stitiye":

"The meridarch Theodorus has enshrined relics of Lord Shakyamuni, for the welfare of the mass of the people"

(Swat relic vase inscription of the Meridarkh Theodoros).

This inscription represents one of the first known mention of the Buddha as a deity, using the Indian bhakti word Bhagavat ("Lord", "All-embracing personal deity"), suggesting the emergence of Mahayana doctrines in Buddhism.

Finally, Buddhist tradition recognizes Menander as one of the great benefactors of the faith, together with Asoka and Kanishka.

Buddhist manuscripts in cursive Greek have been found in Afghanistan, praising various Buddhas and including mentions of the Mahayana Lokesvara-raja Buddha. These manuscripts have been dated later than the 2nd century CE. (Nicholas Sims-Williams, "A Bactrian Buddhist Manuscript").

Some elements of the Mahayana movement may have begun around the 1st century BCE in northwestern India, at the time and place of these interactions. According to most scholars, the main sutras of Mahayana were written after 100 BCE, when sectarian conflicts arose among Nikaya Buddhist sects regarding the humanity or super-humanity of the Buddha and questions of metaphysical essentialism, on which Greek thought may have had some influence: "It may have been a Greek-influenced and Greek-carried form of Buddhism that passed north and east along the Silk Road" (McEvilly, "The shape of ancient thought").

The Kushan Empire (1st–3rd century CE)

The Kushans, one of the five tribes of the Yuezhi confederation settled in Bactria since around 125 BCE when they displaced the Greco-Bactrians, invaded the northern parts of Pakistan and India from around 1 CE.

By that time they had already been in contact with Greek culture and the Indo-Greek kingdoms for more than a century. They used the Greek script to write their language, as exemplified by their coins and their adoption of the Greek alphabet. The absorption of Greek historical and mythological culture is suggested by Kushan sculptures representing Dionysiac scenes or even the story of the Trojan horse and it is probable that Greek communities remained under Kushan rule.

The Kushan king Kanishka, who honoured Zoroastrian, Greek and Brahmanic deities as well as the Buddha and was famous for his religious syncretism, convened the Fourth Buddhist Council around 100 CE in Kashmir in order to redact the Sarvastivadin canon. Some of Kanishka's coins bear the earliest representations of the Buddha on a coin (around 120 CE), in Hellenistic style and with the word "Boddo" in Greek script.

Kanishka also had the original Gandhari vernacular, or Prakrit, Mahayana Buddhist texts translated into the high literary language of Sanskrit, "a turning point in the evolution of the Buddhist literary canon" (Foltz, Religions on the Silk Road)

The "Kanishka casket", dated to the first year of Kanishka's reign in 127 CE, was signed by a Greek artist named *Agesilas*, who oversaw work at Kanishka's stupas (caitya), confirming the direct involvement of Greeks with Buddhist realizations at such a late date.

The new syncretic form of Buddhism expanded fully into Eastern Asia soon after these events. The Kushan monk Lokaksema visited the Han Chinese court at Loyang in 178 CE, and worked there for ten years to make the first known translations of Mahayana texts into Chinese. The new faith later spread into Korea and Japan, and was itself at the origin of Zen.

Artistic Influences

Numerous works of Greco-Buddhist art display the intermixing of Greek and Buddhist influences, around such creation centres as Gandhara. The subject matter of Gandharan art was definitely Buddhist, while most motifs were of Western Asiatic or Hellenistic origin.

The Anthropomorphic Representation of the Buddha

Although there is still some debate, the first anthropomorphic representations of the Buddha himself are often considered a result of the Greco-Buddhist interaction. Before this innovation, Buddhist art was "aniconic": the Buddha was only represented through his symbols (an empty throne, the Bodhi tree, the Buddha's footprints, the prayer wheel).

This reluctance towards anthropomorphic representations of the Buddha, and the sophisticated development of aniconic symbols to avoid it, seem to be connected to one of the Buddha's sayings, reported in the Digha Nikaya, that discouraged representations of himself after the extinction of his body.

Probably not feeling bound by these restrictions, and because of "their cult of form, the Greeks were the first to attempt a sculptural representation of the Buddha" (Linssen, "Zen Living"). In many parts of the Ancient World, the Greeks did develop syncretic divinities, that could become a common religious focus for populations with different traditions: a well-known example is the syncretic God Sarapis, introduced by Ptolemy I in Egypt, which combined aspects of Greek and Egyptian Gods. In India as well, it was only natural for the Greeks to create a single common divinity by combining the image of a Greek God-King (The Sun-God Apollo, or possibly the deified founder of the Indo-Greek Kingdom, Demetrius), with the traditional attributes of the Buddha.

Many of the stylistic elements in the representations of the Buddha point to Greek influence: the Greco-Roman toga-like wavy robe covering both shoulders (more exactly, its lighter version, the Greek *himation*), the contrapposto stance of the upright figures, the stylicized Mediterranean curly hair and top-knot apparently derived from the style of the Belvedere Apollo (330 BCE), and the measured quality of the faces, all rendered with strong artistic realism. A large quantity of sculptures combining Buddhist and purely Hellenistic styles and iconography were excavated at the Gandharan site of Hadda. The 'curly hair' of Buddha is described in the famous list of 32 external characteristics of a Great Being (mahapurusa) that we find all along the Buddhist sutras. The curly hair, with the curls turning to the right is first described in the Pali canon of the Smaller Vehicle of Buddhism; we find the same description in e.g. the "Dasasahasrika Prajnaparamita".

Greek artists were most probably the authors of these early representations of the Buddha, in particular the standing statues, which display "a realistic treatment of the folds and on some even a hint of modelled volume that characterizes the best Greek work. This is Classical or Hellenistic Greek, not archaizing Greek transmitted by Persia or Bactria, nor distinctively Roman" (Boardman).

The Greek stylistic influence on the representation of the Buddha, through its idealistic realism, also permitted a very accessible, understandable and attractive visualization of the ultimate state of enlightenment described by Buddhism, allowing it reach a wider audience: "One of the distinguishing features of the Gandharan school of art that emerged in northwest India is that it has been clearly influenced by the naturalism of the Classical Greek style. Thus, while these images still convey the inner peace that results from putting the Buddha's doctrine into practice, they also give us an impression of people who walked and talked, etc. and slept much as we do. I feel this is very important.

During the following centuries, this anthropomorphic representation of the Buddha defined the canon of Buddhist art, but progressively evolved to incorporate more Indian and Asian elements.

A Hellenized Buddhist Pantheon

Several other Buddhist deities may have been influenced by Greek gods. For example, Herakles with a lion-skin (the protector deity of Demetrius I) "served as an artistic model for Vajrapani, a protector of the Buddha" (Foltz, "Religions and the Silk Road"). In Japan, this expression further translated into the wrath-filled and muscular Nio guardian gods of the Buddha, standing today at the entrance of many Buddhist temples.

According to Katsumi Tanabe, professor at Chuo University, Japan (in "Alexander the Great. East-West cultural contact from Greece to Japan"), besides Vajrapani, Greek influence also appears in several other gods of the Mahayana pantheon, such as the Japanese Wind God Fujin inspired from the Greek Boreas through the Greco-Buddhist Wardo, or the mother deity Hariti inspired by Tyche.

In addition, forms such as garland-bearing cherubs, vine scrolls, and such semi-human creatures as the centaur and triton, are part of the repertory of Hellenistic art introduced by Greco-Roman artists in the service of the Kushan court.

Greco-Buddhism and the Rise of the Mahayana

The geographical, cultural and historical context of the rise of Mahayana Buddhism during the 1st century BCE in northwestern India, all point to intense multi-cultural influences: "Key formative influences on the early development of the Mahayana and Pure Land movements, which became so much part of East Asian civilization, are to be sought in Buddhism's earlier encounters along the Silk Road" (Foltz, Religions on the Silk Road).

As Mahayana Buddhism emerged, it received "influences from popular Hindu devotional cults (bhakti), Persian and Greco-Roman theologies which filtered into India from the northwest"

Conceptual Influences

Mahayana is an inclusive faith characterized by the adoption of new texts, in addition to the traditional Pali canon, and a shitt in the understanding of Buddhism.

It goes beyond the traditional Theravada ideal of the release from suffering (dukkha) and personal enlightenment of the arhats, to elevate the Buddha to a God-like status, and to create a pantheon of quasi-divine Bodhisattvas devoting themselves to personal excellence, ultimate knowledge and the salvation of humanity.

These concepts, together with the sophisticated philosophical system of the Mahayana faith, may have been influenced by the interaction of Greek and Buddhist thought:

The Buddha as an Idealized Man-god

The Buddha was elevated to a man-god status, represented in idealized human form: "One might regard the classical influence as including the general idea of representing a man-god in this purely human form, which was of course well familiar in the West, and it is very likely that the example of westerners' treatment of their gods was indeed an important factor in the innovation... The Buddha, the man-god, is in many ways far more like a Greek god than any other eastern deity, no less for the narrative cycle of his story and appearance of his standing figure than for his humanity" (Boardman, "The Diffusion of Classical Art in Antiquity").

The supra-mundane understanding of the Buddha and Bodhisattvas may have been a consequence of the Greek's tendency to deify their rulers in the wake of Alexander's reign: "The god-king concept brought by Alexander (...) may have fed into the developing bodhisattva concept, which involved the portrayal of the Buddha in Gandharan art with the face of the sun god, Apollo" (McEvilley, "The Shape of Ancient Thought").

The Bodhisattva as a Universal Ideal of Excellence

Lamotte (1954) controversially suggests (though countered by Conze (1973) and others) that Greek influence was present in the definition of the Bodhisattva ideal in the oldest Mahayana text, the "Perfection of Wisdom" or *prajna paramita* literature, that developed between the 1st century BCE and the 1st century CE. These texts in particular redefine Buddhism around the universal Bodhisattva ideal, and its six central virtues of generosity, morality, patience, effort, meditation and, first and foremost, wisdom.

Philosophical Influences

The close association between Greeks and Buddhism probably led to exchanges on the philosophical plane as well. Many of the early Mahayana theories of reality and knowledge can be related to Greek philosophical schools of thought. Mahayana Buddhism has been described as the "form of Buddhism which (regardless of how Hinduized its later forms became) seems to have originated in the Greco-Buddhist communities of India, through a conflation of the Greek Democritean-Sophistic-Skeptical tradition with the rudimentary and unformalized empirical and skeptical elements already present in early Buddhism" (McEvilly, "The Shape of Ancient Thought", p503).

- In the Prajnaparamita, the rejection of the reality of passing phenomena as "empty, false and fleeting" can also be found in Greek Pyrrhonism.
- The perception of ultimate reality was, for the Cynics as well as for the Madyamikas and Zen teachers after them,

only accessible through a non-conceptual and non-verbal approach (Greek "Phronesis"), which alone allowed to get rid of ordinary conceptions.

- The mental attitude of equanimity and dispassionate outlook in front of events was also characteristic of the Cynics and Stoics, who called it "Apatheia"
- Nagarjuna's dialectic developed in the Madhyamika can be paralleled to the Greek dialectical tradition.

Cynicism, Madhyamika and Zen

Numerous parallels exist between the Greek philosophy of the Cynics and, several centuries later, the Buddhist philosophy of the Madhyamika and Zen. The Cynics denied the relevancy of human conventions and opinions (described as *typhos*, literally "smoke" or "mist", a metaphor for "illusion" or "error"), including verbal expressions, in favour of the raw experience of reality. They stressed the independence from externals to achieve happiness ("Happiness is not pleasure, for which we need external, but virtue, which is complete without external" 3rd epistole of Crates). Similarly the Prajnaparamita, precursor of the Madhyamika, explained that all things are like foam, or bubbles, "empty, false, and fleeting", and that "only the negation of all views can lead to enlightenment". In order to evade the world of illusion, the Cynics recommended the discipline and struggle ("askcsis kai machc") of philosophy, the practice of "autarkia" (self-rule), and a lifestyle examplified by Diogenes, which, like Buddhist monks, renounced earthly possessions. These conceptions, in combination with the idea of "philanthropia" (universal loving kindness, of which Crates, the student of Diogenes, was the best proponent), are strikingly reminiscent of Buddhist Prajna (wisdom) and Karuna (compassion).

Greco-Persian Cosmological Influences

A popular figure in Greco-Buddhist art, the future Buddha Maitreya, has sometimes been linked to the Iranian yazata (Zoroastrian divinity) Miera who was also adopted as a figure in a Greco-Roman syncretistic cult under the name of Mithras. Maitreya is the fifth Buddha of the present world-age, who will appear at some undefined future epoch. According to Foltz, he "echoes the qualities of the Zoroastrian Saoshyant and the Christian Messiah" (Foltz). However, in character and function, Maitreya does not much resemble either Mitra, Miera or Mithras; his name is more obviously derived from the Sanskrit *maitri* "kindliness", equivalent to Pali *metta*; the Pali (and probably older) form of his name, Metteyya, does not closely resemble the name Miera.

The Buddha Amitabha (literally meaning "infinite radiance") with his paradisiacal "Pure Land" in the West, according to Foltz, "seems to be understood as the Iranian god of light, equated with the sun". This view is however not in accordance with the view taken of Amitabha by present-day Pure Land Buddhists, in which Amitabha is neither "equated with the sun" nor, strictly speaking, a god.

10

Buddhism in Bhutan

Bhutan, officially the Kingdom of Bhutan is a small landlocked country in South Asia, located at the eastern end of the Himalayas and bordered to the south, east and west by the Republic of India and to the north by the People's Republic of China. Bhutan is separated from the nearby country of Nepal to the west by the Indian state of Sikkim, and from Bangladesh to the south by West Bengal.

Bhutan existed as a patchwork of minor warring fiefdoms until the early 17th century, when the area was unified by the Tibetan lama and military leader Shabdrung Ngawang Namgyal, who fled religious persecution in Tibet and cultivated a separate Bhutanese identity. In the early 20th century, Bhutan came under the influence of the British Empire, followed by Indian influence upon Indian independence.

In 2006, *Business Week* magazine rated Bhutan the happiest country in Asia and the eighth-happiest in the world based on a global survey. Bhutan's landscape ranges from subtropical plains in the south to the Sub-alpine Himalayan heights in the north, with some peaks exceeding 7,000 metres (23,000 ft).

The state religion is Vajrayana Buddhism, and the population of 691,141 is predominantly Buddhist, with Hinduism the second-largest religion. The capital and largest city is Thimphu. After centuries of absolute monarchy, Bhutan held its first democratic elections in March 2008. Bhutan is a member of the United Nations and the South Asian Association for Regional Cooperation

(SAARC); it hosted the sixteenth SAARC summit in April 2010. The total area of the country is currently 38,816 square kilometres (14,987 sq mi).

BUDDHIST CONCEPTS

Karma

Karma in Buddhism is the force that drives samsara—the cycle of suffering and rebirth for each being. Good, skilful deeds (Pali: "kusala") and bad, unskilful (Pali: "akusala") actions produce "seeds" in the mind which come to fruition either in this life or in a subsequent rebirth. The avoidance of unwholesome actions and the cultivation of positive actions is called sila (from Sanskrit: "ethical conduct").

In Buddhism, karma specifically refers to those actions (of body, speech, and mind) that spring from mental intent ("cetana"), and which bring about a consequence (or fruit, "phala") or result ("vipaka").

In Theravada Buddhism there can be no divine salvation or forgiveness for one's karma, since it is a purely impersonal process that is a part of the makeup of the universe. Some Mahayana traditions hold different views.

For example, the texts of certain Mahayana sutras (such as the *Lotus Sutra,* the *Angulimaliya Sutra* and the *Nirvana Sutra*) claim that reciting or merely hearing their texts can expunge great swathes of negative karma.

Some forms of Buddhism (for example, Vajrayana) regard the recitation of mantras as a means for cutting off previous negative karma. The Japanese Pure Land teacher Genshin taught that Amida Buddha has the power to destroy the karma that would otherwise bind one in samsara.

Rebirth

Rebirth refers to a process whereby beings go through a succession of lifetimes as one of many possible forms of sentient life, each running from conception to death. Buddhism rejects the concepts of a permanent self or an unchanging, eternal soul, as it is called in Hinduism and Christianity. According to Buddhism there ultimately is no such thing as a self independent from the rest of the universe (the doctrine of anatta). Rebirth in subsequent existences must be understood as the continuation of a dynamic, ever-changing process of "dependent arising" ("pratityasamutpada") determined by the laws of cause and effect (karma) rather than that of one being, transmigrating or incarnating from one existence to the next.

Each rebirth takes place within one of five realms according to Theravadins, or six according to other schools. These are further subdivided into 31 planes of existence:

1. Naraka beings: those who live in one of many Narakas (Hells)
2. Preta: sometimes sharing some space with humans, but invisible to most people; an important variety is the hungry ghost
3. Animals: sharing space with humans, but considered another type of life
4. Human beings: one of the realms of rebirth in which attaining Nirvana is possible
5. Asuras: variously translated as lowly deities, demons, titans, antigods; not recognized by Theravada (Mahavihara) tradition as a separate realm
6. Devas including Brahmas: variously translated as gods, deities, spirits, angels, or left untranslated.

Rebirths in some of the higher heavens, known as the Suddhavasa Worlds (Pure Abodes), can be attained only by skilled Buddhist practitioners known as ananamis (non-returners). Rebirths in the arupa-dhatu (formless realms) can be attained only by those who can meditate on the arupajhanas, the highest object of meditation.

According to East Asian and Tibetan Buddhism, there is an intermediate state (Tibetan "Bardo") between one life and the next. The orthodox Theravada position rejects this; however there are passages in the *Samyutta Nikaya* of the Pali Canon (the collection of texts on which the Theravada tradition is based), that seem to lend support to the idea that the Buddha taught of an intermediate stage between one life and the next.

BUDDHIST TERMINOLOGY AND DOCTRINE

There is no word corresponding exactly to the English terms "rebirth", "metempsychosis", "transmigration" or "reincarnation" in the traditional Buddhist languages of Pali and Sanskrit: the entire process of change from one life to the next is called *punarbhava* (Sanskrit) or *punabbhava* (Pali), literally "becoming again", or more briefly *bhava*, "becoming", while the state one is born into, the individual process of being born or coming into the world in any way, is referred to simply as "birth" (*jati*). The entire universal process that gives rise to this is called *samsara*.

Within one life and across multiple lives, the empirical, changing self not only objectively affects its surrounding external world, but also generates (consciously and unconsciously) its own subjective image of this world, which it then lives in as 'reality'. It lives in a world of its own making in various ways. It "tunes in" to a particular level of consciousness (by meditation or the rebirth it attains through its karma) which has a particular range of objects-a world-available to it. It furthermore selectively notices from among such objects, and then processes what has been sensed to form a distorted interpretive model of reality: a model in which the 'I am' conceit is a crucial reference point. When nibbana is experienced, though, all such models are transcended: the world stops 'in this fathom-long carcase'.

Historical Context

The Buddha lived at a time of great philosophical creativity in India when many conceptions of the nature of life and death were proposed. Some were materialist, holding that there was no existence that the self is annihilated upon death. Others believed in a form of cyclic existence, where a being is born, lives, dies and then is re-born, but in the context of a type of determinism or fatalism in which karma played no role. Others were "eternalists", postulating an eternally existent self or soul comparable to that in Christianity: the atman survives death and reincarnates as another living being, based on its karmic inheritance. This is the idea that has become dominant (with certain modifications) in modern Hinduism.

The Buddha's concept was distinct, consistent with the common notion of a sequence of lives over a very long time but constrained by two core concepts: that there is no irreducible self tying these lives together (*anatta*) and that all compounded things are subject to dissolution, including all the components of the human person and personality (*anicca*). The story of the Buddha's life presented in the early texts does not allude to the idea of rebirth prior to his enlightenment, leading some to suggest that he discovered it for himself. The Buddha's detailed conception of the connections between action (karma), rebirth and causality is set out in the twelve links of dependent origination.

Ideas of Rebirth

There are many references to rebirth in the early Buddhist scriptures. These are some of the more important; Mahakammavibhanga Sutta (Majjhima Nikaya 136); Upali Sutta (Majjhima Nikaya 56); Kukkuravatika Sutta (Majjhima Nikaya 57); Moliyasivaka Sutta (Samyutta Nikaya 36.21); Sankha Sutta (Samyutta Nikaya 42.8).

Some English-speaking Buddhists prefer the term "rebirth" or "re-becoming" (Sanskrit: *punarbhava*; Pali: *punabbhava*) to "reincarnation" as they take the latter to imply a fixed entity that is reborn. It is said to be the "evolving consciousness" (Pali: *samvattanika vinnana,* M.1.256) or "stream of consciousness" (Pali: *vinnana sotam,* D.3.105). that reincarnates. The early Buddhist texts make it clear that there is no permanent consciousness that moves from life to life. The lack of a fixed self does not mean lack of continuity. In the same way that a flame is transferred from one candle to another, there is a conditioned relationship between one life and the next: they are neither identical nor completely distinct.

While all Buddhist traditions seem to accept some notion of rebirth, there is no unified view about precisely how events unfold after the moment of death. The medieval Pali scholar Buddhaghosa labelled the consciousness that constitutes the condition for a new birth as described in the early texts "rebirth-linking consciousness" (*patisandhi*). Some schools conclude that karma continued to exist and adhere to the person until it had worked out its consequences. For the Sautrantika school each act "perfumed" the individual and led to the planting of a "seed" that would later germinate as a good or bad karmic result. Theravada Buddhism generally asserts that rebirth is immediate while the Tibetan schools hold to the notion of a bardo (intermediate state) that can last up to forty-nine days. This has led to the development of a unique 'science' of death and rebirth, a good deal of which is set down in what is popularly known as *The Tibetan Book of the Dead*.

Theravada Buddhism generally denies there is an intermediate state, though some early Buddhist texts seem to support it. One school that adopted this view was the Sarvastivada, who believed that between death and rebirth there is a sort of limbo in which beings do not yet reap the consequences of their previous actions but may still influence their rebirth. The death process and this intermediate state were believed to offer a uniquely favourable opportunity for spiritual awakening.

Rebirth as Cycle of Consciousness

Another view of rebirth describes the cycle of death and birth in the context of consciousness rather than the birth and death of the body. In this view, remaining impure aggregates, skandhas, reform consciousness.

Buddhist meditation teachers suggest that observation reveals consciousness as a sequence of conscious moments rather than a continuum of awareness. Each moment is an experience of an individual mind-state such as a thought, a memory, a feeling or a perception. A mind-state arises, exists and, being impermanent, ceases, following which the next mind-state arises. Thus the consciousness of a sentient being can be seen as a continuous series of birth and death of these mind-states. Rebirth is the persistence of this process.

In the practice of Vipassana meditation, the meditator uses "bare attention" to observe the endless round of mind-states without interfering, owning or judging. This limits the power of desire which, according to the second noble truth of Buddhism, is the cause of suffering (*dukkha*) and leads to *Nirvana* (*nibbana*, vanishing (of the self-idea)).

MIND AND METAPHYSICS

Dialectics and the No-self View

A common stylistic feature of the Buddhist canonical literature is the use of similes and parables, of which perhaps the best known is the simile of the raft. In the *Middle Length Discourses*, the Buddha is seen explaining to an old man that his body of teachings is like a raft: it serves the purpose of crossing over (viz., from the shore of afflictions to that of nirvana) and should be abandoned once the crossing has been effected.

The simile of the raft marks the pragmatic (Jayatilleke (1963, 357) calls it 'utilitarian') approach of the Buddha's teachings, and is also suggestive of a core aspect of Buddhist praxis: the notion of expedient means (*upaya kausalya*). Ganeri has recently proposed that we identify the nature of Buddha's discourses as being essentially protreptic, similar to the Stoic exhortation which invites the adept to reconsider and rethink her ethical and metaphysical position. Thus, the notion of expedient means—this specifically Buddhist protreptic—operates as a cautionary device against the tendency to assume that Buddhist doctrines may be seen as articulating a particular type of metaphysics whose principles are to be examined without any appeal to context or target audience.

It is primarily in response to the Buddha's use of expedient means (and the expansion of the Buddhist canonical literature with the advent of Mahayana sutras) that Abhidharma traditions develop the hermeneutics of two truths: depending on scholastic affiliation, doctrinal positions are henceforth classified as either in need of interpretation (*neyartha*) or as already possessing the definitive meaning (*nitartha*).

The hermeneutics of two truths is central to Madhyamaka dialectics and its deconstructive analysis of key metaphysical concepts, including those of causation, essence, and the self. In the *Fundamental Wisdom of the Middle Way* (*Mulamadhyamakakarikas*;

hereafter MMK), Nanarjuna extends the notion that phenomena lack intrinsic existence (*svabhava*) to apply to the self, which is usually conceived in dependence upon the five aggregates (MMK, IX, 12).

While considering various ways of conceiving of the self (viz., as distinct from the psychophysical aggregates, as unchanging, as a unifying principle, or as an agent), Nanarjuna concludes that none of them actually make sense on account of the fact that nothing can be said to be prior to the cognitive activities of seeing, hearing, etc. (MMK, IX, 7, 10). A metaphysical self, conceived as an abiding and substantive entity, is therefore inconceivable. However, the mistaken apprehension of a self in a stream of causally interconnected cognitive events does not preclude endorsing a conventional notion of self for ordinary individuals who lack a proper understanding of actions and their consequences.

Indeed, Aryadeva (ca. 150 C.E.), an immediate disciple of Nanarjuna, invokes the expedient means device to endorse precisely such a view: for certain classes of individuals adherence to a conventional view of self is more profitable than the denial of self. The no-self view, claims Aryadeva, is primarily reserved for those of a superior disposition, who alone can grasp the definite meaning of the Buddha's teachings. However, ultimately the Buddha's teachings are interpreted as endorsing not any specific view, but rather the relinquishing of all views—which is only possible in a non-positional awareness that captures the paradoxical nature of the Madhyamaka dialectic.

Realism

Although all Abhidharma schools admit the ultimate reality of *dharmas*, only the Vaibhacika (or Sarvastivada) School contends that *dharmas* exist in all three temporal dimensions (past, present, and future). The main arguments for this view are found in the *Vijnanakaya* and the *Maha-Vibhasa*, as well as in Vasubandhu's *Abhidharmakosa*, where they are systematically debated and refuted. In all, three types of arguments are put forward to support the notion that the past and future basic units of existence (*dharmas*) are presently real:

1. The argument from cognition: Past and future *dharmas* exist because of our ability to make past and future events the object of our cognitive awareness.
2. The dispositional argument: The presence of dispositions (as habituations resulting from past intentional acts) implies that past and future *dharmas* associated with these dispositions must be presently manifest.
3. The causal argument: past *dharmas* must be real and present for otherwise they would lack causal efficacy in bringing about a present effect.

A plausible rationale for the Sarvastivadin's assertion of the continuing existence of past and future *dharmas* concerns the first and third arguments: it is impossible to conceive of a non-existent intentional object or the causal efficacy of a non-existent *dharma*. Given the principle of momentariness, which states that things exist only as point instants, it would be impossible to explain the arising of a particular type of cognitive awareness in the absence of an already existing preceding cause. Cognitive awareness, which arises in dependence upon the object and the corresponding sense faculty, would lack support if past *dharmas* were unreal. In his commentary to the verse portion of the *Treasury of Higher Knowledge*, Vasubandhu explains the standpoint of the Sarvastivadin as follows:

Cognitive awareness (*vijnana*) occurs only if the objective correlate exists, not otherwise. If past and future were nonexistent then the object of cognitive awareness would be a nonexistent cognitive support (*alambana*). Therefore consciousness would not occur if its objective support does not exist. Furthermore if the past is nonexistent then how could there be in the future the effect of good and bad deeds? For the present cause of its fruition no longer exists at the time when the effect arises. Therefore the Vaibhacika maintain that past and future exist.

For the Vaibhacikas the justification for maintaining the existence of *dharmas* in all three temporal dimensions is provided by their causal theory of cognition: since cognitive awareness cannot arise in the absence of an objective support, the cognition must be causally related to the object. The object, therefore, must be real, for nonexistent objects lack causal efficacy.

Nominalism

Nominalism is primarily associated with a specific philosophical position adopted by the Buddhist philosophers of the logico-epistemological tradition concerning the ontological status of universals. However, long before the development of Buddhist Nominalism, Buddhist philosophers had adopted what might be properly termed as a nominalist stance in regards to the nature of composite entities, including persons. Thus, discussions about the ontological status of the various elements of experience in the early Abhidharma traditions were already framed by the distinction between things that existed substantively (*dravyasat*) versus those that had only nominal or conventional existence (*prajnaptisat*).

In the celebrated dialogue between the Buddhist philosopher Nanasena and King Milinda, we come across one of the first references to the notion that an individual exists only as an appellation or conventional designation (Pali *pannatti*, Skt, *prajnapti*). As Nanasena declares in response to the King's question about who he is or what is he known as: "Nanasena and so on— is only a generally understood term, a designation in common use. For there is no permanent individuality (or self) involved in the matter". Nanasena's claim frames the nominalist tendency that is already at work in the Buddhist canonical literature: just as words such as 'chariot' are used only when certain parts are arranged together to form a spatio-temporal entity we ordinarily designate as such, so also an individual (*satto*) is nothing but a conventional designation that applies to the five aggregates.

Although Abhidharma philosophical views on the kinds of entities that have only nominal existence range widely, it is generally agreed that persons or individuals are always to be taken as nothing more than merely conventional designations established on the basis of the five aggregates, the domains of perceptual activity, and their respective elements. Note, however, that Abhidharma philosophers do not deny the physical reality of aggregated entities and persons. Indeed, materiality or form (*rupa*), which is also one of five collections of aggregates, is generally considered to be an external, non-mental reality. Rather, the two-tiered approach to the existence of phenomena, which distinguishes between substantial and nominal existents, is meant to reject not the existence of extra mental entities proper, but rather the existence of all partite entities such as chairs, pots, and tables.

In the Abhidharma ontology only the atoms that compose the four elements are ultimately real. Thus, the theory of two levels of existents implies a philosophical perspective that is best described as reductionism. On this view, only partless entities (i.e., atoms) can be said to properly exist. The property-particulars of phenomenal experience (the *svalakcanas*) are real only insofar as their atomic configurations provide a causal basis for the arising of perceptual apprehension. But the Buddhist reductionist, as Siderits (2003, 13 and *passim*) has clearly argued, is not an eliminativist. Unlike the eliminative materialist who regards conventional, folk-psychological discourse about persons as unsupported by, say, neuroscientific data (and thus is willing to dispense with a theory of persons altogether), the Buddhist reductionist merely points to the conventional nature of persons as ordinarily conceived. Whether we consider the view of Buddhist personalists such as the Vatsiputriyas (or Pudgalavadins), who hold that persons non-reductively supervene upon the psychophysical aggregates, or that of Buddhist reductionists who treat persons as conventional designations, a theory of persons is retained.

Idealism

The Yogacara school, which is associated with the works of the half-brothers Asanga and Vasubandhu, its founders and principal exponents, is often identified by later Buddhist doxographers as the Mind-only or Cognition-only School (*Cittamatra* or *Vijnaptimatra*), on account of its internalist epistemology. In texts such as Vasubandhu's *Twenty Verses: A Demonstration on Existence of Consciousness Only* (*Vimsatika Vijnaptimatratasiddhi*; hereafter VVS) and Dignana's *Investigation of the Cognitive Support* (*Alambanaparikca*; and its *Vrtti*; hereafter APV) we are presented with a metaphysical picture of cognitive awareness or consciousness as the only ultimately existing reality.

In the *Twenty Verses*, Vasubandhu offers an elaborate defence of idealism. His arguments may be summarized as follows: Because non-existing entities can be consciously apprehended, consciousness must have ontological priority (VVS I, 1). The typical realist objection to an assertion of this sort concerns the causal function of perception: indeed, if mental content can be said to consciously arise without any reference to external objects, then why does it arise at a specific time and place and not everywhere and at any given moment? (VVS *ad* 2) In his response, Vasubandhu appeals to the dream argument: objects in a dream appear as having determined spatio-temporal coordinates without there being any correspondence to external realities. As he explains, dream objects arise in dependence upon the transformation of residual impressions (*vasanas*), stock examples of which include the phenomenon of nocturnal emission of semen (VVS *ad* 3–4).

Similarly, to the objection that cognition must have a basis (*ayatana*) for its arising, Vasubandhu responds by appealing to the theory of seeds in the mental stream: the physical object and the cognitive faculty which together provide the basis for the arising of a particular type of cognitive awareness are now seen as an object-oriented cognitive aspect and its internal representation. It only seems as though a patch of colour and the visual system which processes it are the basis for colour qualia. In reality, claims Vasubandhu, it is the residual traces (viz., the transforming seeds) in the mental stream that take the form of tangible object and tactile sense (VVS *ad* 9).

A stronger objection, however, pertains to certain aspects of doctrine: if consciousness has the capacity to appear as bearing the characteristics of material objects, then what purpose do canonical teachings about the material bases for the arising of consciousness serve? The answer to the second objection is twofold: first, Vasubandhu appeals to the hermeneutical strategies of Buddhist schools such as Madhyamaka and Yogacara, which distinguish between direct and indirect meaning (thus interpreting earlier teachings as having only an implied meaning (*neyartha*), which is only made explicit (*nitartha*) in the latter texts of the Mahayana, and in particular of the Yogacara tradition); second,

Vasubandhu, relies on the dual aspect theory of cognition with its internalist perspective (which regards the appearance of objectual aspects in cognition as the result of residual traces stemming from the receptacle consciousness).

However, Vasubandhu's most compelling proof for idealism appeals to the method of mereological reduction: wholes, being merely collections of minimal parts, do not actually exist as perceived. But wholes, which are extended objects, must necessarily be made of parts, the ultimate building blocks of which are the atoms. And since atoms, conceived as partless point-instant are ultimately insubstantial, the realist argument for the existence of material objects as conglomerates of parts must be false (VVS *ad* 11–14; for detailed discussion of some of these arguments.

Vasubandhu's refutation of the reality (and causal efficacy) of external objects *as spatio-temporal entities* raises some important mereological issues and has a number of consequences for perception:

a. For an external entity to be an object of cognition it must (i) either be a whole (*avayavin*) made of parts but be more than its parts put together, (ii) or be a non-combined set of contiguous atoms, (iii) or be a combined set of cohesive atoms.
b. Vasubandhu rejects both wholes and combined sets (whether cohesive or merely contiguous). Wholes are rejected by appealing to the Buddhist reductionist principle which says that only the component parts of an entity are real (aggregated wholes, on this view, are not).
c. The rejection of combined sets rests on the refutation of Vaibhacika atomism. For the Vaibhacika, who are realists, atoms are both indivisible and also capable of aggregation (specifically, in sets of seven atoms, with one at the centre, and the other six arranged so as to correspond to the six cardinal points).
d. In his refutation of atomism, Vasubandhu explains that for combinations of atoms to form partite aggregated entities, the atoms would have to be contiguous, and as contiguous atoms would be confounded with one another. Two or

more atoms in contact would appear to have parts, which is by definition impossible (since atoms are partless entities). Thus, connection among atoms implies loss of indivisibility, and since atoms by definition cannot have (connection enabling) parts, so too aggregated wholes must lack connection among their constitutive parts (it is assumed that the connecting relation is transitive).

e. For Vasubandhu, thus, an ontology of impartite atoms cannot explain connection. In other words, the reduction of compounded entities to their component parts, and of those parts to their own pars, is not logically supported by atomism. Thus, Vasubandhu concludes (VVS *ad* 11) that admitting the existence of partless entities as the ultimate building blocks of reality would make it in effect impossible to explain the specific natures of aggregated phenomena. Consequently, only partite entities exist.

f. Other objections to atomism include the argument from mutual obstruction: lacking parts, an atom could obstruct other atoms from impinging on it, leading to the unwarranted conclusion that all atoms could occupy the same region of space.

g. Thus, neither composite entities made of indivisible parts, nor the indivisible parts themselves can provide a basis for cognitive awareness. Physical objects (the collection of mid-size dry goods that populate the realist's ontology) cannot exist as perceived and must therefore be a product of conceptual elaboration (*vikalpa, kalpana*).

h. Since atoms either alone or combined cannot provide a basis for cognitive awareness, the perception of aggregated entities must be the product of imagination (*parikalpa*).

i. The division of perception into direct (*nirvikalpa,* a bare awareness without any discrimination) and indirect (*savikalpa,* what we ordinarily call a percept, involving some level of cognitive determination of the object), helps clarify Vasubandhu's argument: at the level of bare awareness there is no perception of composite entities; at the level of discriminating awareness perception reveals a world of objects as wholes with specific properties. Indirect perception, arises at a moment when the external cause that occasioned the perceptual experience is not longer present.

j. So by invoking the momentary nature of phenomena, and the two-tier process of perception, Vasubandhu is able to demonstrate that the determinate objects of awareness in fact lack an external cognitive support.

In his *Investigation of the Cognitive Support* Dignana takes up, as the title suggests, one of the specific issue debated by Vasubandhu in his *Twenty Verses*: what exactly should count as an object of cognition? Dignana's definition of the cognitive support invokes the principle of the concomitance of cause and effect (*karyakaranabhava*).

Thus, for an object to count as a support (*alambana*) for cognitive awareness it must (i) produce a cognition, and (ii) that cognition must take the form of the object. In large measure Dignana follows Vasubandhu's line of argumentation in his refutation of the realistic atomism of the Vaibhacikas (and of the Nyaya-Vaisesika tradition).

His innovations consist mainly in appealing to the principle of the coexistence of cause and effect and to the Yogacara theory of mental aspects.

As proof that internal aspects, which provide a basis for cognition, arise simultaneously with cognition itself, Dignana cites the principle of the concomitance of cause and effect (*karyakaranabhava*): although the causal relation is understood sequentially, by virtue of the necessary dependence of cause and effect, whenever a cause is present its effect must also be present.

The theory of cognitive aspects serves to further demonstrate that it is the appearance of an internally cognizable aspect that is the actual cognitive support.

Because cognitions which arise taking the form of an apparently external object are the determining factor for the arsing of subsequent cognitions, the external object (say, a visible entity) and the sense faculty (visual sense) are merely projective aspects of this initial aspectual cognition (APV *ad* VII b).

Thus, Dignana effectively argues that cognition arises bearing two aspects: that of the object and that of the cognition itself, such that cognition and cognized object are not different: they are both manifestations of cognitive awareness itself.

Whether the Yogacara ontology of mind is idealist or can be interpreted as a type of phenomenalism depends of course on how one interprets one of its key technical concepts: the *vijnapti-matra* (lit. 'cognition only' or 'nothing but cognition.'). May (1971) and Schmithausen (1973) are among the strongest proponents of the idealist interpretation. Schmithausen in particular claims that the idealist formulation arose not out of purely theoretical or doctrinal concerns, but rather as a generalization based on the insights derived from meditative practice. In an innovative metaphilosophical essay on Western idealism as seen through Yogacara eyes, Garfield (1998) argues that idealism is a contrastive ontology, in which mind and mental constituents are assigned a fundamental reality that is denied to external objects. Thus, while Berkeley, Kant, Hegel, Schopenhauer, and Bradley may hold different views on the nature of mind, they all presumably agree on its ontological primacy. Likewise, claims Garfield, regardless of how Yogacarins like Vasubandhu conceive of the mind, to the extent that they ascribe to it any sort of ontological primacy over external objects, they are idealists in this contrastive ontological sense.

Wayman (1965) is perhaps the first scholar to have challenged the idealist interpretation of the Yogacara notion of *vijnapti-matra* routinely advanced by both historical opponents, such as the Madhyamikas and orthodox Brahmanical philosophers, as well as by early generations of Buddhist scholars. His argument is that Yogacarins like Vasubandhu do not really deny the reality of external objects; rather, they simply content that cognitive activity can arise even in the absence of an external object. Wayman's critique has set the platform for an entire generation of scholars who have argued against the idealist interpretation of Yogacara ontology.

There is no general consensus at present on how best to represent the metaphysical position of the Yogacaras: proposals vary from realistic pluralism, to pragmatism, neutral monism, epistemic idealism, to a realist phenomenology on the model of Husserl and Merleau-Ponty. Alternative interpretations present the Yogacara school as a system outlining a "therapeutic course of action (acara) rooted in meditation (yoga)" (Anacker 1984, 194) or as providing an account of the "unconscious structuring of experience".

Phenomenalism

Something analogous to a phenomenalist stance is adopted by the Sautrantikas. Vasubandhu, who in the commentary portion to the *Treasury of Higher Knowledge,* argues from the perspective of the Sautrantikas, provides a phenomenalist account of experience. On this view, form does not refer to the material aspect of an independently existing entity but rather to how it is phenomenally disclosed in perception. Form is thus defined as something that can either be disrupted by impact or as something that opposes resistance (*pratighata*). However, these properties do not extend to the atoms themselves, which form the building blocks of materiality. Although as monadic units the atoms are seen as devoid of any formal properties, as atomic compounds (*sanghatastha, samcita*) the atoms are subject to the same properties of resistance and destruction as any other material entities.

The difficulty of reconciling atomism—a fundamental tenet of Buddhist metaphysics—with the phenomenology of perception is apparent in early Abhidharma debates between Realists (chiefly the Vaibhasikas) and the Phenomenalists (the Sautrantikas). The debate between the Vaibhasikas and the Sautrantikas on the issue of whether the sensible qualities of objects (viz., colour, shape, etc.) supervene on the atoms is a telling point. For the Vaibhasikas, secondary properties such as colour (*varna*) are in fact substances (*dravya*) similar to the four great elements. For the Sautrantikas, colour is a derived property that lacks the elemental nature of primary *dharmas* like fire, water, etc. Rather, secondary properties are treated by the Sautrantikas as potentialities that reside in aggregated entities. Moreover, the Sautrantikas conceive of atoms not as substantial impartite entities, but rather as the most subtle collection of material elements.

On this Sautrantika view, as presented by Vasubandhu, perceived material properties, both primary (e.g., solidity) and secondary (e.g., colour) are in fact emergent properties of subtle collections of elements whose phenomenal properties reflect the constitution and function of the perceptual systems. For instance, fluidity in the case of water may be classified both as a primary property of water atoms and also as a secondary property reflecting a specific configuration of water atoms. The same atoms of water, when configured as ice, may produce the sensation of hardness instead of that of fluidity.

A phenomenal object is such that it affects an individual by occasioning different types of experience. For example, water causes the experience of wetness and fluidity, rocks the experience of resistance or hardness, irregular surfaces the experience of roughness, etc. The material aspect of the experienced object *as experienced,* although arising in dependence upon the activity of the corresponding sense sphere, at the same time obstructs and limits it: a wall limits movement, night restricts vision, etc. This is the typical phenomenological stance: physical entities are mind independent, but we have no way of knowing how they are in themselves apart from the way we perceive and conceive them.

An often quoted passage from the Abhidharma literature reads: "One sees the blue, but one does not see 'it is blue'." This statement captures an essential aspect of Buddhist phenomenalism: indirect perception, rather than providing a definitive picture of the content of non-conceptual awareness, instead distorts and misrepresents this content. The Buddhist preoccupation with the pure datum of experience is in large measure motivated by a deep suspicion of "any sort of theorizing about the world that we experience". This is one of the main reasons why philosophers of the logico-epistemological tradition invite us to go beyond our ordinary language intuitions.

11

Buddhist Texts

There are a great variety of Buddhist texts. Buddhists place varying value on them; attitudes range from worship of the text itself, to dismissal of some texts as falsification of the ineffable truth.

The texts can be categorized in a number of ways, but the most fundamental division is that between canonical and non-canonical texts. The former, including the Sutras (Sanskrit) or Suttas (Pali), are held to be, literally or metaphorically, the actual words of the Buddha.

The latter are the various commentaries on canonical texts and other treatises on the Dharma, as well as collections of quotations, histories, grammars, etc.

However, it should be borne in mind that many divisions are arbitrary, and some texts fall between categories, or can be associated with more than one category. Many later Chinese scriptures were explicitly not of Indian origin, but were widely accepted as valid sutras on their own merits by Chinese and East Asian Buddhists of the Mahayana ('YXN) tradition.

Recently an important archaeological discovery was made, consisting of the earliest known Buddhist manuscripts, recovered from somewhere near ancient Gandhara in northwest Pakistan. These fragments, written on birch bark, are dated to the 1st century and have been compared to the Dead Sea scrolls in importance. Donated to the British Library in 1994, they are now being studied in a joint project at the University of Washington.

THE MEANING OF BUDDHISM

The teaching founded by the Buddha is known, in English, as Buddhism. It may be asked, who is the Buddha? A Buddha is one who has attained Bodhi; and by Bodhi is meant wisdom, an ideal state of intellectual and ethical perfection which can be achieved by man through purely human means. The term Buddha literally means enlightened one, a knower. Buddhists believe that a Buddha is born in each aeon of time, and our Buddha-the sage Gotama who attained enlightenment under the bo tree at Buddh Gaya in India-was the seventh in the succession.

Gotama was born the son of an Indian king on the border of modern Nepal 623 years before Christ. The wise men of the kingdom foresaw that he would become either an emperor or a Buddha, and his father, wanting him to be an emperor, kept him utterly secluded from all unpleasant things, so that he might not become wise by seeing life.

But the gods knew that Gotama must become the Buddha, and so they visited earth in various forms to let him see them. On three successive days, while on his way to the royal park, Gotama saw an old man, a sick man, and a corpse, and thus he learned that men-all men-must suffer and die. On the fourth day he saw a monk; from this he understood that to learn the way of overcoming man's universal sorrow lie must give up worldly pleasures. Accordingly, in his twenty-ninth year, he renounced his kingdom and became an ascetic.

Gotama wandered about the countryside, a seeker after truth and peace. He approached many a distinguished teacher of his day, but none could give him what he sought. He strenuously practiced all the severe austerities of monkish life, hoping to attain Nirvana. Eventually his delicate body was reduced almost to a skeleton. But the more he tormented his body the further away he was from his goal. Realizing the futility of self-mortification, he finally decided to follow a different course, avoiding the extremes of pain and indulgence.

The new path which he discovered was the Middle Way, the Eightfold Path, which subsequently became part of his teaching.

By following this path his wisdom grew into its fullest power, and he became the Buddha.

As a man Prince Gotama, by his own will, love, and wisdom, attained Buddhahood-the highest possible state of perfection-and he taught his followers to believe that they might do the same. Any man, within himself, possesses the power to make himself good, wise, and happy.

All the teachings of the Buddha can be summed up in one word: Dhamma. It means truth, that which really is. It also means law, the law which exists in a man's own heart and mind. It is the principle of righteousness. Therefore the Buddha appeals to man to be noble, pure, and charitable not in order to please any Supreme Deity, but in order to be true to the highest in himself.

Dhamma, this law of righteousness, exists not only in a man's heart and mind, it exists in the universe also. All the universe is an embodiment and revelation of Dhamma. When the moon rises and sets, the rains come, the crops grow, the seasons change, it, is because of Dhamma, for Dhamma is the law of the universe which makes matter act in the ways revealed by our studies of natural science.

If a man will live by Dhamma, he will escape misery and come to Nirvana, the final release from all suffering. It is not by any kind of prayer, nor by any ceremonies, nor by any appeal to a God, that a man will discover the Dhamma which will lead him to his goal. He will discover it in only one way-by developing his own character. This development comes only through control of the mind and purification of the emotions. Until a man stills the storm in his heart, until he extends his loving-kindness to all beings, he will not be able to take even the first step toward his goal.

Thus Buddhism is not a religion at all, in the sense in which the word is commonly understood. It is not a system of faith or worship. In Buddhism, there is no such thing as belief in a body of dogma which must be taken on faith, such as belief in a Supreme Being, a creator of the universe, the reality of an immortal soul, a personal savior, or archangels who are supposed to carry out the will of the Supreme Deity. Buddhism begins as a search for truth. The Buddha taught that we should believe only that which is true in the light of our own experience, that which conforms to reason and is conducive to the highest good and welfare of all beings. Men must rely on themselves. Even though he may "take refuge in Buddha," the expression used when a man pledges himself to live a righteous life, he must not fall victim to a blind faith that the Buddha can save him. The Buddha can point out the path, but he cannot walk it for us.

The truth which the Buddhist sees when he looks around him is the truth of cause and effect. Every action, no matter how insignificant, produces an effect; every effect in its turn becomes a, cause and produces still further effects. It is meaningless to inquire for a First Cause. A First Cause is inconceivable; rather, cause and effect are cyclical, and this universe when it dies and falls apart will give rise to another universe, just as this one was formed from the dispersed matter of a previous universe. The origin of the universe, like that of every individual person or thing in it, is dependent on the chain of previous causes, which goes on and on in an endless cycle of birth, death, and rebirth. This is the principle of dependent origination.

What of the soul? The Buddha taught that there is no soul or self, and he used the metaphor of the cart. If you take away the wheels and axles, the floorboards and sides, the shafts, and all the other parts of the cart, what remains? Nothing but the conception of a cart, which will be the same when a new cart is built. So the uninterrupted process of psychophysical phenomena moves from life to life. Each life passes instantaneously in death to a new life, and the new life is the effect of the causes in the old life. A candle flame at this instant is different from the flame that burned an instant ago, yet the flame is continuous.

Thus in the chain of interdependent causation all phenomenal existence is constantly changing. The elements combine and recombine with no underlying substance, or soul, to give them permanence. This is the Wheel of Life. The main cause of the restlessness, the suffering, which is the lot of beings turning on the Wheel of Life, is craving or selfish desire for existence, and it is this desire which sets the life force in motion. Desire is manifested in action. This action is in reality volition or will power, which is responsible for the creation of being. It is called karma in Sanskrit, but in the Pali language, which the Buddha spoke and in which all the Buddhist scriptures were written, it is softened to kamma.

In this universe in which nothing is permanent all change is governed by kamma or the kammic force. Kamma means action. In its general sense, kamma means all good and bad actions. Kamma refers to all kinds of intentional actions whether mental, verbal, or physical, that is, all thoughts, words, and deeds. In its ultimate sense kamma means all moral and immoral volition.

Kamma, though it activates the chain of cause and effect, is not determinism, nor is it an excuse for fatalism. The past influences the present, but does not dominate it. The past is the background against which life goes on from moment to moment; the past and the present influence the future. Only the present moment exists, and the responsibility for using the present moment for good or ill lies with each individual.

Every action produces an effect; it is cause first and effect afterward. We therefore speak of kamma as "the law of cause and effect." If you throw a stone into a pond, the ripples spread out to the shore, but that is not all, for the ripples return inward until they touch the stone again. The effects of our actions come back to us, and as long as our actions are done with evil intent, the waves of effect will come back to us as evil. But if we are kind and keep ourselves peaceful, the returning waves of trouble will grow weaker until they die down and our good kamma will come back to us in blessing.

In the world around us there are many inequalities in the lot of man-some are rich, others are poor, some live full lives, others die young, etc. According to Buddhism, the inequalities which exist are due, to some extent, to environment-which is itself shaped by cause and effect-and to a greater extent to causes, that is kamma, which are in the present, the immediate past, and the remote past. Man himself is responsible for his own happiness and misery. Thus kamma is not fate nor destiny nor blind determinism. Man has a certain amount of free will; he can modify his actions and affect his future. Each act, whether mental or physical, tends to produce its like. If a man does a good deed or thinks a good thought, the effect upon him is to increase the tendencies to goodness in him.

The understanding of kamma gives us power. The more we make the doctrine of kamma a part of our lives, the more power we gain, not only to direct our future, but also to help our fellow beings more effectively. The practice of good kamma, when fully developed, will enable us to overcome evil and even to overcome kamma itself, thus bringing us to our goal, Nirvana.

The principle of dependent origination and the law of kamma provide the background for understanding the nature of rebirth. According to Buddhism, death is "the temporary end of a temporary phenomenon." It is not the complete annihilation of the being, for although the organic life has ceased, the kammic force which hitherto actuated it is not destroyed. Our physical forms are only the outward manifestations of the invisible kammic force. When the present form perishes, another form takes its place according to a good or bad volitional impulse-the kamma that was the most powerful-at the moment before death.

At death the kammic force remains entirely undisturbed by the disintegration of the physical body, and the passing away of the present consciousness creates the conditions for the coming into being of a fresh body in another birth. The stream of consciousness flows on like a river which is built up by its tributaries and dispenses its water to the countryside through which it passes. The continuity of flux at death is unbroken in point of time; there is no breach in the stream of consciousness, and therefore there is no room whatever for an intermediate stage between this life and the next. Rebirth takes place immediately.

The present being, present existence, is conditioned by the way one faced circumstances in the last and in all past existences. One's present character and circumstances are the result of all that one has been up to the present, but what one will be in the future depends on what one does now in the present. The true Buddhist regards death as a momentary incident between one life and its successor and views its approach with calmness. His only concern is that his future should be such that the condition of that life may provide him with better opportunities for perfecting himself. Buddhism teaches that with the practice of meditation and concentration the memory can be trained. By meditation and mind culture one can acquire the power to see one's rebirth as a link, or a succession of links, in a chain of births; one can also acquire the power of looking back into one's previous lives. Not only this, but Buddhism also teaches that with the attainment of Nirvana in this life itself, through enlightenment and true wisdom, one can reach the end of this chain of rebirths.

Nirvana, the state to which all Buddhists aspire, is the cessation of desire and hence the end of suffering. Nirvana in Sanskrit means "the blowing out." It is understood as the extinguishment of the flame of personal desire, the quenching of the fire of life. Among Westerners Nirvana is often thought of as a negative state, a kind of "nothingness." But in the Buddhist scriptures it is always described in positive terms; the highest refuge, safety, emancipation, peace, and the like. Nirvana is freedom, but not freedom from circumstance; it is freedom from the bonds with which we have bound ourselves to circumstance. That man is free who is strong enough to say, "Whatever comes I accept as best."

Nirvana is the dying of the kammic force. The Buddhist ascends to Nirvana through many stages of the Middle Way, the path of wisdom, morality, and control. There is not space enough here even to mention these phases or the various aspects of the regimen recommended by the Buddha in his vast scriptures; but it may be taken for granted that the life of the conscientious Buddhist is full and rich. Through the cycle of rebirths he ascends, he perfects himself, he conquers his cravings through wisdom and love. Slowly the kammic force ebbs away, the flame dies down.

At the root of man's trouble is his primal state of ignorance. From ignorance comes desire, which sets the kammic force in motion. Hence the way to Nirvana lies through knowledge, and we come again full circle to Dhamma, the Buddha's teachings. For in Dhamma, as truth, lies release from ignorance and desire and perpetual change, and the Buddha has shown us the way to truth.

What, then, is the meaning of Buddhism? Ultimately Buddhism, although not strictly speaking a religion, is a systematic exercise in spirituality, certainly one of the greatest ever conceived. It offers the individual a means by which he may fulfill himself through understanding, reaching eventually the plane of the supraperson on which both the self and self-knowledge are no longer useful. Meister Eckhart, the great Christian mystic, said: "The kingdom of God is for none but the thoroughly dead." The Buddhist would agree, though he would probably prefer a less grim way of saying it. Nirvana in life, the peace which "passeth all understanding," is the conquest of life, the discovery of the permanent in its flux of psychophysical accidents and circumstances. The Buddhist believes that through meditation and good hard thought he can follow the Buddha through the successive stages of enlightenment and achieve at last the perfect wisdom which surmounts all need.

But by no means all Buddhists are monks or adepts. What does Buddhism mean for the ordinary person going about his work in the world? All through the Buddha's teaching, repeated stress is laid on self-reliance and resolution. Buddhism makes man stand on his own feet, it arouses his self-confidence and energy. The Buddha again and again reminded his followers that there is no one, either in heaven or on earth, who can help them or free them from the results of their past evil deeds. The Buddhist knows that the powers of his own mind and spirit are enough to guide him in the present and shape his future and bring him eventually to the truth. He knows that he possesses a strength which is ultimately unsurpassable.

Moreover, Buddhism points unequivocally to the moral aspect of everyday life. Though Nirvana is amoral, in the sense that final peace transcends the conflict of good and evil, the path to wisdom is definitely a moral path. This follows logically from the doctrine of kamma. Every action must produce an effect, and one's own actions produce an effect in one's own life. Thus the kammic force which carries us inevitably onward can only be a force for good, that is, for our ultimate wisdom, if each action is a good action.

This doctrine finds its highest expression in metta, the Buddhist goal of universal and all-embracing love. Metta means much more than brotherly feeling or kindheartedness, though these are part of it. It is active benevolence, a love which is expressed and fulfilled in active ministry for the uplifting of fellow beings. Metta goes hand in hand with helpfulness and a willingness to forego self-interest in order to promote the welfare and happiness of mankind.

It is metta which in Buddhism is the basis for social progress. Metta is, finally, the broadest and intensest conceivable degree of sympathy, expressed in the throes of suffering and change. The true Buddhist does his best to exercise metta toward every living being and identifies himself with all, making no distinctions whatsoever with regard to caste, color, class, or sex.

In addition, of course, the teachings of the Buddha are a prime cultural force in Oriental life, just as the Bible is the ultimate source of much Western art and thought. The Buddhist scriptures are larger and more detailed than the Christian Bible, however, and in translation would fill a dozen volumes. In Pali, the language of the scriptures, the Buddha's teachings are called Tripitaka, which means "The Three Baskets."

Vinaya Pitaka, "The Basket of Discipline," consists of five books which expound the rules of monastic life. Sutta Pitaka, "The Basket of Discourses," is a collection of discussions, stories, poems, and proverbs, written in simple language, imparting all the precepts of practical Buddhism. The third basket, Abhidhamma Pitaka, or "Basket of Ultimate Things," deals with epistemological, metaphysical, and psychological matters and is of interest mainly to trained philosophers.

Thus the Tripitaka offers cohesive guidance at every level of intellectual, ethical, and spiritual activity. The Buddha's word is light, a lamp for Burma-and for everyone.

CANONICAL TEXTS

These are, in some way or other, texts associated with Gautama, the historical Buddha. Different schools, however, are not always in agreement about which texts are canonical, and the various recensions of the Buddhist Canon contain widely varying numbers and types of texts. Broadly speaking, the texts come in three types:

- sutras (i.e. discourses)

- vinaya (relating to the rules of monastic discipline)
- abhidharma (analytical texts).

Together these three make up what is known in Sanskrit as the Tripitaka and in Pali as the Tipitaka. Both the sutras and the vinaya of every Buddhist school contain a huge variety of documents including discourses on the Dharma, commentaries on other teachings, cosmological and cosmogonical texts, stories of the Buddha's previous lives, and various lists.

The Theravada and other Nikaya schools believe, more or less literally, that these texts contain the actual words of the Buddha. The Theravada canon, also known as the Pali Canon after the language it was written in, contains some four million words.

Later texts, such as the Mahayana Sutras, are also considered by Mahayanists to be the word of the Buddha, but transmitted either in secret, via lineages of mythical beings (such as the nagas), or revealed directly from other Buddhas or bodhisattvas. Some 600 Mahayana Sutras have survived in Sanskrit, or in Chinese and/ or Tibetan translation. The most complete Mahayana Canon is in Chinese, though it was originally in Sanskrit. It contains texts from many strands of earlier tradition.

The earliest Mahayana texts were composed in a 'Middle Indo-Aryan' language which was Sanskritised during the Gupta era when Sanskrit became the official language of the Indian court. Most of the Mahayana sutra texts are composed in what is called Buddhist Hybrid Sanskrit, a Middle Indo-Aryan Prakrit with ornaments and flourishes designed to imitate Sanskrit. Some later Buddhist texts, particularly those originating at the university at Nalanda, were composed in true Sanskrit.

The Tibetan canon, which belongs to the various schools of Tibetan Vajrayana Buddhism, in addition to containing the earlier three classes of texts, also contains the tantric texts and commentaries on them.

The division of texts into the traditional three yanas may obscure the process of development that went on. For instance, there are so-called *proto-Mahayana* texts, such as the Ajitasena Sutra, which are missing key features that are associated with

Mahayana texts. Some Pali texts also contain ideas that later became synonymous with the Mahayana. Some Mahayana texts are also thought to display a distinctly tantric character, particularly some of the shorter Perfection of Wisdom Sutras. An early tantra, the Mahavairocana Abhisambodhi Tantra, is also known as the Mahavairocana Sutra.

Some Buddhist texts evolved to become a virtual canon in themselves, and are referred to as *vaipulya* or extensive sutras. Scholars think, for instance, that the Golden Light Sutra constellated around the celebrated third chapter. The Avatamsaka Sutra is another example of a single Sutra made up of many other sutras, many of which, particularly the Gandhavyuha Sutra still circulate as separate texts. The Avatamsaka Sutra and the White Lotus Sutra are associated with the idea of the Ekayana or One Vehicle.. The texts claim to unify all the teachings that have come before into a greater whole.

Shingon Buddhism developed a system which assigned authorship of the early sutras to Gautama Buddha in his physical manifestation, of the *Ekayana* sutras to the Buddhas as Sambhoghakaya, and the Vajrayana texts to the Buddha as Dharmakaya.

Non-canonical Texts

Non-canonical or semi-canonical texts have been important from very early in Buddhism. Extensive commentaries exist in Pali for the Pali Canon and in Tibetan, Chinese and other East Asian languages.

Important examples of non-canonical texts are the Visuddhimagga, or *Path of Purification*, by Buddhaghosa, which is a compendium of Theravada teachings that include quotes from the Pali Canon. The Milinda Panha (Pali: Milinda), or *Questions of Milinda,* sometimes included in the Pali Canon is a popular condensation of the Dharma in the form of a dialogue between the Buddhist sage Nagasena and the Indo-Greek King Menander.

The treatise *Awakening of Faith in the Mahayana* (attributed by the faithful to Ashvaghosa) strongly influenced Mahayana doctrine and inspired numerous commentaries authored by early Chinese and Korean Buddhist teachers. Shantideva's *Bodhicaryavatara* has been influential in both Mahayana and Vajrayana, and his Shikshasamucaya contains references to texts which are no longer extant in any other form.

The Platform Sutra of Huineng might be considered a semi-canonical text; it is one of a very few texts not thought to be spoken by the Buddha that has the label "sutra." One should note, however, that this distinction may be an artifact of translation; in the original Chinese, the Platform Sutra is a *jing*, a term that may be translated as "sutra", but is also applied to a variety of other classic texts, such as the Daodejing and the Shi Jing.

In the Platform Sutra, Hui Neng gives an autobiographical account of his succession as Zen Patriarch, as well as teachings about Zen theory and practice. The Zen and Ch'an school in particular rely on non-canonical accounts of Zen masters lives and teachings, for example the *Blue Cliff Record*.

Tibetan Buddhism has a unique and special class of texts called terma. These are texts which were supposedly composed but hidden to be rediscovered at some later date.

Termas are discovered by a terton, whose special function it is to discover these texts. Some termas are hidden in caves or similar places, but a few are said to be 'mind termas' which are 'discovered' in the mind of the terton. The Nyingma school has a large terma literature. Many of the terma texts are said to have been written by Padmasambhava, who is particularly important to the Nyingmas. Probably the best known terma text is the so-called "Tibetan book of the dead", the Bardo thodol.

Other types of non-canonical texts which have been important are the histories of Buddhism in Sri Lanka, the Dipavamsa and Mahavamsa.

Texts of the Early Schools

Although many versions of the texts of the early Buddhist schools exist, the only complete canon to survive is the Pali Canon of the Theravadin school, which preserved the texts in the Pali language. Also large parts of the Sarvastivada and Dharmaguptaka texts are extant.

The Pali literature divides into roughly three periods. The early, or classical, period begins with the Pali Canon itself and ends with the Milindha-panha about the turn of the Christian era.

After a period of being in comparative disuse or decline, Pali underwent a renaissance in the 4th or 5th century with the help of Buddhaghosa, and this period lasted until the 12th Century. The third period coincides with major political changes in Burma and lasted for some time in Sri Lanka, and much longer in Burma.

The other (parts of) extant versions of the Tipitakas of early schools include the agamas, which includes texts of the Sarvastivada and the Mahasanghika. Parts of the canon of the Dharmaguptaka can be found amongst the Gandharan Buddhist Texts. Several early Vinaya Pitakas (from various schools) are also kept in the Chinese (Mahayana) Canon.

Vinaya

The vinaya literature is primarily concerned with aspects of the monastic discipline. However, vinaya as a term is also contrasted with Dharma, where the pair (Dhamma-Vinaya) mean something like 'doctrine and discipline'. The vinaya literature in fact contains a considerable range of texts. There are, of course, those which discuss the monastic rules, how they came about, how they developed, and how they were applied. But the vinaya also contains some doctrinal expositions, ritual and liturgical texts, biographical stories, and some elements of the "Jatakas", or birth stories.

Paradoxically, the text most closely associated with the vinaya, and the most frequently used portion of it, the *Pratimoksha,* is in itself not a canonical text in Theravada, even though almost all of it can be found in the canon.

Six complete vinayas survive:

- Theravada, written in Pali
- Mula-Sarvastivada, written in Sanskrit, but surviving complete only in Tibetan translation
- Mahasanghika, Sarvastivada, Mahishasika, and Dharmagupta, originally in Sanskrit, but only surviving in Chinese translation.

In addition, portions survive of a number of vinayas in various languages.

The *Mahavastu* compiled by the Lokottaravadin sub-school of the Mahasanghika was perhaps originally the preamble to their vinaya that became detached; hence, rather than dealing with the rules themselves, it takes the form of an extended biography of the Buddha, which it describes in terms of his progression through ten bhumis, or stages. This doctrine was later taken up by the Mahayana in a modified form as Vasubandhu's Ten Stages Sutra.

Sutta

The Suttas (in Sanskrit, *Sutra*) are mostly discourses delivered by the Buddha or one of his close disciples. They are all, even those not actually spoken by him, considered to be 'Buddhavacana' or the word of the Buddha, just as in the case of all canonical literature. The Buddha's discourses were perhaps originally organised according to the style in which they were delivered; there were originally nine, but later twelve, of these:

- Sutra: prose discourse
- Geya: mixed prose and verse discourse
- Vyakarana: explanation, analysis
- Gatha: verse
- Udana: inspired speech
- Ityukta: beginning with 'thus has the Bhagavan said'
- Jataka: story of previous life
- Abhutadharma: concerning wonders and miraculous events
- Vaipulya either 'extended discourses' or 'those giving joy' (cf Mahayana Texts)
- Nidana: in which the teachings are set within their circumstances of origin
- Avadana: tales of exploits
- Upadesha: defined and considered instructions.

The first nine are listed in all surviving agamas, with the other three added in some later sources. In Theravada, at least, they are regarded as a classification of the whole of the scriptures, not just suttas. The scheme is also found in Mahayana canons. However, some time later a new scheme of organisation was imposed on the canon, and it is this scheme which most people are familiar with. The scheme organises the suttas into:

Long Discourses

These range in length up to 95 pages. The Pali Digha Nikaya contains 34 texts, including the Mahaparinibbana Sutta and the Brahmajala Sutta. The Dirghagama of the Dharmagupta also survives in Chinese translation and contains 30 sutras.

Medium-length Discourses

These are the rest of the suttas of any length, and the Pali Majjhima Nikaya has 152 suttas. The Madhyamagama of the Sarvastivada containing 222 sutras survives in Chinese translation.

Connected Discourses

This grouping consists of many short texts connected by theme, setting, or interlocutor. The Pali Samyutta Nikaya contains more than 2,800 suttas. The Samyuktagama of the Sarvastivada containing only 1,300 sutras survives in Chinese translation.

Numbered Discourses

Suttas which have the same number of doctrinal items containing over 2,300 suttas in the Pali Anguttara Nikaya. The Chinese canon contains an Ekottaragana which is thought to belong to the Mahasanghika school originally.

Miscellaneous Texts

Not all schools had this category, but the Pali Khuddaka Nikaya has several well-known and loved texts, including:

- the Dhammapada: a collection of sayings and aphorisms.
- The Udana : a collection of inspired sayings in verse usually with a prose introduction that sets a context of sorts for the saying.
- The Sutta nipatta: along with the Dhammapada and the Udana, the Suttanipatta is thought to represent the earliest

strata of the written canon. Many of the features of later texts, such as numbered lists of teachings, or complex doctrinal categories, are not present.

- Theragatha and Therigatha two collections of biographical verse related to the disciples of the Buddha (male and female respectively.)
- Jataka: the so-called 'birth stories' which recount former lives of the Buddha. These remain popular in many forms of Buddhism.

Many of these texts are available in translation as well as in the original language. The Dhammapada, for instance, has a Pali version, three Chinese versions, a Tibetan version, and a Khotanese version.

Abhidharma

Abhidharma (in Pali, *Abhidhamma*) means 'further Dharma' and is concerned with the analysis of phenomena. It grew initially out of various lists of teachings such as the 37 Bodhipaksika-dharmas or the 37 Factors leading to Awakening. The Abhidharma literature is chiefly concerned with the analysis of phenomena and the relationships between them.

The Theravada Abhidhamma survives in the Pali Canon. Though it is regarded as the word of the Buddha, modern scholarship has shown that it developed much later, and most of the literature is the product of the two centuries after Ashoka (1st Century CE). Outside of the Theravada monasteries the Pali Abhidharma texts are not well-known.

A Sarvastivada Abhidharma composed in Sanskrit, survives in Chinese and Tibetan traditions. Though the Theravadin Abhidhamma is well preserved and best known, it should be noted that a number of the early Eighteen Schools each had their own distinct Abhidharma collection with not very much common textual material.

Not all schools accepted the Abhidharma as canonical. The Sautrantika, for instance, held that the canon stopped with the vinaya and sutras. The rejection by some schools that dharmas (i.e.

phenomena) are ultimately real, which the Theravada Abhidhamma, for instance, insists, is thought to be an important factor in the origin of the Mahayana.

Non-canonical Texts

The first important, non-canonical text is probably the *Milinda panha* (literally *The Questions of Milinda*). This text is in the form of a dialogue between Nagasena, and the Indo-Greek King Menander (Pali: Milinda). It is a compendium of doctrine, and covers a range of subjects. It is included in some editions of the Pali Canon. The Pali texts have an extensive commentarial literature that remains largely untranslated.

These are largely attributed to Buddhaghosa. There are also sub-commentaries or commentaries on the commentaries.

Buddhagosa was also the author of the *Visuddhimagga*, or *Path of Purification*, which is a manual of doctrine and practice according to the Theravada school.

MAHAYANA TEXTS

Perfection of Wisdom Texts

These deal with prajna (wisdom or insight). Wisdom in this context means the ability to see reality as it truly is. They do not contain an elaborate philosophical argument, but simply try to point to the true nature of reality, especially through the use of paradox.

The basic premise is a radical non-dualism, in which every and any dichotomist way of seeing things is denied: so phenomena are neither existent, nor non-existent, but are marked by sunyata, emptiness, an absence of any essential unchanging nature.

The Perfection of Wisdom in One Letter illustrates this approach by choosing to represent the perfection of prajna with the Sanskrit/Pali short *a* vowel — which, as a prefix, negates a word's meaning (e.g., changing *svabhava* to *asvabhava*, "with essence" to "without essence"; cf. *mu*); which is the first letter of Indic alphabets; and which, as a sound on its own, can be seen as the most neutral/basic of speech sounds (cf Aụm and bija).

Many sutras are known by the number of lines, or slokas, that they contained.

Edward Conze, who translated all of the Perfection of Wisdom sutras into English, identified four periods of development in this literature:

1. 100BCE-100CE: Ratnagunasamcayagatha and the Astasaharika (8,000 lines)
2. 100-300CE: a period of elaboration in which versions in 18,000, 25,000, and 100,000 lines are produced. Possibly also the Diamond Sutra
3. 300-500CE : a period of condensation, producing the well known Heart Sutra, and the Perfection of Wisdom in one letter
4. 500-1000CE : texts from this period begin to show a tantric influence.

The Perfection of Wisdom texts have influenced every Mahayana school of Buddhism.

Saddharma-pundarika

The earlier teachings are said to be 'skilful means' in order to help beings of limited capacities. Notable for the (re)appearance of the Buddha Prabhutaratna, who had died several aeons earlier, because it suggests that a Buddha is not inaccessible after his parinirvana, and also that his life-span is said to be inconceivably long because of the accumulation of merit in past lives. This idea, though not necessarily from this source, forms the basis of the later Trikaya doctrine. Later associated particularly with the Tien Tai in China (Tendai in Japan) school and the Nichiren schools in Japan.

Pure Land Sutras

There are three major sutras that fall into this category: the Infinite Life Sutra, also known as the Larger Pure Land Sutra; the Amitabha Sutra, also known as the Smaller Pure Land Sutra; and the Contemplation Sutra, or Visualization, Sutra. These texts describe the origins and nature of the Western Pure Land in which the Buddha Amitabha resides.

They list the forty-eight vows made by Amitabha as a bodhisattva by which he undertook to build a Pure Land where beings are able to practise the Dharma without difficulty or distraction. The sutras state that beings can be reborn there by pure conduct and by practices such as thinking continuously of Amitabha, praising him, recounting his virtues, and chanting his name. These Pure Land sutras and the practices they recommend became the foundations of Pure Land Buddhism, which focus on the salvific power of faith in the vows of Amitabha.

The Vimalakirti Nirdesha Sutra

Composed some time before 150CE., the Bodhisattva Vimalakirti appears in the guise of a layman in order to teach the Dharma. Seen by some as a strong assertion of the value of lay practice. Doctrinally similar to the Perfection of Wisdom texts, another major theme is the Buddhafield (Buddha-kshetra), which was influential on Pure Land schools. Very popular in China and Japan where it was seen as being compatible with Confucian values.

Samadhi Sutras

Amongst the very earliest Mahayana texts, the Samadhi Sutras are a collection of sutras which focus on the attainment of profound states of consciousness reached in meditation, perhaps suggesting that meditation played an important role in early Mahayana. Includes the Pratyutpanna Sutra and the Shurangama-samadhi Sutra.

Bibliography

Anesaki, Masaharu: *Nichiren, the Buddhist Prophet,* Cambridge, Harvard University Press, 1916.

Bhattacharyya, Dilip : *Bhutan: The Himalayan Paradise,* New Delhi: Oxford and IBH, 1975.

Candragomin, S. : *Difficult Beginnings: Three Works on the Bodhisattva Path,* Boston, MA: Shambhala, 1985.

Chang, Garma C. C.: *The Hundred Thousand Songs of Milarepa,* Boulder, Shambhala, 1979.

Chaterjee, Suman : *Buddhism : The Way to Wisdom,* Cyber Tech Pub, Delhi, 2009.

Cole, Alan : *Mothers and Sons in Chinese Buddhism,* Stanford, CA: Stanford University Press, 1998.

Coomaraswamy, Ananda K. : *Buddha and the Gospel of Buddhism,* Munshiram Manoharlal, 2003.

Dargyay, Eva M.: *The Rise of Esoteric Buddhism in Tibet,* Delhi, Motilal Banarsidass, 1977.

Dayal, Har: *The Bodhisattva Doctrine in Buddhist Sanskrit Literature,* London, Kegan Paul, 1932.

George, Christopher S.: *The Candamaharosana Tantra,* New Haven, American Oriental Society, 1974.

Georges, B.J. : *Recognizing Reality: Dharmakirti's Philosophy and Its Tibetan Interpretations,* Albany, NY: State University of New York Press, 1997.

Goodman, Steven D. and Ronald M. Davidson : *Tibetan Buddhism: Reason and Revelation,* Albany, NY: State University of New York Press, 1992.

Gregory, Peter N. : *Buddhism in the Sung,* Honolulu, HI: University of Hawaii Press, 2002.

Gross, Rita M.: *Buddhism after Patriarchy: A Feminist History, Analysis, and Reconstruction of Buddhism,* Albany, SUNY Press, 1993.

Gupta, K. : *Buddhism in Mathura : A Detailed Study of Buddhist Tradition, Archaeology and Art,* Bharatiya Kala Prakashan, Delhi, 2009.

Harris, Ian : *Cambodian Buddhism : History and Practice,* Munshiram Manoharlal, 2010.

James C. Jodo Shinshu : *Shin Buddhism in Medieval Japan,* Bloomington, IN: Indiana University Press, 1989.

Johnson, Willard: *Poetry and Speculation of the Rg Veda,* Berkeley, University of California Press, 1980.

Keown, Damien: *The Nature of Buddhist Ethics,* New York, St. Martin's Press, 1992.

Lamrimpa, Gen : *Calming the Mind: Tibetan Buddhist Teachings on Cultivating Meditative Quiescence,* Ithaca, NY: Snow Lion, 1995.

Maillard, Monique : *Buddhism in Afghanistan and Central Asia,* Leiden: E.J. Brill, 1976.

Matthew, T. : *The Tibetan Assimilation of Buddhism: Conversion, Contestation, and Memory,* New York: Oxford University Press, 2002.

Nanamoli, Bhikkhu: *The Life of the Buddha,* Kandy, Buddhist Publication Society, 1972.

Naudou, Jean: *Buddhists of Kashmir,* Delhi, Motilal Banarsidass, 1980.

Philip Denwood : *Tibetan Art: Towards a Definition of Style,* London: Laurence King/Alan Marcuson, 1997.

Ramanan, K. V.: *Nagarjuna's Philosophy as Presented in Maha-Prajnaparamita-Sastra,* Delhi, Motilal Banarsidass, 1978.

Ricard, Matthieu : *The Life of Shabkar: The Autobiography of a Tibetan Yogin,* Albany, NY: State University of New York Press, 1994.

Sarkisyanz, E.: *Buddhist Backgrounds of the Burmese Revolution,* The Hague, Martinus Nijhoff, 1965.

Strachan, Paul: *Pagan: Art and Architecture of Old Burma,* Whiting Bay, Scotland: Kiscadale Publications, 1989.

Takakusu, Junjiro: *The Essentials of Buddhist Philosophy,* Honolulu, Office Appliance Co., 1956.

Taylor, J. L.: *Forest Monks and the Nation-state,* Singapore: Institute for Southeast Asian Studies, 1993.

Thaye, Jampa : *The Garland of Gold: The Early Kagyu Masters in India and Tibet,* Bristol: Ganesha Press, 1990.

Williams, Paul: *The Reflexive Nature of Awareness,* London, Curzon, 1997.

G

Great Renunciation, 83.

H

Hindu Philosophies, 27.

M

Mahayana Buddhist Influence, 209.

Mahparinirvna Sutra, 171, 173.

N

Nirvna, 171, 172, 173, 174, 175.

P

Pessimism of Buddha, 89.

Philosophy of Buddhism, 149.

Political Traction, 230.

S

Shin Buddhism, 42, 43, 44.

Slavery, 96, 97, 98, 99.

Social Criticism, 136, 137, 144.

T

Teachings of the Buddha, 81, 126, 177, 284, 290.

Tibetan Buddhism, 38, 51, 57, 66, 103, 104, 105, 106, 107, 108, 198, 199, 209, 227, 228, 229, 230, 266, 293.

Tibetan Culture, 52, 207, 208.

Tibetan Mountain Gods, 200, 202.

❑❑❑

Index

A

Amitabha, 42, 99, 100, 101, 102, 103, 162, 163, 191, 229, 250, 263, 299, 300.
Aspects of Faith, 105.
Atheism of Buddha, 85.

B

Buddha, 1, 2, 3, 6, 8, 9, 10, 13, 14, 15, 17, 18, 20, 21, 23, 31, 33, 34, 36, 37, 38, 39, 40, 41, 42, 43, 44, 45, 46, 47, 48, 49, 50, 52, 53, 55, 56, 57, 58, 59, 62, 64, 65, 68, 69, 71, 74, 75, 76, 77, 78, 79, 81, 82, 85, 86, 88, 89, 90, 92, 93, 94, 95, 97, 98, 99, 100, 101, 102, 103, 106, 108, 121, 125, 126, 127, 128, 129, 130, 145, 146, 149, 150, 151, 152, 153, 154, 155, 158, 159, 161, 162, 163, 164, 165, 171, 172, 173, 174, 175, 176, 177, 178, 179, 181, 186, 188, 189, 190, 191, 192, 193, 195, 210, 222, 224, 225, 228, 229, 232, 237, 238, 239, 240, 242, 243, 244, 247, 251, 255, 256, 257, 258, 259, 260, 261, 262, 263, 265, 267, 270, 282, 283, 284, 285, 286, 288, 289, 290, 291, 292, 293, 295, 297, 299, 300.
Buddhist Ethics, 6, 121, 122, 123, 124, 127, 128, 132, 136.
Buddhist Philosophical Doctrines, 156.
Buddhist Philosophy, 64, 133, 138, 150, 159, 192, 195, 262.
Buddhist Terminology, 267.
Buddhist Texts, 19, 60, 104, 105, 137, 141, 148, 150, 232, 257, 268, 269, 282, 291, 292.

C

Canonical Texts, 282, 292, 293.
Chinese Buddhism, 51, 214, 250.

D

Dalit Buddhist Movement, 53.
Dhamma Philosophy, 151.

E

Economic Ethics of Buddhism, 133.
Egoism of Buddha, 92.
Ethics of Buddhism, 121, 131, 132, 133.